NON-CIRCULATING

THE MERTON ANNUAL

8

THE MERTON ANNUAL

Studies in Culture, Spirituality, and Social Concerns

THE MERTON ANNUAL publishes articles about Thomas Merton and about related matters of major concern to his life and work. Its purpose is to enhance Merton's reputation as a writer and monk, to continue to develop his message for our times, and to provide a regular outlet for substantial Merton-related scholarship. THE MERTON ANNUAL includes as regular features reviews, review-essays, a bibliographic survey, interviews, and first appearances of unpublished, or obscurely published, Merton materials, photographs, and art. Essays about related literary and spiritual matters will also be considered. Manuscripts and books for review may be sent to any of the editors.

EDITORS

Michael Downey
Theology Department
Bellarmine College
2001 Newburg Road
Louisville, KY 40205-0671

George A. Kilcourse
Theology Department
Bellarmine College
2001 Newburg Road
Louisville, KY 40205-0671

Victor A. Kramer
English Department
Georgia State University
University Plaza
Atlanta, GA 30303-3083

Volume editorship rotates on a yearly basis.

ADVISORY BOARD

THE MERTON ANNUAL

Studies in Culture, Spirituality, and Social Concerns

Volume 8   **1995**

Edited by

Michael Downey

A Liturgical Press Book

THE LITURGICAL PRESS
Collegeville, Minnesota

1   2   3   4   5   6   7   8   9

The Merton Annual

Volume 8	1995

Michael Downey
Collision Course 101:
The Monastery, the Academy, and the Corporation ix

* * *

Thomas Merton, O.C.S.O.
Foreword by Patrick Hart, O.C.S.O.
A Balanced Life of Prayer 1

* * *

Parker J. Palmer
Contemplation Reconsidered: The Human Way In 22

Paul J. Wadell, C.P.
The Human Way Out:
The Friendship of Charity as a Countercultural Practice 38

* * *

Roy D. Fuller
The Virtuous Teacher: Thomas Merton's Contribution
to a Spirituality of Higher Education 59

Julia Ann Upton, R.S.M.
Humanizing the University:
Adding the Contemplative Dimension 75

Gloria Kitto Lewis
Learning to Live:
Merton's Students Remember His Teaching 88

Thomas Del Prete
Culture and the Formation of Personal Identity:
Dilemma and Dialectic in Thomas Merton's Teaching   105

* * *

Thomas F. McKenna, C.M.
A Voice in the Postmodern Wilderness:
Merton on Monastic Renewal   122

Matthias Neuman, O.S.B.
Revisiting *Zen and the Birds of Appetite*
after Twenty-five Years   138

Claire Badaracco
Animated Outsiders:
Echoes of Merton in Hampl, Norris, Dillard, and Ehrlich   150

* * *

Edited by Christine M. Bochen
Translations by Roberto S. Goizueta
Time of Transition:
A Selection of Letters from the Earliest Correspondence
of Thomas Merton and Ernesto Cardenal   162

* * *

Conducted by Michael Downey
Edited by Andrew Hartmans
Daughter of Carmel; Son of Cîteaux: A Friendship Endures
An Interview about Thomas Merton
with Angela Collins, O.C.D.   201

* * *

Victor A. Kramer
Thousands of Words: A Bibliographical Review   221

* * *

REVIEWS

Douglas Burton-Christie
Witness to Freedom: Letters in Times of Crisis
  By Thomas Merton   246

Erlinda G. Paguio
A Catch of Anti-Letters
  By Thomas Merton and Robert Lax   254

Joann Wolski Conn
Thomas Merton in Search of His Soul:
A Jungian Perspective
  By Robert G. Waldron   258

Irwin H. Streight
Watch with Me and Six Other Stories of the
Yet-Remembered Ptolemy Proudfoot and His Wife,
Miss Minnie, Née Quinch
  By Wendell Berry   262

Rick Axtell
Disarming the Heart: Toward a Vow of Nonviolence
  By John Dear   264

Michael Johmann
My Song Is of Mercy
  By Matthew Kelty   271

Matthew Kelty, O.C.S.O.
Brother and Lover: Aelred of Rievaulx
  By Brian Patrick McGuire   274

* * *

Contributors   277

Index   281

Collision Course 101:
The Monastery, the Academy,
and the Corporation

Michael Downey

Had he not met an untimely death in 1968 at age fifty-three, Thomas Merton might have enjoyed celebrating eighty years of life on January 31, 1995. Festivities marking his eightieth were low-key compared to the celebrations which marked the twenty-fifth anniversary of his death. Two of the twenty-fifth anniversary celebrations provided rich fare in the way of insights on Merton's life and legacy. The first of these took the form of a symposium of discussion and reflection held from October 15–17, 1993, at St. John's University in Jamaica, New York. Some of the papers from the symposium entitled "The Vocation of the Cultural Critic" have already been published in *The Merton Annual*, volume 7. The present volume includes two papers from the St. John's symposium: Thomas Del Prete's "Culture and the Formation of Personal Identity: Dilemma and Dialectic in Thomas Merton's Teaching"; and Thomas McKenna's "A Voice in the Postmodern Wilderness: Merton on Monastic Renewal." Both attend to the ambiguous character of culture which thereby necessitates rigorous assessment so that it might contribute to authentic human flourishing.

Bellarmine College in Louisville, Kentucky, home of the Thomas Merton Center, celebrated the twenty-fifth anniversary throughout the academic year 1993–1994. The highpoint of the Merton Year was a conference held from March 17–19, 1994 entitled " 'The Human Way Out': The Contemplative Dimension." Parker Palmer's "Contemplation Reconsidered: The Human Way In" and Paul Wadell's "The Human Way Out: The Friendship of Charity as a Countercultural Practice" were two keynote addresses that oriented participants to explore the contemplative dimension of various spheres of life. The volume includes four other papers given at the Bellarmine conference: Roy Fuller, "The Virtuous Teacher: Thomas Merton's Contribution to a Spirituality of Higher Education"; Julia Upton, "Humanizing the University: Adding the Contemplative Dimension"; Matthias Neuman, "Revisiting *Zen and the Birds of Appetite* after Twenty-five Years"; and Claire Badaracco, "Animated Outsiders."

Gloria Kitto Lewis's "Learning to Live: Merton's Students Remember His Teaching" is a unique contribution to the volume. An interview-based essay, this is the only paper in the volume that did not have a dress rehearsal in one of the twenty-fifth anniversary conferences. Lewis's interviews demonstrate that Merton was not only a teacher but also a mentor and friend to his students at Gethsemani, rounding out and complementing some of the themes addressed in the other contributions. It also serves as a gentle reminder that Merton's school was the monastery and not the halls of the academy.

The editors of *The Merton Annual* have avoided gathering papers around a predetermined theme. It is somewhat surprising, then, to see the extraordinary convergence of themes found in this collection. Without trying to pin down the rich array of insights offered here, it is worthwhile to note that the fruits of two of the twenty-fifth anniversary celebrations provide fresh insights which enable us to see more clearly the connections among three seemingly disparate ways of life: that of the educator, the contemplative, and the cultural critic. In Merton they appear to be intrinsically related.

The title of Julia Upton's "Humanizing the University" is itself indicative of the hazards faced these days by those who teach and learn at the levels of higher education. Heirs to the monasteries of earlier epochs, the universities of the High Middle Ages became the seedbed for the very best expressions of culture. In our own day colleges and universities are gradually relinquishing their responsibility to educate the whole person in service of the human and humanizing community. Knowledge and understanding are often reduced to the transmission of technical information judged to be useful and practical; the education of the whole person reduced to skills training and job preparation. The values of academic culture are being squelched in colleges and universities today as administrators of educational institutions take on the role of corporate executive officers, breeding a corporate culture whose values fly in the face of those of academic life and educational integrity. The creation of a corporate culture in place of an academic community is no less characteristic of many private, Catholic, and denominational colleges and universities than of secular and state-affiliated educational institutions. Far too often college and university presidents, once vibrant examplars of a cultivated intellect, now function as managers of a corporation providing an "educational product" for consumers in the marketplace.

Merton consistently raised a critical voice in the face of those "modern" institutions all too prone to depersonalization and dehumanization. Systems of education were not exempt from his critique. The basis of Merton's critique lies in a recovery of the contemplative dimension of everyday living. This provides the grounds for the recognition that authentic education of the whole person is an activity by which God is glorified.

As Parker Palmer intimates, perhaps it is only the recovery of the deepest reserves of the contemplative spirit which might serve as an antidote to the pragmatic preoccupations that propel our educational systems. In the simplest of terms, contemplation is the nonpragmatic regard for others, for created things, and for God. In a culture such as ours which is driven by narcissism, restlessness, and bottom-line pragmatism, it seems that the vocation of the teacher is closely linked to that of the cultural critic. And this vocation requires that one offer a sustained critique of the educational establishment-become-corporation. The teacher must constantly critique the college or university that has become untethered from the academic values and integrity that lie at the heart of any and all approaches to educating the whole person in knowledge, freedom, and love.

Paul Wadell's essay offers insight regarding the constituent elements of friendship as a countercultural practice. Two feature items in this volume offer further insight on Merton the man and monk by way of two of his friends: Ernesto Cardenal and Angela Collins. We are pleased to include here both sides of the correspondence between Merton and Ernesto Cardenal, from a time of critical importance in Merton's vocational struggle. Cardenal's letters to Merton are available here for the first time in English, translated from the Spanish by Roberto S. Goizueta. The correspondence is introduced by Christine M. Bochen, editor of *The Courage for Truth*, the fourth volume of letters in which many of Merton's letters to Cardenal have been published. Merton's capacity for the friendship of charity is also seen in "Daughter of Carmel; Son of Cîteaux: A Friendship Endures." Having read the letters of Thomas Merton to Sr. Angela Collins, O.C.D., in *The School of Charity*, the third volume of letters edited by Patrick Hart, I became interested in knowing more about this Carmelite nun who had been Prioress of the Carmelite Monastery in Louisville. In the course of my interview with Sister Angela it became clear why Merton sought her counsel, and why she became his friend and confidante. I here acknowledge my gratitude to Sister Angela and the Carmelite nuns of the Carmelite Monastery in Savannah, Georgia, for the warm and gracious hospitality extended to me during my visits to the Savannah Carmel where this interview was conducted.

Victor A. Kramer's "Thousands of Words" provides a thorough survey of 1994 publications pertinent to Merton, with attention to the five volumes of his letters, particularly the fifth and final volume, *Witness to Freedom: Letters in Times of Crisis*, edited by William Shannon.

The volume concludes with reviews of seven books, selected by George Kilcourse.

One of the unique contributions of *The Merton Annual* is its publication of previously unpublished or lesser known published works by Thomas Merton. It is a delight to include in the opening pages of this volume a little known essay of Merton's entitled "A Balanced Life of Prayer." Patrick Hart has provided a foreword which gives helpful orientation to the piece.

Michael Downey
Editor, *The Merton Annual 8* (1995)

A Balanced Life of Prayer

By Thomas Merton, O.C.S.O.
Foreword by Patrick Hart, O.C.S.O.

Foreword

On Trinity Sunday, 1951, Thomas Merton, or Father Louis as he was known in the monastery, having lived the Cistercian life for nearly a decade, was named Master of the Scholastics by Dom James Fox, the first to be so designated in the history of Gethsemani. This appointment followed the completion of the Annual Visitation on May 5 by the Father Immediate, Dom Louis de Gonzague le Pennuen, Abbot of Gethsemani's Motherhouse of Melleray in Brittany (France). With twenty-six temporary professed choir monks in formation, it became necessary to have a Father Master appointed to attend this "flock" within the community of Gethsemani.

Father Louis had been giving conferences to the novices since his ordination on the Feast of the Ascension in 1949, so when these novices made temporary vows, they moved out of the novitiate and became more identified with the solemnly professed choir monks. Father Louis's responsibility was to look after these fledgling monks, give them individual spiritual direction, and monitor their monastic and theological training. At that time the choir monks were automatically destined for the priesthood, so all the studies necessary for their ministry would have to be provided by competent monks of the Gethsemani community.

When Merton became Master of the Scholastics (or Students), he plunged into the task with great enthusiasm, as can be seen from

1

his journals of that period (*The Sign of Jonas,* New York: Harcourt Brace, 1953), and in the letters that have more recently been published, especially his letters on religious renewal and spiritual direction (*The School of Charity,* New York: Farrar, Straus, Giroux, 1990) where he often writes of his spiritual flock and something of the blessings as well as the burdens involved in the task.

One of the recently rediscovered works written during this period, "A Balanced Life of Prayer," was obviously based on some of his conferences to the novices and junior professed, in which he mapped out a general program of monastic life and prayer, applicable to both monks and those dedicated to the spiritual journey among the laity. It was published as a pamphlet and dedicated "in respectful gratitude to Rev. Father Paul Philippe, O.P." (Trappist, Ky.: Abbey of Gethsemani, 1951). Father Philippe had been invited to Gethsemani to give conferences on the Christian life of prayer. One of his strong emphases was that Cistercian monks should be trained within the Cistercian tradition, and that the Cistercian Fathers (and Mothers) be made available to young monks in formation.

Father Louis, with enormous energy and great ability with languages, was providentially prepared to undertake such a ministry. He had already been giving conferences to the novices for two years using the four "Cistercian evangelists," Bernard of Clairvaux, William of St.-Thierry, Guerric of Igny and Aelred of Rievaulx, among others. Merton, more than anyone before him, used the Migne Patrology texts of the Cistercian tradition as a preparation for his classes. Since he kept very complete notes of these conferences on monastic orientation, we have copies of his working notebooks which he had mimeographed for the sake of the young monks, and which he circulated to other English-speaking monasteries, especially the daughterhouses of Gethsemani. It was the earliest beginnings of what would develop later as "Cistercian Studies." (Cistercian Publications has contracted with the Merton Legacy Trust to bring out twelve volumes of Merton's Monastic Orientation Notes.)

"A Balanced Life of Prayer" was well-received and became very popular when it first appeared in late 1951, but for several decades it has been totally inaccessible. Following the suggestion of my golden jubilarian confrere, Brother Nivard Stanton, who incidentally was one of Merton's first students in 1951, it was decided to reissue this early work in *The Merton Annual.* We are grateful to the trustees of the Merton

Legacy Trust for approving this reprint, and to the editors of *The Merton Annual* for making it available again after all these years.

The work is divided into four parts beginning with "The Object of the Life of Prayer" where Merton quotes Paul's exhortation to the Thessalonians: "Pray without ceasing." This was taken up by the earliest monastic tradition of the Desert Fathers with Cassian in particular. Merton compared praying with breathing: "Prayer is as important for the life of the soul as breathing is for the life of the body." That is why we are instructed in the Gospel of Luke "to pray always and never give up." Merton relied here as elsewhere on John's basic text: "God first loved us." His entire prayer life can be considered a response to God's initiative.

Merton is practical in his approach to a life of prayer, and in the second part points out the obstacles and ways in which they may be overcome. He sees prayer as a spiritual activity of the highest order, engaging mind, soul and will. I will resist giving a commentary on Merton's own commentary on these obstacles, since they are spelled out so clearly in the following pages.

A word should be said about the third part of this pamphlet which deals with the subject of "Public Prayer and Sacrifice." Merton quotes extensively from Pope Pius XII's encyclicals *Mediator Dei* and *Menti Nostrae*, where the Christian is encouraged to pray with the entire Church, the Mystical Body of Christ, in public worship, especially the Eucharist. But really the entire sacramental life of the Church must be embraced by the Christian. This does not mean that there should be a rift between public and private prayer in the life of the Christian or the monk. Ideally one should complement the other. Merton would have more to say on this subject later on in his monastic life, especially in his monograph on "Action and Contemplation in St. Bernard of Clairvaux." (See *Thomas Merton on St. Bernard*, Kalamazoo: Cistercian Publications, 1980.)

The final section on "Mental Prayer and Contemplation" continues and develops this line of thought, which would occupy Merton's attention for years to come. Although he became a champion of the contemplative life and encouraged it in monks who were disposed for this kind of quiet resting in God, he also believed in the need for prayer in community, and for the monk this meant the Divine Office and the Eucharist. He saw liturgical prayer and mental or contemplative prayer as complementary, not opposed to each other.

Dedicated in respectful gratitude to
Rev. Father Paul Philippe, O.P.

A BALANCED LIFE OF PRAYER[1]

1—The Object of the Life of Prayer

St. Paul told the Thessalonians to "pray without ceasing" (I Thess. 5:17). At first that sounds rather hard, especially when we reflect that this is not a counsel but a commandment which cannot be ignored. And yet it is really quite simple. It is just as if Our Lord told us "You must keep on breathing, or else you will die." The only difference is this: breathing is instinctive, prayer is not. But by rights prayer ought to be just as instinctive as breathing.

Prayer is as important for the life of the soul as breathing is for the life of the body. That is why the Gospel tells us "we ought always to pray and never to give up" (Luke 18:1).

If Adam had never fallen, prayer would have been second nature to us. But Christ, the New Adam, has raised up the whole human race to a heavenly life, restoring to man the grace which Adam lost and endowing our souls with the theological virtues and Gifts of the Holy Ghost which are the "organs" or faculties of our new supernatural being. By means of these faculties we can learn gradually to inhale and exhale in a manner that is inexpressibly wonderful because it is divine. For then we shall constantly be breathing with the very "breath" of God, that is to say we shall receive into our souls the "spiration" of the Holy Spirit, and we shall mystically "breathe" this Divine Spirit of Love back into God, since the Father and the Son, dwelling within us, "breathe" forth their mutual love in our souls. Their love for us becomes our love for them.

We are united to God as St. Bernard says, by the bond which unites the Father and the Son, Let us take courage then, and sing with

---

[1] Editor's Note: This text is published as it originally appeared. I have made no changes in the text. I have respected the integrity of Merton's writing and have avoided trying to make his language more gender inclusive. M.D.

the Psalmist: "I opened my mouth and gasped for breath because I longed for thy commandments" *Aperui os meum et attraxi spiritum, quia mandata tua desiderabam* (Psalm 118:131). It is theologically correct to apply this line to the thought we have just expressed, because the ardent desire to do the will of God is what draws the "breath" of the Holy Spirit of Love to enliven our souls.

It is by prayer that we lay open our souls to God and seek to "breathe" His life. The supreme object of prayer is the fulfilment of God's Will.

A Practical Ideal

Someone will protest that this ideal is all very well for Carmelite Nuns and Cistercians, but what does it have to do with Laymen absorbed in business? With politicians, and with men of war?

They are the ones who most of all need to pray. The chaos of modern society is the result of our godlessness. The disintegration of our world is the corruption of a dead body that has lost the life of prayer.

The light of God enlightens every man who comes into this world. What does that mean? It means that there never was and never will be a man born who was not designed, by God, to become a saint. His plan for each human soul is sanctity, beatitude, union with God in heaven, perfect vision, perfect love, perfect happiness. This fulfilment exceeds everything that is due to nature or imaginable by nature. "No eye has ever seen and no ear has ever heard the things that God has prepared for those who love Him, and it has not even entered into the heart of man to imagine what they are like" (I Corinthians 2:9).

Why is it that men do not become saints? Not because God does not give them the grace to do so, but because they neglect the grace He gives them. In order to become saints, they have only to desire sanctity with an efficacious desire that embraces the God-given means to that end. The first and most fundamental expression of this desire is: *prayer*.

His Holiness Pope Pius XII has insisted on this in a recent document which will rank among the most important to have proceeded from the Holy See in our times. *Menti Nostrae* (Sept 23, 1950) is addressed primarily to the Catholic Priesthood but its teachings can also be applied, with only slight modification, to all Christians. An important section of this letter of the Holy Father once again reproves the "heresy of action" which is one of the characteristic evils of our time. His Holiness defines the "heresy of action" as the activity "which is not based on the help of grace and *does not make constant use of the means, necessary to the pursuit of sanctity,* given us by Christ."

One of the most important of these means is prayer.

Sanctity Should Be Normal

A life of sanctity and even in some sense a life of contemplation ought to be the normal development of our baptismal vocation. Let no one think such a claim is exaggerated. Pope Pius XII says explicitly in his Encyclical *Mediator Dei* that: *"The ideal of the Christian life is that each one be united to God in the closest and most intimate manner."* The context explains that this is the whole reason for the complex liturgical life of the Catholic Church. At the beginning of *Menti Nostrae* His Holiness also points out that perfect charity which embraces all the virtues and constitutes sanctity or Christian perfection, ought to be the object of the constant striving of every man. The Holy Father says: "In whatever circumstances a man is placed he should direct his intentions and his actions toward this end." This is a sweeping statement. It allows of no exceptions. It includes everyone, from the cloistered nun to the busy housewife, the priest, the lawyer, the doctor, the mechanic, the farmer. No one is excepted. No moment of man's life is excluded from this law. At all times, no matter where we are and what we are doing, our intentions should be at least virtually directed toward the perfect union of love with God, and all our actions should be carrying us forward, in some way or other, toward that end. This does not mean that we can no longer lead ordinary lives. But our work, our duties and all our interests must be transfigured by a supernatural intention, divinized by charity so that even our most common and routine actions can become a sacrifice of praise to God.

There is only one way in which this can be done: *by a life of prayer.*

2—Obstacles to the Life of Prayer— How to Overcome Them

There are many obstacles to the life of prayer. One of the most important of these is *ignorance.* So many people do not really know what prayer is.

They know that when they were children their mothers taught them to kneel down and recite some words before going to bed. They vaguely remember that something in their nature told them instinctively that this was a good and fitting thing to do. Yet later on they forgot to do it any more.

At other times they wander into a church and hear groups of people saying the Rosary together or reciting other vocal prayers. It seems to be a good thing. But yet the meaning of it all does not quite register, as the saying goes.

What is the trouble? Prayer cannot properly be understood if we see only the surface, the accidentals. The essence of prayer does not consist in kneeling down or assuming some other position, nor does it even consist in reciting certain set forms of words. Still less is the value of prayer measured by the amount of time you spend on your knees or by the number of words you recite.

There are two popular definitions of prayer. One that it is a "lifting of the mind and heart to God" and the other that it is "asking God for things that are for our good." Both of these really come to the same thing. We cannot ask God intelligently for anything unless we lift our minds and hearts to Him and we cannot raise our souls to Him without asking Him at least to hear us and to receive our prayer!

Intelligence and Love

First of all, prayer is a spiritual activity. This activity engages the highest faculties of our soul, our mind and our will. To be valid, prayer must be intelligent and it must be an act of sincere love. Already we can see that prayer is one of the most perfect actions a man can perform. When we pray properly we are exercising our intelligence and we are working with our will. This cannot be done without interior discipline. The more we practice prayer the stronger do these higher faculties become, and so they regain their lost control over the passions which are the root of all prejudice and of all error. Thus, in the natural order alone, the true practice of prayer would be sufficient to elevate and purify the soul to some extent. But this presupposes that prayer is really *prayer* and not pious automatism, or mere exterior formalism, or, worse still, an act of blind superstition. These dangers must all be obviated by the constant striving for *intelligent attention* and for a sincere, earnest and fervent *intention* of the will.

One of the greatest works a man can perform is to devote his life to the constant purification of the thought and love which go to make up his interior life. In so doing, he offers the best that is in him to God. And besides, since man's body and soul form a single vital unit, a reasonable person, we cannot elevate our minds and hearts to God without also at the same time consecrating to Him our bodies and the work of our hands. What is more, when our work belongs to God it consecrates to Him everything that we work with. Thus the man of prayer not only sanctifies himself but sanctifies everything around him, and makes the whole world resound with the praise of its Creator.

Divine Grace

So far we have considered only the human agent at work in prayer. We have spoken as if prayer were an act man performed all by himself and as if God were a distant and silent listener. Actually, this is not enough. The prayer of a Christian must be strictly supernatural. That is to say it must be a *divine* activity produced in us, with our free cooperation, by God's grace. St. Paul tells us that the Holy Spirit not only teaches us how to pray but actually prays in our souls with movements of desire that are like deep, unheard sighs in the secret places of the soul. These cries of the Divine Spirit in the depths of our being are rendered in the familiar Douay translation of the Bible by a rather baffling expression: "For we know not what we should pray for as we ought; but the Spirit Himself asketh for us with unspeakable groanings" (Romans, 8:26). Some who do not grasp the import of this quaint turn of phrase never recognize in themselves the sweet and profound inspirations of love and desire with which Divine grace touches their souls and awakens them to pray.

If prayer proceeds from grace, that is from the divine power that floods our souls when they become Temples of God and shine with the light of His presence, grace must also make use of other instruments or faculties. These "faculties" are the infused virtues, especially the theological virtues of faith, hope and charity. Faith is a habit which elevates our intelligence in a mysterious manner to a level far above our own nature so that we can grasp the mysteries which God alone reveals because He alone contemplates their infinite intelligibility. Hope and love endow our wills with supernatural power and make us cling to God with our whole being, so that we become "one spirit" with Him (I Cor. 6:17).

The amazing consequence of all this is that as soon as the soul is inspired to pray, *it can be morally certain of the presence and action of God within itself.*

St. Paul assures us that we cannot even call upon the Name of Jesus with meritorious sentiments of love and trust unless the Holy Spirit inspires us to do so. Now the Holy Spirit is present wherever He acts, and in any case this inspiration is only attributed to the Holy Spirit, being, in actual fact, common to the Three Divine Persons. Hence no matter how terrible your state may seem to be, no matter how bitterly you are attacked by temptations, and no matter how perturbed your imagination may be with dark thoughts and terrifying images, no matter what may have been your past sins, you could not call upon the Redeemer with love and faith unless God were at work within you, pouring grace into your soul and moving you to pray. It follows that at such a time, God is making Himself intimately present to you in the operation of His grace. If you turn to Him and receive the love He offers you, you have placed your foot upon the narrow path that leads straight upward to the summit of sanctity. But you must be prepared to continue the long journey and to overcome many obstacles before you reach the goal.

Nevertheless, remember that you could not begin to love God unless God had first loved you. St. John tells us so explicitly: "In this is charity: not as though we had loved God, but because He hath first loved us and sent His Son to be a propitiation for our sins" (I John, 4:10).

The Parable of The Sower

In the Parable of the Sower, Jesus compares this good beginning to the sowing of a seed. Many men feel the impulse to pray. There is no man who reaches the age of reason and does not at some time or other feel impelled to turn to God. But many reject this inspiration. No doubt a large number fail to go on with prayer because they have no idea what it is all about. The vast majority of mankind is plunged in almost total ignorance of the things of God. That is why Jesus said that some of the seed fell by the wayside, and was snatched up by birds—the devils carry it away. This is the trouble with minds that are blinded by prejudice or superstition or else held in complete captivity by falsity and attachment to sin.

At other times, the inspirations of grace and the seed of the divine word fall upon souls that are like rock. They are to some extent willing to receive God's truth. They at least expose their minds to some book or some radio sermon. They consider it for a moment and find that it has a certain appeal. But they do not allow the seed to take root. Why is this? Because they weigh God's truth in the balance of purely natural considerations. They will listen to a sermon if it is well-preached and they will read a book if it is a best-seller. But the trouble is they listen to any good speaker and they read all the best sellers. They accept, with complete indifference, all kinds of contradictory doctrines provided they happen to be in fashion at the moment. Ours is a society in which the Truth is only sometimes fashionable.

But the greatest tragedy is that of men who are capable of leading lives of prayer but never do so. They are intelligent. They have good will and they lead good and even religious lives. It may be that they even consecrate themselves to God. But they do not take the trouble to develop their supernatural "talents." They do not cultivate the good ground of their soul. It becomes overgrown with thorns and weeds and the seed of God's word is choked to death by business, pleasures and all the cares and anxieties which preoccupy the children of this world.

Asceticism

It is hard work to keep our souls clear of these weeds. But we are obliged to do so if we wish to preserve the divine life within us and bear fruit for the glory of God in lives of prayer.

Our most important work in life is the job of keeping our souls and their faculties clear and unobstructed so that they can always, under all circumstances, respond to God's grace. Our life of prayer must always, at the same time, be a life of sacrifice. Otherwise our prayer will easily degenerate into routine and formalism. Thought will give place to mere habit, attention will be lost in distractions, love will cool and turn into indifference.

However, if we seek to overcome all these defects by a mere violent application of our will, by the miltiplication of more prayers, by longer periods of prayer coupled with mental exertion we shall not do much to remedy matters.

It is very necessary for religious people to be on their guard against sentimentality. Some people do not know the difference between sentimentality and love, or the distinction between love and charity. Love is a movement of the will toward an object that is at least apparently good. Love is objective and concrete. Charity is supernatural love, prompted by divine grace and terminating in God Himself, who is the Infinite Good. Charity too is supremely concrete and objective. *Sentimentality* on the other hand is a weak, superficial emotion in which the will is not really directed to a definite object but rather rebounds from the object, and turns inward upon itself in order to feast on feelings and imagination.

When this definition of sentimentality is understood, we can see that it is an extremely dangerous thing. Sentimentality makes human love selfish, insipid and maudlin. It tends to destroy charity at its very roots. Sentimentality is essentially ego-centric and therefore futile, but charity, which is the very essence of spiritual life and of perfection, involves the complete gift of ourselves to the Infinite God. The sentimental mind gradually succumbs to a vicious inclination to substitute the *imaginary* for the *real*. Religious sentimentalism pretends to love God, pretends to pray, but actually exhausts the soul in futile emotions and in the cult of sweet interior feelings without any real self-sacrifice, humility, or consideration for one's neighbor.

Balance and Freedom

Intelligence and love are the hall-marks of true spirituality. Intelligence brings order and balance into everything we do. Our first concern should be to make use of the best means to liberate all our capacities to pray, to give ourselves room to develop. A life of prayer must, like every other life, receive constant and sufficient nourishment. It must have room to expand and grow. It must be rich, deep, spontaneous and, in the best sense, free. But freedom is incompatible with anarchy. It requires direction. For all these elements we can do no better than consult the mind of the Church herself.

The Modern Popes have constantly insisted on the need for *balance* and *fullness* in the Catholic's life of prayer. The word "catholic" means "universal," "all-embracing." *Catholic prayer should then allow full expression to every genuine religious need of the human soul.*

Now every man is at the same time an individual person and a member of society. He is therefore instinctively impelled to worship God both as an individual and as a member of society. Furthermore, he belongs to more than one society. The Church has never sought to force men into a mould. The Church is practically the only Body in the world today that has a complete awareness of and respect for the dignity of the human person as well as a full understanding of the needs of particular local and national groups. A balanced life of prayer must therefore be one in which a man is able:

(1) To pray to God in the universally valid public prayer of the Mystical Body of Christ, a prayer based on the eternal truths of dogma and centered in the supremely efficacious redemptive action of the Liturgical Mysteries;

(2) To pray to God publicly according to the needs and the situation of a particular time, race, nation, region, and so forth;

(3) To arrive at the most intimately personal communion with God in the solitude of his own heart.

The first need is satisfied by the *Liturgy,* above all by the *Holy Mass.* The second need is satisfied by *non-liturgical* devotions, both public and private (for instance devotions to St. Anne, in Quebec; pilgrimages to St. James of Compostella in the Middle Ages; devotion to Our Lady of Fatima in the twentieth century, etc.). The third need, which is usually the least recognized, demands to be satisfied by *mental prayer, contemplation* and a life of sustained personal union with God.

A Dangerous Error

Pius XII has characterized as "false, insidious and pernicious" the error of those who taught that there was no place in the life of prayer for what they called "subjective piety" (groups 2 and especially 3 above). This error wanted to make us believe that the *only* kind of prayer worthy of consideration was liturgical public prayer, and that one could not reconcile this public prayer with individual asceticism and contemplation. Pius XII says: "Unquestionably liturgical prayer is *superior in excellence* to private prayers but this does *not at all imply contrast or incompatibility* between these two kinds of prayer." (*Mediator Dei*)

3—Public Prayer and Sacrifice

Pope Pius XII reminds us, in *Mediator Dei,* that man has a fundamental duty to orientate his entire being and his life to God. This orientation is obligatory not only for each individual but for every level of human society and for mankind at large. Personal life, family life, civic life, and every aspect of human existence is bound by the natural law to be centered upon God the Creator of all life and the source and guarantee of all order. Failure to obey this law, which is implanted in us as one of the deepest needs of human nature, results in the terror and carnage of a time like our own.

This orientation of man to God means three things: the acknowledgment of His supreme authority, the submissive acceptance of His Truth and complete obedience to His divine Law. Now although these obligations are binding upon us by our very nature, nature alone does not adequately fulfil them. This is because all men are now living, in actual fact, in a supernatural order in which these obligations exceed the capacities of our nature. The mission of the Church on earth is to bring all men and all human society to a life centered in God. This she does by her teaching authority, by her judiciary power and above all by her work of sanctification. This is centered in the public prayer and the Sacramental Life of the Church which finds its highest expression in the Holy Sacrifice of the Mass.

Transformation in Christ

As Pius XII says, the orientation of mankind to God is fully achieved only when "Christ lives and thrives as it were in the hearts of men and when men's hearts are fashioned and expanded as though by Christ." *(Mediator Dei)* This implies something more than the adaptation of men's minds to the doctrine of Christ, for Christianity is more than a doctrine. The fullest expression of the ideal proposed to us by the Church is nothing less than mystical *transformation* in Christ. The chief means of this transformation is Christ's Holy Sacrifice.

When they declare that we must strive after the most intimate union with God and orientate our whole lives towards Him, the Encyclicals of Pius XII are not proposing a vague ideal. The meaning of this terminology is quite precise and the means to arrive at this end are well defined. The foundation of the life of prayer is *active participation* in the Holy Sacrifice of the Mass.

Some people think that "active participation" in the Mass means busily leafing through a missal in order to follow the priest at the altar. It is quite true that the use of a missal should normally be a great *help* towards this active participation. But neither the use of a missal nor participation in a dialogue-Mass constitutes the essence of true active participation in the Holy Sacrifice.

There are two ways in which we actively participate in a sacrifice: as *priests* and as *victims*. Only the Sacrament of Holy Orders can give us the power to share in the strict sense in the priesthood of Christ at Mass. The priest consecrates the Sacred Species in the Person of Christ, acting as an instrument of God, because his soul is marked with an indelible character conforming it to the soul of Christ as priest. But all the faithful are priests in a broad sense because their *baptismal character* conforms them to Christ and they are able to offer the Holy Sacrifice by uniting their intentions with those of the priest.

Besides participating in the Mass as priests we have not only the privilege but the *obligation* of participating in it as victims. This, says Pius XII, is necessary if the sacrifice is to have its full effect. *(Mediator Dei)* In *Menti Nostrae* the Holy Father insists, in the strongest terms, that the priest has a special obligation to unite himself with Christ as victim and offer himself to the heavenly Father in union with Jesus on the altar.

This conformity with Christ as priest and victim is the very essence of liturgical contemplation. Without it, liturgy is an empty form or at best an academic and social function. What does this conformity mean in practice? The very heart of the Liturgical year is Holy Week, when the Church celebrates the institution of the Holy Mysteries and the Redemptive Sacrifice of Christ on the Cross. All through Holy Week the liturgy resounds with the words of St. Paul: *"Let this mind be in you* which was also in Christ Jesus . . . Who emptied Himself, taking the form of a servant . . . and humbled Himself becoming obedient unto death, even to the death of the Cross"* (Philippians 2:5-8). These words are a concise expression of what it means to participate actively in the sacrifice of Christ. This participation means *conforming our minds and hearts* ("Let this mind be in you") to the obedience and the humility and the total self-oblation of our Divine Redeemer in His death on the Cross for love of us. Active participation in the liturgy is therefore not mere artistic appreciation of the prayers and chant and ceremonies; it is the gift of ourselves in union with the Sacrifice on the Altar, in an act which involves the practice of the highest virtues and above all of perfect charity. Mass is the early Christian *Agape* or feast of love. We know that we have truly taken active part in it not when we have savored the beautiful prayers but when we come forth from the Church inspired with deep contrition for our sins, filled with the resolution to lead new lives for love of Christ and above all united to our neighbors in sincere and unselfish love. Pius XII says, in clear and simple words: "All the elements of the liturgy would have us reproduce in our hearts the likeness of the Divine Redeemer through the mystery of the Cross." *(Mediator Dei)*

Humility and Obedience

The orientation of the faithful to God means, in actual practice, that they must all make the Mass the most important thing in their lives and direct their strivings in the most concrete possible way to union with the Crucified Savior. Pius XII says this most explicitly in *Menti Nostrae*. The priest "must orient his life towards that sacrifice in which he must needs offer and immolate himself with Christ." In an earlier paragraph, Pope Pius XII explained just what was the essence of this self-immolation, from an ascetic point of view. Our immolation is above all a sacrifice of our *will*. This is not merely a blind renunciation of liberty, but an enlightened and glorious obedience guided by humility and therefore perfectly conformed to Truth. The Holy Father says: "The spirit of humility illumined by faith, disposes the soul to immolation of the will by means of obedience." *(Menti Nostrae)* It is in this way above all that we reproduce in our souls the likeness of the Redeemer who for our sakes "became obedient unto death."

Thought and Sacrifice

The most effective way of participating in the Liturgy is to follow as intelligently as we can the deep dogmatic meaning of the prayers and rites in order that our hearts may share the dispositions which liturgical prayer is meant to arouse. These dispositions are none other than those of Christ Himself. For Catholic Doctrine teaches that the prayer of the Church is the prayer of Christ. As Pope Pius XII says in *Mediator Dei*, "Through His Spirit in us, Christ entreats the Father." This is merely an echo of St. Paul. It is quite clear then that we should make every effort to understand the liturgy in order that we might "make our own those sentiments in which we are elevated to heaven." *(Mediator Dei)*

It may require effort to enter into the beauties of the liturgy. The prayers of the Missal form the matter for real and serious study. But anyone who undertakes this effort will find himself richly rewarded. The theological content of the Missal, made up as it is of the most beautiful texts of Sacred Scripture and the liturgical compositions of the Church, is one of the greatest treasures we have on earth. To pray with the Church, in the Liturgy, is a guarantee that our prayer is *intelligent* and that our hearts will be protected against the menace of sentimentality. The Liturgy is *never sentimental*. Always calm, objective and serene, it meditates upon the Mysteries of Faith with clear-sighted objectivity. Liturgical prayer is a true school of enlightenment and order. And yet this prayer which by its universality is adapted to all men of every race and century, nevertheless permits each individual to give expression to his deepest personal needs and to arrive at the most intimate contact with God in the secret depths of his own soul. Thus the Liturgy, far from being cold, enkindles in us the purest and most powerful of loves, and strengthens the soul with a charity that will sooner or later effect our complete transformation in Christ.

Non-liturgical Devotions

It should not be necessary to add that there are other forms of devotion which play an integral part in Catholic life. These devotions are non-liturgical. They do not form part of the official public prayer of the Church. Nevertheless everyone knows that the Rosary, for instance, is almost as characteristically Catholic as the Mass itself!

For this reason it would be quite wrong to suppose that non-liturgical devotions are merely an expedient which the Church tolerates in order to satisfy the spiritual needs of those who cannot enter more fully into the meaning of the Liturgy. We cannot believe that the Liturgy alone dispenses a man from these other, simpler devotions which generally attach themselves to some particular aspect or phase of Catholic life. A truly balanced life of prayer demands a certain element of non-liturgical devotion. The Rosary did not exist in the time of the Church Fathers, yet nevertheless they had an intense and simple devotion to the Blessed Virgin Mary. This is proved by their writings in her honor and by the dogmatic declarations of the Council of Ephesus (431 A.D.). There has always existed devotion to our Lady outside the Liturgy, but this devotion takes different forms in different ages.

Non-liturgical devotions are extremely numerous. Some of them are only temporary. Others, like the Rosary, the Stations of the Cross and Benediction of the Blessed Sacrament have finally entered into the permanent heritage of Catholic piety.

The use of non-liturgical devotions must be marked at the same time with *freedom* and with *discretion*. The faithful must be allowed freely to follow their attraction to any devotion approved by Ecclesiastical Superiors. On the other hand, we must take care to test the spiritual value of our attractions to *new devotions* and to restrain a vain and curious multiplication of devotional practices, at the expense of a deep interior life.

In a balanced spiritual life, one or two well established non-liturgical devotions (especially the Rosary) will always play a part. Besides these, the individual will feel attracted to a few particular saints, to the special use of certain prayers and pious practices. This attraction ought to be marked by order and moderation. We must at all costs avoid levity and superficiality in our devotions.

It is to be noticed that the Holy See has issued special warnings, in our time, against the superstitious credulity with which some of the faithful rush to the scene of so-called "apparitions" and "miracles." The true Catholic sense will prompt us to accept all unusual manifestations of the "supernatural" with discreet reserve.

4—Mental Prayer and Contemplation

From what has been said about the Liturgy, it is clear that a fully active participation in the Mass implies some sort of "mental power." Of course, liturgical prayer is essentially vocal prayer. But the vocal prayers of the liturgy are meant to stimulate acts of thought and affection in our hearts which turn into mental prayer and even into contemplation. When the priest leaves the altar, and when the communicant returns from the communion rail, the soul should find itself aflame with light and love, and the normal effect of Holy Communion should be a period of deep absorption in the transforming action of the Blessed Sacrament.

As St. Benedict foresaw, in his great monastic rule (6th century) liturgical prayer tends to prolong itself in private contemplation. But this contemplative effect will be less powerful if we do not understand the message of the liturgical texts. Hence, mental prayer also plays an important part in preparing us for the liturgy. The beginner in the spiritual life ought assiduously to meditate on the prayers of the Missal and above all on the Gospels and Epistles of the various feasts and Sundays. For here he will absorb the word of God which is the true seed of contemplation. Therefore Pius XII says that mental prayer is "the *best means* of preparation before and thanksgiving after Mass (and communion)." *(Menti Nostrae)*

In this particular passage the Holy Father was not referring especially to meditation on the liturgy. He was insisting on the immense importance of mental prayer as such. His remarks are addressed to priests, but they apply to all Christians, though perhaps with somewhat less urgency.

Piux XII insists that without meditation we cannot acquire perfect dominion over ourselves and our senses, we cannot purify our hearts and live true lives of virtue and we cannot generously and faithfully carry out our duties as priests (or as religious or even active Christians). So great is the importance of mental prayer that the Holy Father insists upon it in the strongest possible terms. Here are his words:

"IT MUST THEREFORE BE SAID WITHOUT RESERVATION THAT NO OTHER MEANS HAS THE UNIQUE EFFICACY OF MEDITATION AND IN CONSEQUENCE ITS DAILY PRACTICE CAN IN NO WISE BE SUBSTITUTED FOR." *(Menti Nostrae)*

This declaration is addressed to priests but applies with equal force to all clerics and religious to whom meditation is recommended by the law of the Church. The Catholic layman will also do well to take it to heart.

Everyone should read the passage in the Autobiography of St. Theresa of Avila in which she describes the benefits of mental prayer *(Life, ch. 8)*. She says, among other things, that when a person takes up the practice of meditation, "if that soul perseveres notwithstanding the sins, temptations and falls of a thousand kinds into which the devil leads it, the Lord, I am certain, will bring it to the harbor of salvation."

Now this is not like the specious claims that are sometimes put forth for the recitation of this or that "efficacious prayer." St. Theresa's words have a solid foundation not only in theology but in plain common sense. The true practice of mental prayer fulfils all the conditions that we laid down at the beginning of this essay. It raises the mind to God in thought, unites the heart to Him in love, purifies the whole soul by the action of grace and the theological virtues, enables it to overcome all deliberate sin and disposes it proximately for the gift of mystical contemplation.

What is meditation? St. Thomas and St. Bernard describe mental prayer *(consideratio)* as the "quest for truth" *(inquisitio veritatis)*. Intellectual study is also a quest for truth. But if mental prayer is study and nothing more it will not be of very great profit to the soul. The distinctive element of mental prayer is that it is a search that *springs from love and ends in greater love.* St. Albert the Great points out that "the contemplation of philosophers seeks nothing but the perfection of the one contemplating and it goes no further than the intellect. But the contemplation of the saints is *fired by the love of the One contemplated, that is God.* Therefore it does not come to an end in an act of intelligence but passes on to the will by love." His great disciple, St. Thomas Aquinas, remarks tersely that for this very reason the contemplative's knowledge of the highest truth is a knowledge arrived at, at least on this earth, by the light of burning love: *per ardorem caritatis datur cognitio veritatis* (Commentary on St. John's Gospel, ch. 5).

The mind and will must work together in mental prayer. But they must not seek proficiency in meditation merely for its own sake alone. The Christian contemplative is not interested in simply becoming a disciplined adept, who can confront the evils of life with supreme indifference because he knows how to recollect himself and hold his mind above them. The only function of mental prayer for a Catholic is union with God through Jesus Christ. Now when we look closely at this function we find that the object of mental prayer and the object of liturgical prayer are ultimately one and the same thing: "Let this mind be in you that was also in Christ Jesus." It is perfect conformity with Christ's obedience, love and self-oblation in order that through His Sacrifice we may be united to the Father. Hence the fruits of a good meditation will be much the same as the fruits of active participation in the Sacrifice of the Mass.

The peculiar value of meditation is that it is more *personal* and *private* and therefore allows us to develop in the way that is demanded by our own personal needs, our temperament, character, our work, our surroundings and all the rest.

It is a shame that meditation is sometimes a dreary and stereotyped "exercise." Above all at the time of mental prayer the soul should be allowed all freedom for spontaneous and personal communion with God. Meditation is best practiced in an atmosphere of silence and peace. Solitude is a great help in mental prayer. But each individual ought to find the time and place that is best for him or her. Without prejudice to the schedule prescribed by a religious rule, we can reserve one of our free intervals for the practice of solitary communion with God under the conditions most favorable for our own souls. Many who simply fall asleep when they make their meditation sitting together in chapel would profit greatly by learning to commune with God out under the sky, or alone in their room. It is of course quite obvious that the most fruitful moments of mental prayer will come to us in our private visits to Jesus in the Blessed Sacrament when the chapel is quiet and we are practically alone with Him.

But these factors are external and accidental. The great benefit of mental prayer is that it brings us quickly into communion with the Three Divine Persons dwelling in the depths of our souls. This is the proximate end that we should aim at in all our mental prayer: a vital and loving awareness of the presence of God. We should reflect on these words of St. John of the Cross: "Oh thou soul, most beautiful of creatures, who so ardently longest to know the place where thy Beloved is, that thou mayest seek Him and be united to Him, *thou art thyself that very tabernacle where He dwells,* the secret chamber of His retreat where He is hidden!" (Spiritual Canticle)

The Sacraments, working *ex opere operato,* are the normal means by which this secret presence of God is conferred upon the soul and gains greater possession of our being. Nevertheless, if God comes to dwell in us as in His temple it is above all in order that He may be known and worshipped there. It is a tragedy that so few know how to take advantage of the graces conferred upon them by the Sacraments in order to retire within their hearts and rest in silent adoration of their Divine Guest. Jesus gave us Holy Communion not only in order to refresh and nourish our souls from time to time, but in order that He might feast with us in our hearts in a perpetual banquet of the Spirit. And in this banquet there is no weariness because spiritual joys, unlike those of sense, increase our hunger while we taste of them. This is exactly the opposite to the pleasures of sense which nauseate us when we take our fill. Jesus tells us in the *Apocalypse* of His desire for this intimate and silent communion with souls who give themselves to Him in lives of prayer: "Behold I stand at the gate and knock. If any man shall hear my voice and open to me, I will come in to him and will sup with him, and he with me" (Apoc. 3:20).

The ways of mental prayer do not always lead us through sweetness and consolation. On the contrary, in order to raise us above our nature and enable us to taste the pure joys of mystical union, the Holy

Spirit purifies the soul and detaches our weak human senses from interior consolation. The secret of progress in mental prayer lies above all in the humble acceptance of spiritual dryness and interior trial. But here we are close to the heart of the matter, because in mental prayer, more than any other, the way to perfection is the way of the Cross.

The End

Ex Parte Ordinis—
*Nihil Obstat—*fr M. Paul Bourne, O.C.S.O.
fr M. Maurice Molloy, O.C.S.O.

Censores deputati.
Imprimi Potest
fr M. Dominique Nogues, O.C.S.O.
Abbas Generalis

*

Imprimatur:

✝JOHN A. FLOERSH,
Archbishop of Louisville
July 30th, 1951

Contemplation Reconsidered: The Human Way In

Parker J. Palmer

As I was preparing this essay, I remembered a correspondence Thomas Merton once had with a scholar named Louis Massignon, who had been instrumental in lifting up the life and work of a ninth-century Muslim mystic named al-Hallaj. When Massignon was asked about his scholarship on this mystic, he said that his relation to al-Hallaj was not so much that of scholar to subject as it was "a friendship, a love, a rescue." Massignon did not mean that he had rescued al-Hallaj from historical obscurity but that al-Hallaj had somehow reached out across time to rescue him.

That is how I feel about my own relation to Thomas Merton. I never met Merton and I am not a Merton scholar. I discovered his books only after he had died—I was raised as a mainline Protestant, and we are a little slow in these matters. I simply want to share with you something of what Thomas Merton has given me—this Merton who, at a time when I needed it, reached out to me from beyond the great divide and offered friendship and love and rescue.

My remarks will take us through three "movements." Each of them builds on a quotation from Merton's brilliant essay, "The Inner Experience."[1] The first movement is titled "Self-Impersonation as a Way of Being in the World," the second is "Get a Life," and the third is "God is Shy—and So Am I." The images and insights belong to

---

1. Thomas Merton, "The Inner Experience," in *Thomas Merton: Spiritual Master*, ed. with introduction by Lawrence S. Cunningham (Mahwah, N.J.: Paulist, 1992) 294–356.

Merton; I simply attempt to articulate some of the ways they have illumined my own life-journey to this day.

I. Self-Impersonation as a Way of Being in the World

> Reflect, sometimes, on the disquieting fact that most of your statements of opinions, tastes, deeds, desires, hopes and fears are statements about someone who is not really present. When you say "I think," it is often not you who think, but "they"—it is the anonymous authority of the collectivity speaking through your mask. When you say "I want," you are sometimes simply making an automatic gesture of accepting . . . what has been forced upon you. That is to say, you reach out for what you have been made to want.
>
> Who is this "I" that you imagine yourself to be? An easy and pragmatic branch of psychological thought will tell you that if you can [say] your proper name, and declare that you are the bearer of that name, you know who you are. . . . But this is only a beginning. . . . For when a person appears to know his own name, it is still no guarantee that he is aware of the name as representing a real person. On the contrary, it may be the name of a fictitious character occupied in very active self-impersonation in the world of business, of politics, of scholarship or of religion.
>
> This however is not the "I" who can stand in the presence of God and be aware of Him as a "Thou." For this "I" there is perhaps no clear "Thou" at all. Perhaps even other people are merely extensions of the "I," reflections of it . . . aspects of it. Perhaps for this "I" there is no clear distinction between itself and other objects: it may find itself immersed in the world of objects, and to have lost its own subjectivity, even though it may be very conscious and even aggressively definite in saying "I."[2]

I have been meditating for some days on this remarkable diagnosis of the malaise of modern men and women: we are immersed in the world of objects and we have lost our subjectivity. Merton's words lead to some troubling reflections about a sector of our society in which I do a lot of work, education, a sector that has a tremendous impact on the formation and deformation of our souls. Higher education especially does not worry about our immersion in the world of

2. Ibid., 295–296.

objects—indeed, it is obsessed with the opposite phenomenon. Higher education believes that people are lost in subjectivity and must be brought, kicking and screaming, into the world of objects where, it presumes, personal and social health is to be found.

In our educational establishment we are deeply devoted to the notion that knowledge that is not "objective," that does not make the known into an object, is not knowledge worth having—indeed, is not knowledge at all. We believe that until you know a subject at arm's length, as an objectified "thing," you do not have any real knowledge about it at all. We believe that if young people are not taught to objectify the world they will be lost in narcissism and emotion and irrelevance. In fact, we are profoundly afraid of the very subjectivity to which Merton is calling us. We do not value it the way Merton suggests we should—we flee from it as if from a plague.

I have spent this year teaching undergraduates at a small liberal arts college, teaching a course for seniors on vocational discernment and decision-making. On the first day of class I told my students that they would be writing a series of brief papers in which they recalled their own life experience and reflected upon it. At the end of that first session, a young man came up to me and asked, "In those papers you are asking us to write, is it OK to use the word 'I'?"

I said that I could not imagine how to write an autobiographical paper without using the word "I," and then asked him why he asked. "Because," he said, "in my major department I am downgraded a full grade if the word 'I' appears in a paper." We sell students the myth that a paper that says "I believe" is subjective and suspect, while a paper that says "It is believed" is objective knowledge. We do so, I suspect, because faculty themselves have been trained in graduate programs bent on draining us of our personhood and subjectivity and sense of self so that we will become safe bearers of "objective" knowledge, knowledge that gets transmitted to students untouched by human hands. This is why we have such poor writing coming out of the academy—and why we have so little academic knowledge that is of deep human significance, of real human scale.

I have puzzled a great deal about why our education so frequently turns Merton's insight on its head. Why is it that instead of rescuing people from the world of objects and helping them to recover the authentic self, we ask them to sweep self under the rug and lose themselves in a world of objects? To put it more succinctly, why are we so afraid of subjectivity? The answer that comes to me, slowly but persistently, is that we fear the subjective because subjectivity will draw us into relationships with what we know—and in those relationships we will find *ourselves* challenged and changed rather than being forever able to fancy ourselves as those who will change the world.

The poet Rilke once wrote the stunning line, "There is no place at all that is not looking at you—you must change your life."[3] But in academic life we turn that around and teach students how to objectify the world in a way that prevents it from looking back at us.

We teach biology in a way that lets us look at nature and dissect it and experiment upon it without ever letting nature call us to accountability for our consumptive way of living. We teach political science in a way that lets us look at Third World countries and critique the "mess" they are in without letting those cultures look back at us and critique our distorted First World values. We teach literature with the tools of literary criticism without letting the reader encounter the poem or the novel in a personal way that might make a claim on how he or she is living life. Education of this sort turns out people who are very adept at manipulating the external world of objects but who know nothing about what is going on within their own communities or within themselves.

I travel around the country visiting campuses and talking to students, and I often ask them, "When was the last time you were invited to intersect your own story, your 'little' story, with the 'big' story of the disciplines you are studying?" The most common answer I get is, "Never." The entire agenda of our educational institutions is to sweep the student's "little" story under the rug because it is full of bias and prejudice and error, so that the "big" story of objective truth can replace it—and when this is accomplished we believe we have an educated person. But Merton is telling us that what we really end up with is the pathological personality of our time, someone so lost in the world of objects that he or she has no subjective self and thus ends up as "a fictitious character occupied in very active self-impersonation in the world of business, of politics, of scholarship or of religion." If ever a phrase hit uncomfortably close to home, this is it!

3. Rainer Maria Rilke, "Archaic Torso of Apollo," in Robert Bly, trans., *Selected Poems of Rainer Maria Rilke* (New York: Harper, 1981).

I think often of a particular deformation in my own education that may make my point clearer and weightier. I was educated at some of the best schools in this country about the horrors that go under the name of the Third Reich. I was taught about the murder of six million Jews—and of countless gay and lesbian people and gypsies and people with retardation and protesting Christians and others who did not fit the Nazi mold—but I was taught about all of this in a way that left me with the impression that it had all happened on another planet, to another species. My teachers never said, "Other planet, other species," but they taught me about these things at such objective distance, at such arm's length, that I was left with the sense that none of them had anything to do with my own life, my own experience.

We studied the Holocaust almost exclusively through words and numbers about it. We never looked at the heart-wrenching art created in those camps; we never read the poetry written by the survivors and those who died, and I was well out of school before I saw the photographs of the bodies piled like cordwood at Auschwitz. Why? Because by the canons of objectivism, those data would have been suspiciously subjective. They would have evoked passion and feeling—and to evoke passion and feeling is to destroy the possibility of objective knowledge.

So we stayed with the words and numbers, and my life, as a result, was ethically deformed. Nobody every asked me to intersect the subjective with the objective, my little story with the big story. Nobody ever helped me to understand that the town I grew up in had its own fascist tendencies, to reflect on the fact that the Jews all lived in their own gilded ghetto, two suburbs away. Worse still, nobody ever helped me understand that I have a little Hitler in my own heart—that is, a shadow force that, when the difference between you and me gets too threatening, will attempt to kill you off. I will not do it with a gun or a gas chamber, but with a word, a concept, a dismissive image— "Oh you're just a this or a that. . . ." I will engage in the ultimate objectification, the transformation of a human being into a disposable "thing."

Elie Wiesel has made this point with the power that only a survivor of the death camps can summon:

> How do you describe the sorting out on arriving at Auschwitz, the separation of children who see a father or mother going away, never to be seen again? How do you express the dumb grief of

a little girl and the endless lines of women, children and rabbis being driven across the Polish or Ukrainian landscapes to their deaths? No, I can't do it. And because I'm a writer and teacher, I don't understand how Europe's most cultured nation could have done that. For these men who killed with submachine-guns in the Ukraine were university graduates. Afterwards they would go home and read a poem by Heine. So what happened?[4]

Too many educated people are, as Merton suggests, immersed in a world of objects, lacking authentic subjectivity and engaged in active self-impersonation, living on the outside of their lives and not from the inside out—and our "scientific" mode of education contributes heavily to the pathology. But what amazes me about all this is not only how ethically deforming objectivism is, but how utterly unfaithful it is to the nature of true science as well. The myth of objectivism has nothing to do with real science at all—it has everything to do with the arrogance that leads us to want to believe that we are in charge of the world of objects.

Here is my favorite story from the heart of real science. A year or two ago, the *New York Times* carried a front-page obituary for a woman named Barbara McClintock. McClintock, who died in her early nineties, was arguably the greatest American scientist of the twentieth century and almost certainly the greatest American biologist. As a young woman, McClintock became fascinated with the dynamics of genetic transmission, and she began pursuing hypotheses so outrageous that her science was widely regarded as out of vogue—until she won a Nobel Prize.

When a biographer asked her, late in her life, to describe how she did her great science, McClintock's answer was, "You have to have a feeling for the organism." When the question was pressed further, McClintock, thinking of the ears of corn she had studied for so many years, said, "You must learn to lean into the kernel."[5]

Is this Nobel Laureate saying that objective data and analysis have nothing to do with science? Of course not. But she *is* telling us that science is a profoundly relational activity in which authentic subjectivity is interlaced with rigorous objectivity, a dance of intimacy and

4. From *The Columbia University Dictionary of Quotations* (New York: Columbia University Press, 1993).
5. Evelyn Fox Keller, *A Feeling for the Organism* (New York: Freeman, 1983).

distance which we must learn to do in every dimension of our lives. She is saying that the relation between a geneticist and an ear of corn is not unlike a relationship between two persons—intersubjective, in the deepest sense of that term.

Evelyn Fox Keller, McClintock's biographer, writes a sentence about all of this that I hope I never forget. She says that McClintock, in her relation to ears of corn, achieved the highest form of love—"love that allows for intimacy without the annihilation of difference."[6] What an extraordinary way to assert the same thing that Merton is asserting: if we are to live well, if we are to do science or any other human activity well, we must be liberated from the world of objects and become reconnected with that authentic subjectivity in which both we and the world become real again.

II. Get a Life

> The worst thing that can happen to a person who is already divided up into a dozen different compartments is to seal off yet another compartment and tell him that this one is more important than all the others, and that he must henceforth exercise a special care in keeping it separate from them. That is what tends to happen when contemplation is unwisely thrust without warning upon the bewilderment and distraction of Western man.
>
> The first thing you have to do, before you start thinking about such a thing as contemplation, is to try to recover your basic natural unity, to reintegrate your compartmentalized being into a coordinated and simple whole, and learn to live as a unified human person. This means that you have to bring back together the fragments of your distracted existence so that when you say "I" there is really someone present to support the pronoun you have uttered.[7]

When I first read this selection from "The Inner Experience," I found the opening paragraph deeply insightful—it named everything I have always felt was wrong when "contemplation" is presented as a "fix" or a technique. So when I began reading the second paragraph

---

6. Evelyn Fox Keller, *Reflections on Gender and Science* (New Haven: Yale University Press, 1985) 164.

7. Merton, op. cit., 295.

I thought, "This is great! Now Merton is going to tell me what I have to do in order to have a spiritual life, to recover my authentic self."

Then I read his next words: "The first thing you have to do . . . is to . . . learn to live as a unified human person." I thought, "Right. You bet. Thanks a lot, Tom!" I thought this recovery of self was the pearl of great price that came at the end of long contemplative experience, but here Merton is telling me that it is the first thing I must do before I even think about contemplation!

Then I recalled a remarkable moment in a Merton tape I heard years ago, a tape in which Merton is speaking as novice master to the young monks of Gethsemani. As the tape begins, you can hear the rustling of papers and the sounds of people settling into their chairs. There is a brief silence, and then Merton suddenly blurts out, "Men, before you can have a spiritual life, you've gotta have a life!"

I turned off the tape player at that point while a wave of horror washed over me: "My God, I've got to go out and get a life before I can be spiritual." As I sat there, indicted by that thought, another wave washed over me with the suddenness of insight that comes with a Zen koan: "My God, I've already got a life—and it's a complete mess! It's full of loves and hates, joys and anguish, happiness and defeats! Merton isn't telling me I need to get a different life. He's telling me something much harder—that I must embrace the life I have, the only life I will ever have, as the only true source of my own spirituality."

That, I think, is what Merton is saying in the quote at the beginning of this second movement. Before I can even *think* about contemplation, let alone do it, I must accept the life I have, stop fighting it, embrace the whole of it as the source of my own wholeness. Similar words, words that Merton would have loved, I think, were penned by Florida Scott-Maxwell in *The Measure of My Days*: "You need only claim the events of your life to make yourself yours. When you truly possess all you have been and done . . . you are fierce with reality."[8]

I have a theory that God creates nouns but we create adjectives— which we then use to mess up the lovely nouns God has given us, qualifying them and distorting them beyond recognition. For example, God creates people; then we start piling the adjectives on: male and female people, black and white people, gay and lesbian and straight people, conservative and liberal people, good and bad people. With

8. Florida Scott-Maxwell, *The Measure of My Days* (New York: Knopf, 1979).

the adjectives we make distinctions, usually invidious—and with those distinctions we destroy the essence of created goodness that the original noun embodies.

So God creates the noun "life" and then we louse it up by saying, at some point, "I've got to have a love life," or "I've got to have a professional life," or "I've got to have a successful life," or "I've got to have a spiritual life." I think Merton is calling us back to the nouns that God created in us, back to the givenness and giftedness of our own experience, back to the simplicity and everydayness of our loves and hates, our joys and anguishes, our happinesses and defeats as the source of our deepest treasure—because the adjectives diminish our lives. I am clear that he is telling me, at least, that by seeking a "spiritual" life I may lose the life I have—but by claiming my life as it is I may find what I am seeking, right here, right now.

In earlier years, as I ran headlong after a "spiritual" life, I experimented with different forms of contemplation. I tried techniques beyond number, and none of them worked for me. I finally figured out that I am not a contemplative by intention; I am a contemplative by catastrophe. One of the great gifts of my life has been enough catastrophes that I could have become a world-class contemplative—if I had been paying attention.

Today my definition of contemplation is quite simple: contemplation is any way one has of penetrating illusion and touching reality. If I understand the great mystics correctly, that is what their contemplation was all about: it was not about technique, but about a journey from illusion to reality, a journey that we are given a thousand opportunities to take every day—if we have eyes to see and ears to hear. It is precisely in the ordinary catastrophes of life that we have a chance to distinguish what is real and abiding from what is not.

I think often of a woman I know who is the single mother of a child with severe retardation. This woman does not have an extra five minutes a day to sit cross-legged and chant a mantra, for she must live two lives. If her child is going to move, she must move for him; if her child is going to eat, she must help him eat; if he is going to play, she must be there to play with him.

But despite her lack of "retreat" time, as classically understood, this woman has become a contemplative on the order of Teresa of Avila. In the very raising of her child, she has had to penetrate all the cruel illusions that this society harbors about what makes a human being valuable—things like success and physical beauty and wit—and she has grounded herself in the truth, the reality, that there is an essence of personhood that makes all of us precious just as we are.

If I ask myself when it is in my own life that I penetrate illusion and touch reality, the first answer is "Not often enough." But the second answer is, "When times are tough." Gain and success do not put me into an especially contemplative mood—indeed, they seem to generate more illusions than they penetrate. But failure and loss force me to reflect long and hard on who I am and how I am and where I am, and the result is sometimes a breakthrough into reality.

My father died earlier this year. He was an extraordinary man who surrounded me all my life with love and affirmation and trust—and I am still in the process of penetrating certain illusions about life that I was able to harbor because his presence kept me from having to face the realities behind them. In particular, I am having to deal more directly with the reality called my own mortality which I could somehow evade a bit when my father was still alive.

We moan, sometimes, about the "disillusionments" that come with the hard experiences of life—and if someone comes to us complaining of having been "disillusioned," we tend to put an arm around their shoulders and say, "I'm so very sorry. How can I help?" But if we understood contemplation properly, we would respond quite differently. We would shake their hand, saying, "Congratulations! To be 'dis-illusioned' means that you've just lost another illusion! Tell me, how can I help disillusion you some more?"

In my own life two profound passages of clinical depression have turned out to be times of profound contemplation. There are many different kinds of depression, I think, some of them almost totally biochemical, so I do not mean to generalize about the experience. But my depression was very situational, very much related to choices I had made in my life. I was living the compartmentalized life that Merton describes in the quote at the beginning of this movement—a divided life in which no division ever communicated with any other division.

My life at that time was not like the famous "seven-storey mountain" of Merton's life, but more like a seven-storey apartment building with no stairs and no elevator and no hallways and no telephone system. No communication was going on between the various parts of me, between the good stuff and the bad stuff and all the in-between stuff. I would live out of one or another of those parts at any given time, while hiding the others away, ignoring and denying their existence.

I got great help from a person who said to me, "You seem to keep imaging your depression as the hand of an enemy trying to crush you. Why don't you image it, instead, as the hand of a friend trying to press you down to safe ground on which to stand?" Eventually, I came to understand my depression as a life-giving force bent on demolishing that seven-storey apartment building so that those isolated compartments would have to connect and communicate with one another—so that I would have to move toward wholeness, or die. Wholeness—the movement from self-impersonation to authentic selfhood—is the great gift contemplation can bring, a gift often hard-won through the catastrophes of our lives.

As I bring this movement to a close, I want to note that the gifts contemplation has to offer are not only for individuals but for societies as well. For several years I have been trying to understand the great social movements of our time—the civil rights movement, the women's movement, the liberation of Eastern Europe, the movement for gay and lesbian rights. At the outset of all of these movements, as I understand them, there are people—some now famous, some still obscure—who make a deep inner decision to live "divided no more," people who decide one day that it is no longer tolerable to live one way on the outside while feeling and knowing something completely different on the inside.

I call this "the Rosa Parks decision" because she is so emblematic in our century of the social power of living the undivided life. On December 1, 1955, this forty-two-year-old black seamstress in Montgomery, Alabama, decided that she would no longer sit at the back of the bus, but would sit up front in witness to the fact that she knew herself as a full human being. Years later, someone asked if she had taken that act in order to start the Civil Rights Movement. She said, "I sat down because my feet were tired." Of course, she meant that her heart was tired, her soul was tired, her whole being was tired of living a divided life, of acting as if she were less than fully human.

I have often wondered where people like Rosa Parks get the courage to decide to live divided no more, knowing full well that they will be punished for their acts. From studying her life, and others, I now think I know the answer: that courage comes from realizing that no punishment anyone might ever lay on you could possibly be worse than the punishment that comes from conspiring in one's own diminishment.

The story of Vaclav Havel, the person most responsible for triggering the movement that liberated Czechoslovakia, is parallel to that of Rosa Parks. Years before the so-called "Velvet Revolution" occurred, Havel wrote an open letter of dissent to Gustav Husak, President of Czechoslovakia and head of the Communist Party. Later, when someone asked him if he had written that letter to spark the revolution, Havel answered, "No, I wrote it to keep from committing suicide." It was an act of expressing personal integrity which was taken to change Havel's own life—and ended up changing the world as well.

The words I quoted from Thomas Merton at the beginning of this movement seem daunting, but his advice is actually quite simple and realistic and to the point: "The first thing you have to do, before you start thinking about such a thing as contemplation, is to try to recover your basic natural unity, to reintegrate your compartmentalized being into a coordinated and simple whole, and learn to live as a unified human person." Before we take on anything as complex and challenging as a contemplative life, we need to take on life itself with the simple act of writing that letter of dissent or of sitting at the front of the bus. Once we do, our contemplation will have commenced and nothing will ever be the same.

III. God Is Shy—And So Am I

From what has been said, it is clear that there is and can be no special planned technique for discovering and awakening one's inner self, because the inner self is first of all a spontaneity that is nothing if not free. . . . The inner self is not a part of our being, like a motor in a car . . . It is like life, and it is life: it is our spiritual life when it is most alive. It is the life by which everything else in us lives and moves. . . .

The inner self is as secret as God and, like Him, it evades every concept that tries to seize hold of it with full possession. It is a life that cannot be held and studied as an object, because it is not "a thing." It is not reached and coaxed forth from hiding by any process under the sun, including meditation. All that we can do with any spiritual discipline is produce within ourselves something of the silence, the humility, the detachment, the purity of heart and the indifference which are required if the inner self is to make some shy, unpredictable manifestation of his Presence.[9]

The reason we are so obsessed with technique in our society—in every arena from sex to spirituality—is that we grant all reality and power to the things of the outer world, the world of objects, and "things" always yield to technique. But there is no technique for the inner life because the inner life is not a "thing." It is a world of nearly-invisible truths, of silence and modesty and reticence, whose inhabitants can be encountered only as one is willing to sit quietly and wait for them to come forth. And it is a world of great power, even though our culture ignores and even denies that fact.

Let me illustrate by reflecting for a while on the sources of power in professional life—especially in teaching, the profession I know best—and on how those sources are, or are not, addressed in the way we train professionals. To put it in a nutshell, I am intrigued by the fact that good work in any profession can never be reduced to technique, and yet we prepare people for all the professions with little more than training in technique.

For twenty-five years I have visited schools and colleges around the country, often asking young people, "Who are your great teachers?" The answers I get range all over the map in terms of technique—some great teachers lecture almost non-stop, some do little else but assign a lot of reading and ask a lot of questions, and others fall somewhere in between. The stories I have heard about great teaching have no discernible continuities in terms of technique—but what they do have in common is an emphasis on the qualities of selfhood that great teachers possess and reveal and offer to their students. Students continually say things like, "Professor X is really present when he teaches," or "Professor Y really cares about her subject," or "Professor Z is such a real person—and I would like to be like him some day."

I remember one young woman who said that she could not possibly generalize about her good teachers because they were so different from one another—but she could describe her bad teachers because they were all the same: "Their words float somewhere in front of their faces, like the balloon speech in cartoons." Here is a remarkable, intuitive image of bad teaching—or bad practice in any profession: it hap-

9. Merton, op. cit., 297–298.

pens not simply because of a failure of technique, but because there is a gap between the stuff being taught and the self that is teaching it. Such a teacher is engaged in "active self-impersonation," to use Merton's phrase.

When I hear these stories about the selfhood of good teachers, I marvel again at the fact that our teacher education programs are devoted almost exclusively to technique, and spend little, if any, time helping would-be teachers clarify and confront the self that is the ultimate source of all good work. But rather than merely bemoan that fact, I want to say a few words about a new program for teachers that is attempting to do things differently.

The program is sponsored by a foundation called the Fetzer Institute, which sponsored and helped design the recent Bill Moyers series on public television called "Healing and the Mind." Fetzer is interested in the spiritual dimensions not only of medicine, but of teaching and other professions as well. I am helping them develop the program for teachers, which we have come to call the "Teacher Formation Program."[10]

Just a month and a half before our first, experimental event, a weekend retreat called "The Courage to Teach" aimed at K–12 teachers in central Michigan, we sent out about a couple hundred brochures to as many school principals; we did not have a mailing list of teachers, and we were fearful that the brochures might get buried on the desks of those busy administrators. The brochure said that this retreat would not be about technique or about curriculum reform or about budgetary issues—it would be about the inner life of the teacher, and especially about recovering the heart to teach in these discouraging times for public education.

Within a week or two, we found ourselves overwhelmed with inquiries and applications, including those from principals who wanted to know why this was for teachers only! We selected twenty-two teachers from the one hundred who sent in applications, and we walked together through a three-day retreat of real depth and power. These teachers—many of whom had been at their craft for one or two decades—told us that never before in their careers had they been invited to share and explore and develop their inner lives. Instead, they

10. Information about the Teacher Formation Program can be obtained from The Fetzer Institute, 9292 W. KL Ave., Kalamazoo, MI 49009.

had usually been subjected to a promotion for the "method-of-the-month" that promised to make everything better, or had been berated for being such poor stewards of public funds and public trust.

What we did at the retreat, of course, was to try to create the conditions that would invite, from the group and from each individual, "something of the silence, the humility, the detachment, the purity of heart and the indifference which are required if the inner self is to make some shy, unpredictable manifestation of God's Presence." That is, we approached each other, and our professional lives, with the respect that is due to the dignity and the mystery of the human soul—a respect that seems sorely lacking in the way we train professionals and, not surprisingly, in the way professionals then treat the people whom they are supposed to serve.

In the development of the Teacher Formation Program (which draws heavily on Merton's insights into the nature of spiritual formation), we have been trying consciously to avoid the "manufacturing metaphor" of doing education (or spiritual formation) and turning, instead, to an "agricultural metaphor." The manufacturing model is the dominant one in our society, a model that assumes that the "stuff" we are working with—i.e., the human being—is raw material with little value until we add our technique and our labor to shape it into something worthwhile. This is, of course, a violent way to do anything, and it results in the spread of violence throughout our society.

But the agricultural model is one that respects the a priori reality and fecundity and integrity of the seed—the seed of true self. In this model we know that our task is not to "make" something happen, but to provide the conditions under which the seed can grow. We know that sometimes the weather works for us, and sometimes against us, and we must develop the patience to co-create with whatever weather we get. We know that we cannot force the crop, but must learn how to await the shy, unpredictable springing of the green, and then learn how to nurture it into fuller growth and hearty maturity.

I think again of Rilke, who was in so many ways a soul-mate to Thomas Merton. Rilke wrote, "Love is this—that two solitudes border, protect, and salute one another."[11] He was warning us against the invasive and violent notion we have of how to "love" each other

---

11. Rainer Maria Rilke, *Letters to a Young Poet*, trans. by Stephen Mitchell (New York: Vintage, 1984) 78.

into shape (even if it kills us), spreading the good news that we can best help bring each other into fullness of life by creating quiet and attentive spaces where the God-image that is in us can finally emerge. I give thanks for the life of Thomas Merton, which was lived so deeply in such a space, and for the message of healing and hope that his voice still speaks to us out of the eternal silence.

The Human Way Out:
The Friendship of Charity
as a Countercultural Practice

Paul J. Wadell, C.P.

God has a dream for the world, and God's dream is real and beautiful. God's dream is for absolutely everyone of us to grow to fullness of life and well-being through justice, compassion, and love. God's dream is for all of us to live together in harmony and peace and benevolence, not injustice, violence, and hostility. God's love wish for the world is to bind us together in friendship, care, and mutual affection.

But God's dream is under assault. Something is happening in our society today that is frightening. There seems to be a breakdown in all the things that make life together possible. When we look around we see so many people angry with one another. We see people who have completely forgotten what it means to care for others or how to live with even minimal thoughtfulness. We see so much random cruelty and meanness, so much hatred and viciousness. It really does seem, as Leopold Bloom says in James Joyce's *Ulysses*, that we live in a world "in which everybody is eating everybody else."

We are faced today with a crisis of dehumanization. There are the dehumanizing forces of violence, whether that violence be physical, verbal, psychological, or economic. There are the dehumanizing forces of selfishness and individualism which overlook the centrality of justice and the common good. We are dehumanized through consumerism and materialism, through exploitative and manipulative relationships, and through a kind of moral agnosticism which suggests there are no sure values through which our human dignity is sustained and our spirits perfected. We are dehumanized through the fatal patterns of excessive wealth for some and debilitating poverty for others, in the sad and tragic cycles of family breakdown, and in the growing number of people who seem to be expendable. Is it any wonder people today are losing heart? Are we surprised that the modern maladies of the soul with which we struggle are apathy, a dangerous sense of resignation and defeat, cynicism, and sometimes even hopelessness?

Over thirty years ago in one of *The Cold War Letters*, Thomas Merton spoke of "the human way out."[1] In confronting the fatal patterns of his time, Merton searched for a more truthful and hopeful way of envisioning life. He decried the "sickening inhumanities that are everywhere in the world" and refused to be complacent before them: "They are too awful for human protest to be meaningful,—or so people seem to think. I protest anyway, I am still primitive enough, I have not caught up with this century."[2] In another of *The Cold War Letters* written at New Year's 1962, Merton wrote poignantly of an hour of crisis before which Christians, and all people of good will, must do everything possible to find a way to peace. In a passage remarkably appropriate for our times, Merton said:

> I don't want to waste your time philosophizing. But I do want to say this one thing. We are in an awfully serious hour for Christianity, for our own souls. We are faced with necessity to be very faithful to the Law of Christ, and His truth. This means that we must do everything that we reasonably can to find our way peacefully through the mess we are in. This is becoming harder and harder every day and success seems less and less likely. Yet we remain responsible for doing the things that "are for our peace." . . .
>
> We have to try to some extent to preserve the sanity of this nation, and keep it from going berserk which will be its destruction, and ours, and perhaps also the destruction of Christendom. . . .
>
> I wanted to say these few things, as we enter the New Year. For it is going to be a crucial year, and in it we are going to have to walk sanely, and in faith, and with great sacrifice, and with an almost impossible hope.[3]

1. William H. Shannon, "The Year of the 'Cold War Letters,'" *Toward an Integrated Humanity: Thomas Merton's Journey*, ed. M. Basil Pennington (Kalamazoo: Cistercian Publications, 1988) 166–177.

2. Thomas Merton, *Seeds of Destruction* (New York: Farrar, Straus, Giroux, 1964) 279.

3. Ibid., 266–267.

If we are not to be destroyed by the pathologies of our time, we must do the same. What I want to suggest is that one way to "find our way peacefully through the mess we are in" is by recovering the practice of friendship; however, I have a particular kind of friendship in mind. It is not the friendship of cordial relations and passing acquaintances, but the substantive and challenging friendship of charity.

Thomas Aquinas defined charity as friendship with God and all those God loves, sinners and saints, angels as well as enemies. For him, charity is more than kindness; indeed, charity is a transformative way of life constituted by distinctive virtues such as forbearance, compassion, justice, mercy, and peace. Based on practicing the ways of God, charity is a way of life in which people bear one another's burdens, help and support one another, care for one another, and offer forgiveness when necessary. The human way out of the "sickening inhumanities that are everywhere in the world" lies in embracing the life of charity, and understanding this friendship with God and neighbor not as a cozy, complacent relationship, but as a distinctive social and ecclesial practice powerful and hopeful enough to overcome our crisis of dehumanization by demonstrating that people can live together in benevolence, joy, and peace.

To substantiate this claim, I want to consider four points: (1) what in our culture works against the kind of friendships we need for authentic human living; (2) Aristotle's understanding of virtue friendships and their role in the moral life; (3) Aquinas's description of charity as friendship with God; and (4) why the life of charity challenges our understanding of who is our neighbor, calls us to a different understanding of power, and commits us to being a reconciling and peaceful presence in the world.

I. Cultural Impediments to Friendship

The moral and spiritual life requires friendships of depth, substance, and endurance, but it is exactly these kinds of relationships that cannot be presumed today. We live in a culture that misunderstands, trivializes, and often subverts friendship. How can we build our moral and spiritual lives on friendship when our culture subtly encourages us to use others, claiming them as friends when they are advantageous, abandoning them when they are not? Furthermore, what passes for friendships in our culture are often not friendships at all because they are not relationships capable of bettering the self. They may be relatively superficial acquaintances, passing relationships, or worse, manipulative, unhealthy partnerships in which persons are diminished and sometimes destroyed. Even at their best, such friendships may not be constituted around the kinds of substantive goods necessary for the most promising development of the self. Friendship is a moral skill which demands at least minimal generosity and thoughtfulness, a capacity to care, and at least sufficient justice to recognize how we are obliged to respond to the needs and well-being of others, something not easily presumed in a culture as individualistic as our own.

Rodney Clapp addresses this in his article "The Celebration of Friendship" where he argues that "friendship has become a difficult, even counter-cultural practice" because of a variety of social and cultural forces which sabotage the good and abiding relationships we need for the moral and spiritual life.[4] One of those social forces is consumerism. We live in a culture that is aggressively materialistic, urging us to believe we need things more than we need people. This cultural narrative tells us that we are liberated through what we own, not through friendship, and our identity is measured by our possessions, not by the richness of our loves. People formed by a consumerist society lack the deeper spiritual resources necessary for friendship, particularly justice, genuine benevolence, compassion, and availability. If we believe what we own matters more than whom we love, we will hardly be unselfish enough to seek the good of another for her own sake or to find joy in spending ourselves for her well-being, which is exactly what good friendships require.

In a consumer society, friends are just another commodity to pick up or dispose of as we see fit, novelties that are quickly displaced when something new and more interesting comes along.[5] If our identity is

4. Rodney Clapp, "The Celebration of Friendship," *The Reformed Journal* (August 1989) 11–13.

5. Merton makes a similar point in his essay "Love and Need: Is Love a Package or a Message?" He argues that in our market economy, love and friendship are viewed as an exchange whose sole purpose is the fulfillment of one's needs. When a friend is no longer capable of satisfying those needs, the relationship ends and a new one is sought. See "Love and Need: Is Love a Package or a Message?" *Love and Living*, eds. Naomi Burton Stone and Patrick Hart (New York: Bantam, 1979) 27.

primarily formed by the consumerist narrative of our culture, we will
lack the qualities and dispositions necessary to relate to others on a
deeper level or to be friends in a genuinely humanizing way. Even
more tragically, we will be blind to our need for others because we
will have been fooled by the fantasy that our salvation lies in the clut-
ter of our possessions, rather than in the joy that comes from loving
and being loved.

In his essay "Love and Need: Is Love a Package or a Message?"
Merton makes a similar point. He argues that the language and categories of a market economy have so permeated our culture, including
our understanding of relationships, that we have come to think of
"ourselves and others not as *persons* but as *products*."[6] Love is a form
of salesmanship through which we strive to make ourselves desirable
to others, and this is only possible if we appear to others as worthwhile products through whom they will be fulfilled. "We unconsciously think of ourselves as objects for sale on the market," Merton
writes. "We want to be wanted. We want to attract customers."[7]

But like any product that will soon be surpassed by something
better, our appeal, or another's for us, can only be fleeting. No relationship is lasting because no single person can forever satisfy our
needs; hence, when our needs are no longer being fulfilled, we look
for a more stimulating and exciting product. When friendships and
relationships are viewed on the model of a market exchange, Merton
notes, "We do not give ourselves in love, we make a deal that will
enhance our own product, and therefore no deal is final. Our eyes are
already on the next deal—and this next deal need not necessarily be
with the same customer. Life is more interesting when you make a
lot of deals with a lot of new customers."[8] In a profoundly insightful
passage, Merton describes what happens to love, and hence friendship, when it is seen as nothing more than a market exchange:

> This concept of love assumes that the machinery of buying
> and selling of needs and fulfillment is what makes everything run.
> It regards life as a market and love as a variation on free enter-
> prise. You buy and you sell, and to get somewhere in love is to
> make a good deal with whatever you happen to have available.

6. Ibid., 26.
7. Ibid.
8. Ibid.

In business, buyer and seller get together in the market with their needs and their products. And they swap. The swapping is simplified by the use of a happy-making convenience called money. So too in love. The love relationship is a deal that is arrived at for the satisfaction of mutual needs. If it is successful it pays off, not necessarily in money, but in gratification, peace of mind, fulfillment. Yet since the idea of happiness is with us inseparable from the idea of prosperity, we must face the fact that a love that is not crowned with every material and social benefit seems to us to be rather suspect. Is it really *blessed?* Was it really a *deal?*[9]

Second, true friendship will be impossible if the self is understood to find life not, as Merton wrote, in making a gift of ourself to others,[10] but by dominating and controlling them. In *Theology and Social Theory*, John Milbank argues convincingly that since the Enlightenment and the rise of capitalism there has been a radical shift in our understanding of the self that has critical repercussions for friendship. Instead of believing that selfhood and identity are established through love, our culture suggests they are constituted through owning and controlling, but here the ownership and dominion is extended beyond possessions to persons.[11] In such a system friendship has no place at all because people are seen more as adversaries than friends. Self-identity is not determined by our relationship with God and our neighbors, but by what and who we are able to dominate and control; in short, our identity is proportionate to our power, but here power is understood not in terms of service, justice, or love, but in terms of mastery over one's self, one's possessions, and others. We thrive not when we are friends, but when we manipulate and control.

There is something brutal and inescapably violent in this understanding of the self because it fundamentally argues that identity requires oppression. It is a vision of life that sees human beings locked in ceaseless competitive struggle as everyone seeks to dominate others. It is a world in which people come to life through self-love and self-assertion, not gentleness, mercy, and sacrifice. Here we grow not when we endorse others, raise them up, and love them in joyful self-

---

9. Ibid., 27–28.

10. Ibid., 25.

11. John Milbank, *Theology and Social Theory: Beyond Secular Reason* (Oxford: Basil Blackwell, 1990) 12–13.

forgetfulness, but when we are able to manipulate, maneuver, and exploit.

This is not a world in which real friendship is possible or even desired because the otherness of people is seen as something to overcome or control, not as something we are blessed to receive. Too, it is not a world in which people can live together in the kind of harmony and peace necessary for friendship because there is too much violence and division and cruelty to achieve anything more than the false and shaky peace that comes when the strong subdue the weak. This is the world not of blessed and saving friendship love, but of the barbaric nihilism which inevitably marks a culture in which power is the ultimate idol.[12]

No wonder so many people live shoulder-to-shoulder, but their lives hardly touch. No wonder that for many there is physical proximity, but no spiritual connectedness, no mingling of souls or unity of spirit. With these understandings of the self dominating our culture, for many people today life, in Ignace Lepp's haunting phrase, is nothing more than "a mere juxtaposition of solitudes."[13] This should not astonish us. If we live in a society shaped by ideologies of consumerism and materialism, radical individualism, and dynamics of self-assertion and domination, it is not surprising that we have lost the art of friendship and forgotten what friendship, in the richest and most promising sense, entails.

Our understanding of friendship, as well as its possibilities, is connected to our understanding of self. The narrative of our modern culture devalues and subverts friendship because of how it defines the self through consumerism, individualism, and domination. What we lack today is a philosophy of self adequate for a healthy and flourishing moral and spiritual life, as well as a social and political life defined by a strong commitment to a common good. I want to suggest not only that a particular understanding of friendship, namely, the friendship defined through charity, offers a much more promising understanding of the self for overcoming our crisis of dehumanization, but also that it is absolutely essential.

Thus, in order to sustain an argument for friendship as key to "the human way out" we must adopt a countercultural understand-

12. Ibid., 326–434.
13. Ignace Lepp, *The Ways of Friendship* (New York: Macmillan, 1966) 15.

ing of the self. We must reject the model of the self governed by consumerism, individualism, and domination, and retrieve from Aquinas the model of *caritas* in which to be a self is to live in friendship with God and neighbor. However, before considering why the Thomistic notion of friendship is countercultural to our modern age, I want to examine briefly Aristotle's understanding of virtue friendships and their role in our humanization, first because they will contribute something vital to "the human way out," and second because it is in them that so much of Aquinas's treatment of charity's friendships, however different, is rooted.

II. Virtue Friendships and Their Role in the Moral Life

Aristotle identified three kinds of friendship, each distinguished by whatever goods or purposes bring the friends together and explain the life of the friendship. There are friendships of usefulness or advantage, friendships of pleasure, and friendships of character or virtue.[14] Of the three, however, only friendships of virtue and character pass the test of friendship in every way; Aristotle said they alone are friendships in the most "perfect and complete sense."[15] Character friendship's moral excellence is derived from the purpose which identifies the friendship, namely, a mutual love for virtue and a mutual desire to become good.

Aristotle argues that friendships of character are the deepest and most permanent and worthiest because they are constituted by the best and most excellent of goods: a shared desire to develop together the qualities of character and virtue that are most perfecting of human beings. Since Aristotle believed there was nothing more humanizing than goodness and nothing more perfecting than the virtues, these relationships will be the most crucial and indispensable for life. They are the friendships in which people who want to be good can become good. Too, the explicit purpose of virtue friendships is to work for the moral well-being of one's friend, and for Aristotle this is to love her or him truly.[16]

14. John M. Cooper, "Aristotle on Friendship," *Essays on Aristotle's Ethics*, ed. Amelie Oksenberg Rorty (Berkeley: University of California Press, 1980) 303.
15. Aristotle, *Nicomachean Ethics*, trans. Martin Ostwald (Indianapolis: Bobbs-Merrill, 1962) 1157b33.
16. *NE*, 1156b6–25.

For Aristotle the moral life is unavoidably a cooperative enterprise, "a jointly pursued life,"[17] because we need others to create a way of life in which growth in virtue and the development of character are possible.[18] Friendship is indispensable to the moral life for Aristotle precisely because the virtues are shared activities. They are not disconnected pieces of behavior, isolated acts which occasionally engage us, but comprise an ongoing way of life in which people joined in a partnership of the good come to understand what the virtues are and how they need to be expressed. Contrary to our dominant cultural understandings, Aristotle could never conceive of happiness or a good life as something we could achieve on our own; rather, by their very nature as shared activities, the virtues require "a life in companionship with others."[19] Put simply, good friendships are schools of virtue.

And so Aristotle is saying much more than friendship makes the virtues more interesting and pleasant; he is claiming that friendship makes the life of virtue *possible*. He agrees that we need friends "only to provide what we are unable to provide ourselves,"[20] but exactly his point is that the one thing we cannot offer ourselves is virtue. Virtue friendships are more than conveniences; they are indispensable moral enterprises because the only way for us to come in touch with the good is through lasting relationships with people who share our love for the good and are committed to helping us grow in it. As Nancy Sherman observes, virtue friendships provide "the very form and mode of life" within which we grow in goodness and achieve happiness.[21]

Virtue comes to us in friendships with good people. It is this mutual, communal seeking of the good that makes us good; in fact, it is truer to say in this mutual, communal seeking of the good we make one another good because at least to some extent virtue is mediated through the love exchanged among friends. By seeking goodness for

17. Nancy Sherman, *The Fabric of Character: Aristotle's Theory of Virtue* (Oxford: Clarendon, 1989) 131.

18. Aristotle captures this when he writes that friendship "is some sort of excellence or virtue, or involves virtue, and it is, moreover, most indispensable for life" (*NE*, 1155a3–4). And again, "We may also get some sort of training in virtue or excellence from living together with good men, as Theognis says" (*NE*, 1170a11–12).

19. Sherman, *The Fabric of Character*, 127.

20. *NE*, 1169b8.

21. Sherman, *The Fabric of Character*, 127.

one another and encouraging each other in virtue, the friends are transfigured in goodness themselves. Thus, it is not surprising that by the
end of the *Nicomachean Ethics* friendship has emerged as the crucial
context for acquiring, exercising, and flourishing in the virtues. It is
the moral community in which those who love the good come together
in a shared life so they may actually become good.[22] Too, it is the moral
community most essential for making and keeping us human.

If virtue friendships figure so significantly in the moral life, then
certainly such persons must be chosen carefully and wisely. As Nancy
Sherman writes, ''in choosing a character friend, we select 'another
self' (*NE* 1170b–7), who shares a sense of our commitments and ends,
and a sense of what we take to be ultimately 'good and pleasant' in
living. We choose another to be a partner in the joint pursuit of these
ends.''[23] Such a person cannot be chosen haphazardly because his or
her impact on our character and moral development will be profound.
We are looking for someone whose values and concerns are fundamentally in agreement with our own, someone who shares our ideals,
aspirations, and principles, and especially someone who agrees with
us on what a truly good and worthwhile life involves. Even to discover
who might be best suited for this kind of relationship requires time,
testing, much reflection, and prudence.[24] Once chosen, the friend
makes one's moral life a partnership, a joint adventure in which the
friends mutually deliberate about what their life together means and
how it can best be pursued.[25]

This analysis of Aristotle's ethics may seem far removed from
Aquinas's vision of the Christian moral life as charity, but actually they
are closely connected. In many respects Aristotle provides the foundation on which Aquinas constructs his account of the moral life. For
instance, like Aristotle, Aquinas has a normative understanding of the
good life and a normative understanding of a good person. Too, like
his Athenian predecessor, transformation was at the heart of the moral
life for Aquinas. Both believed morality involved change and growth
through the virtues; indeed, they insisted that without the virtues we
could hardly remain human because apart from them we were bound

22. See Paul J. Wadell, *Friendship and the Moral Life* (Notre Dame: University
of Notre Dame Press, 1989) 63.
23. Sherman, *The Fabric of Character*, 131–32.
24. Ibid., 132.
25. Ibid., 135.

to be corrupted. And both insisted that this transformation of the self in virtue was not something we could possibly achieve alone, but something attempted in the crucible of virtue friendships.

Nonetheless, for all their similarities, there are considerable and important differences. Aristotle gave a privileged place to friendship in his schema of the moral life, but ironically only the privileged could partake of it. As Aristotle saw it, the best and most necessary of friendships were possible only for politically free *men*; women, children, and slaves were excluded. Too, while Aristotle did not believe human beings could be friends with the gods because the gods were too unlike us, Aquinas argued that without friendship with God we could not truly be human at all.

Thus, for Aquinas, Aristotle is useful but limited. As we shall see, Aquinas radically re-envisions what the moral life is about. In his account of charity as friendship with God, he explodes the boundaries Aristotle put on what the best friendships might be, what they are seeking, and who could enjoy them. For as Aquinas saw it, the most crucial and blessed of friendships was not with politically free men, but with God, and they were seeking happiness not in Athens, but in the kingdom of God in fellowship with the saints. And most importantly, unlike Aristotle, Aquinas believed it was a happiness open to all. If our crisis of dehumanization is to be overcome and a truly human way out discovered, it will be through the hopeful, challenging, and joyous life of charity.

III. Charity as Friendship with God

Charity is friendship with God and all those God loves. It is what the Christian life of grace is all about. Charity is something more than kindness and acts of thoughtfulness; indeed, it is sharing in the very life and goodness of God so intimately that eventually we enjoy union with God. Friendship with God is the vocation all share: however, far from being a cozy, complacent relationship, it is the daunting challenge to be transformed in order to live God's life now.

Charity is friendship with God, and that friendship is a life of never-ending conversion and deep change of heart, a metamorphosis so complete that those who enter charity go from being sinners to saints. Charity contains both the great hope and the great challenge of the Christian life. Charity's hope is that through grace and love we

can enjoy a life together with God now, a kinship of hearts so intimate that we can become for God who God has always been for us,
a friend, a source of happiness and delight. Charity's challenge is that
the only way for us to enter the life of God is by undergoing a radical
reconstruction of ourself through repentance, contrition, forgiveness,
grace, and virtue.[26]

Aquinas believed God calls us to share in the life of the Trinity
in this world now and in the reign of God to come.[27] He saw us not
primarily as fallen, but summoned, creatures who, despite whatever
frailty and weakness, were relentlessly and ingeniously loved by God
and called to union with God. Aquinas interpreted the whole of history as an endless chronicle of God reaching out to us in love and
friendship, healing and restoring us through grace, leading and
redeeming us in Christ, sanctifying and strengthening us in the Spirit.
God's foremost desire, Aquinas believed, is to share with us his happiness and perfection, and to do so by drawing us into his life. Yes,
God loves all things, but he loves us uniquely and passionately with
the special love marked out for friends. Yes, God loves everything that
is, Aquinas reasoned, but he loves us as friends, wanting for us all
the goodness and happiness that is himself.[28] The message of charity
is that God is in love with us, making us his friends.

This view of the Christian life was consistently affirmed by
Thomas Merton. He knew that God's befriending love is the foundation of our life and that we have life only insofar as we are known and
loved by God; in fact, for Merton our life *is* a never-ending act of friendship with God, of knowing and loving God and being known and loved
by God in return.[29] In *The New Man* Merton says authentic human
existence "is nothing else but a participation in the life, and wisdom,
and joy and peace of God Himself," adding that this friendship relationship is our "supreme freedom" and "most perfect fulfillment."[30]

26. For a fuller treatment of charity as friendship with God see Paul J. Wadell,
The Primacy of Love: An Introduction to the Ethics of Thomas Aquinas (New York: Paulist,
1992) 63–78, and Paul J. Wadell, *Friends of God: Virtues and Gifts in Aquinas* (New
York: Peter Lang, 1991) 1–49.

27. Brian Davies, *The Thought of Thomas Aquinas* (Oxford: Clarendon, 1992) 207.

28. *Summa Theologiae*, I–II, 110,1.

29. Thomas Merton, *Contemplative Prayer* (New York: Herder and Herder,
1969) 104.

30. Thomas Merton, *The New Man* (New York: Farrar, Straus, and Cudahy,
1961) 48.

Like Aquinas, Merton realized our self-realization is a measure of our union with God, and that we live "not when we pause to reflect upon our own self as an isolated individual entity," but when "we center our whole soul upon the God Who is our life."[31]

For both Aquinas and Merton the life of friendship with God that is charity begins in the outpouring of grace into our hearts and, interestingly, both describe this grace as an invitation to friendship, an appeal to share in the very friendship life of God. Aquinas speaks of charity as the gift by which God shares with us his happiness and sees our life as an ever deepening participation in this happiness.[32] Merton says simply, "Grace is friendship with God,"[33] but understands this gift not as something static, but as the dynamic and unfolding process by which the baptized are transformed and sanctified through friendship with God, eventually acquiring the likeness to God necessary for mystical union.[34]

The grace that makes friendship with God possible must initially heal, restore, and rehabilitate a nature living more at enmity with God than in friendship. Aquinas describes this succinctly by saying the grace that comes with charity is "a certain habitual gift, by which spoiled human nature is healed, and once healed, is raised up to perform works which merit eternal life."[35] That is quite a turnabout, but describing grace as a *habitual* gift captures well the fact that charity is essentially new life, indeed, a radically transformed life constituted by grace and forgiveness, and deepened and nurtured through the virtues and the sacraments, particularly baptism, the Eucharist, and reconciliation. Through the grace of charity we are reconciled to God and to one another, we become sharers in God's life, companions of the Trinity, and find freedom in making God's ways our own. Thus, charity is a distinctive *habitus*, a radically new way of life constituted by unique habits and practices which require considerable discipline and training, but their transformative effects are stunning. As Thomas puts it, through the *habitus* of charity, erstwhile sinners find themselves "performing works which merit eternal life."

31. Ibid., 122.
32. *ST*, I–II, 23,1, 24,2.
33. Merton, *The New Man*, 42.
34. Ibid., 165–223.
35. *ST*, I–II, 109,9.

His point is that charity ought to make a concrete, discernible difference in our lives; indeed, we misunderstand charity if we receive it and remain unchanged, or if we think it calls for exactly the same patterns of living we knew when we were fallen. The life of charity does not mean *more of the same* because charity empowers us to live, however incompletely, a godlike life now.[36] Charity is a summons to a new kind of life, a life that is essentially a resurrection to new and better possibilities. This does not mean that a life of friendship with God takes us out of the world, but it definitely does mean that it calls us to live in the world differently, acting according to who we truly are, fallen ones who, thanks to love, are now the friends of God.

A life lived in company with God opens us to new and better moral possibilities. Aquinas calls these the acts or effects of charity and names them joy, peace, mercy, kindness, almsgiving, and fraternal correction.[37] They are characteristics of those whose lives have been transformed by friendship with God. Far from being accidental, joy, peace, mercy, kindness, almsgiving, and fraternal correction collectively describe a new way of being, a different kind of life, born from friendship with God. These are the practices, the habitual ways of being and acting, which characterize those whose lives have been transfigured in charity. They are also the practices that respond to the crisis of dehumanization by making life together possible.

Collectively, these habits of charity represent a distinctive way of life. But it is important to note that in many respects they also represent a countercultural way of life. They are virtues which unmask and challenge the usual ways we go about life. Joy, peace, mercy, kindness, almsgiving, and fraternal correction do not characterize the dominant social patterns of our world. Instead of genuine joy, we often see superficial happiness and artificial satisfactions. Instead of peace, we see so many conflicted hearts and a very conflicted world, a world that seems intent to live by violence, turmoil, and endless bloody hostilities. Instead of kindness, we see too much cruelty and selfishness. And instead of fraternal correction, we too often see a tolerance which masks a deeper indifference in people who do not care enough to challenge one another or to call one another to what is best.

---

36. Davies, *The Thought of Thomas Aquinas*, 271–272.
37. *ST*, II–II, 28–33.

The life of charity is a different kind of witness: indeed, it is a sign of contradiction and perhaps even a threat to many of the reigning ideologies of our time. Charity is a way of life characterized not by violence and division and vindictiveness, but by justice, harmony, mutuality, and peace.[38] Charity is a distinctive way of life rooted in the conviction that if all of us are called to live together in friendship with God and with one another, then peace, not violence, is the truth of things, and this peace is rooted in a way of life marked by care, forbearance, cooperation, generosity, forgiveness, and love. Far from being a single virtue, charity is a contrasting way of life founded on the ways of God revealed in Christ and empowered by the Spirit. Charity is not wishful thinking, it is a counter-history begun in a deliberate way of life committed to living God's ways now. In its pledge to witness God's friendship to all people through joy, kindness, mercy, and peace, the community of charity does not escape the world but recreates it. In its commitment to love who God loves *as* God loves them, the community of charity is the world's true hope. As both Aquinas and Merton knew, there is no more human way out.

IV. Embracing the Life of Charity Today

What would it mean to embrace the life of charity today? I want to suggest that charity commits us to a way of life characterized by three things, each of which is essential to countering the dehumanizing forces of our times: (1) a much more inclusive vision of who is our neighbor; (2) a much more life-giving understanding of power; and (3) a commitment to be a reconciling and peaceful presence in the world.

First, what about charity's understanding of who is our neighbor? Charity is the most radical and demanding love of all because charity, Aquinas says, means we are to love whomever God loves and love them because God loves them.[39] But God loves everybody, even our enemies, sinners as well as saints, and so, Aquinas reasoned, should we.[40] His point was simple but stunning: We are summoned to love

38. These ideas were suggested to me in John Milbank's *Theology and Social Theory,* 380–434. Although Milbank focuses on Augustine's *City of God,* a parallel argument can be made with Aquinas's understanding of the life of charity.

39. *ST,* II–II, 25,1.

40. *ST,* II–II, 25,6,8.

everyone who is connected to God, and of course everybody is. We are obliged to love everyone who is a friend of God, but his point is precisely that charity makes everyone a friend of God. The fellowship of charity is no small community. It is the one place where there is room for everybody.

In a world where there seems to be increasingly less openness to differences, in a world where hate crimes are increasing, and in a world torn apart by ethnic divisions and racism, there will be no human way into any kind of hopeful future unless visions of mistrust and hostility are replaced by the vision of charity. Charity is the kind of truthful vision necessary for justice and peace. Through the vision of charity our eyes are opened to recognize absolutely everyone as brother or sister to us and, most importantly, as fellow friend of God. We have a deep and ineradicable kinship with every man and woman of every time and place because through charity all of us share the same source of life and the same destiny in glory. Before we risk loving anyone, God has loved us all first, has befriended us, and has called us *together* to enter the divine life. Community really is the truth of humanity; all of us really are members one of another.

This vision of charity is key to the "human way out" because only in charity do we find a vision truthful and expansive enough to recognize that absolutely everyone is our neighbor, not just now but for eternity. Charity says our neighbor is whoever shares with us the fact of being loved by God and called to God's happiness. But God gives this gift to everyone, which is why charity explodes our normal understanding of who is our neighbor. Charity bursts open the boundaries of community far beyond what we normally think. The fellowship of charity embraces everyone who has been loved and befriended by God. It tells us our fellowship with one another is based on God's friendship with all of us, a point echoed by Merton in *No Man Is an Island* when he comments that the "universal basis for friendship" with all peoples is the fact that all of us are loved by God.[41]

Charity makes all of us sisters and brothers. It says no one can ever really be a stranger to us, no one truly an outsider, because like ourselves they are members of the fellowship of God's friendship.[42]

41. Thomas Merton, *No Man Is an Island* (New York: Harcourt, Brace and Co., 1955) 11.

42. Merton makes the same point when he writes, "Every other man is a piece of myself, for I am a part and member of mankind. Every Christian is part

The community of charity is inherently countercultural because it is open to everybody, and it is open to everybody because its basis is not nationality or race or gender or religion, but God's befriending love. Charity is the love running through life, the love which says the starting point for relating rightly to everyone is to see them as one like ourselves, one who has been made by God a sharer in the divine life. If we are to find a human way out of our crisis of dehumanization, particularly the crisis of injustice, we must make charity's vision our own.

Second, charity calls us to a much more life-giving understanding of power. In her recent book *The Power of the Cross*, Sally B. Purvis argues that there are two starkly different models of power. The first she calls "power as control."[43] Here power is the ability to control and manipulate through domination. This kind of power is inherently unjust and essentially violent, first because it works directly against the power of justice to reconstruct the world in right relationships, and secondly because it consistently violates the basic demand of justice that we respect the dignity of others and in every instance give them their due.[44] As long as this understanding of power is endorsed, there is no way to escape the "sickening inhumanities" Merton despised.

But there is a "human way out" if we endorse the second model of power which Purvis calls "power as life."[45] Power as life is God's power, a power revealed in the seeming weakness of the crucified Christ, a power, St. Paul tells us (1 Cor 1:18-25) that looks absurd and foolish to most, but is the power and wisdom of God by which all things are saved. God's power working through charity is absolutely countercultural because it expresses itself not in domination and oppression, not in violence and division, but in life-giving acts of mercy, kindness, and benevolence. This is the power of compassion, the power

---

of my own body, because we are members of Christ. What I do is also done for them and with them and by them. What they do is done in me and by me and for me. But each one of us remains responsible for his own share in the life of the whole body. Charity cannot be what it is supposed to be as long as I do not see that my life represents my own allotment in the life of a whole supernatural organism to which I belong." *No Man Is an Island*, xxii.

43. Sally B. Purvis, *The Power of the Cross: Foundations for a Christian Feminist Ethic of Community* (Nashville: Abingdon, 1993) 19–36.

44. *ST*, II-II, 58,1.

45. Purvis, *The Power of the Cross*, 37–54.

of mutual enhancement, the power of sharing in suffering and increasing happiness. It is not the power to dominate, but the power to bless and to serve. Too, power as life is essentially just because its steadfast aim is not to diminish, but to safeguard and enhance the well-being of others. It is a model of power which reminds us that other people matter and we cannot be indifferent to their lives whether they be nearby or oceans away. Unlike power as control, power as life recognizes no one is expendable and no one can be ignored.

Merton had a similar understanding of the power of charity. In *The New Man* he describes charity as an *imitatio Christi*, and says when we imitate the love of Christ, particularly in his passion and death, we practice a love powerful enough to overcome evil and all the destructiveness it brings.[46] In *No Man Is an Island*, Merton says the aim of charity's love is to make us an instrument, not an obstacle, "of God's Providence" in the lives of others.[47] We are to use the power of our love to do for them whatever God seeks. We are, Merton says, to be "sacraments" of "the mysterious and infinitely selfless love God has for them," and "ministers" of God's Spirit.[48] For Merton, the distinctive life-giving power of charity is to love others as God loves them, never seeking to dominate or control, but using the power of love to help them be who God wants them to be."[49] In this respect, true power is benevolence, the capacity and the desire to seek what is best for another in every possible way; in Christian language, Merton hints, it is to "seek the life of the Spirit of God" in the hearts of all people.[50]

Finally, the life of charity calls us to be a reconciling and peaceful presence in our world. In a world which so many are determined to keep broken, in a world where divisions often abide and hurts are never healed, the community of charity works to put all the broken pieces back together again by practicing the healing love of forgiveness and peace.

Think of the passage in Ephesians 4:31–5:2. There Paul tells the Christian community to "get rid of all bitterness, all passion and anger, harsh words, slander, and malice of every kind." Paul says leave all that behind and refuse to be ruled by it. Instead, Paul says, "be kind

---

46. Merton, *The New Man*, 193.
47. Merton, *No Man Is an Island*, 7.
48. Ibid., 8.
49. Ibid., 168.
50. Ibid., 7.

to one another, compassionate, and mutually forgiving, just as God has forgiven you in Christ.''

What is Paul telling us? He says be a reconciling presence in the world. Be imitators of the God who forgives and seeks peace. Be part of a community of mercy and life. There is surely something counter-cultural and provocative about that way of life, but is there anything more hopeful?

The greatest contribution the community of charity can make to the world is to pledge to be the people who live not by the debilitating power of bitterness and anger and resentment, and not by the destructive fantasies of violence, but by the uplifting powers of forgiveness, reconciliation, patience, tolerance, and peace. By refusing to let the hurts and divisions of life prevail, by refusing to lose our freedom to bitterness and cynicism, and by refusing to let broken relationships stay that way, we show that reconciliation, not division, is the truth of things, that peace is possible, and that love really is stronger than death.

People who practice charity's friendship are mindful of the power they have. They know in our everyday actions we can divide or we can make whole, we can bring death or we can bring life. If we pledge ourselves to reconciliation and peace, we become people who refuse to pass on the violence. This is a compelling countercultural witness and it is a choice we have everyday. When we are hurt we can pass on the hurt, adding a little more grief to the world, or we can forgive it. When we are wounded by another's cruelty, we can respond by seeking vengeance, or we can practice a much more creative and powerful love, the love of forgiveness and peace. As friends of God and friends of one another, even our enemies, we are called each day to make the choice not to pass on the violence, but to defuse it through forgiveness and peace.

Nothing could be closer to the thought of Thomas Merton. In ''Christian Humanism'' Merton says, ''The dynamic of Christian love is a dynamic of forgiveness,'' adding that the power of this special love is ''to transform evil into good.''[51] In ''The Climate of Mercy,'' an essay written in honor of Albert Schweitzer, Merton reminds us that we who have been ''liberated'' by God's mercy are to show the same mercy and forgiveness to others; in fact, the essential mission of the

---

51. Thomas Merton, ''Christian Humanism,'' *Love and Living*, 130.

Church is to continue the mercy of God shown us in Christ. We are "to keep alive on earth the irreplaceable climate of mercy, truth, and faith in which the creative and life-giving joy of reconciliation in Christ always not only remains possible but is a continuous and ever-renewed actuality."[52]

For Merton, mercy was not weakness or submission, and it certainly was not complacency; rather, mercy is the power that "heals in every way. It heals bodies, spirits, society, and history. It is the only force that can truly heal and save."[53] In fact, Merton saw "evangelical mercy" as a social force, a transformative power to renew the world by witnessing the kingdom of God.[54] The world would not be saved by fear and threats, and it certainly, Merton knew, would not be saved by weapons of war. The ultimate life-saving power is Christian mercy because it alone is capable of overcoming divisions, ending hostilities, and restoring genuine peace. In a particularly moving passage, Merton reflects on the power of Christian mercy in a world surrounded by weapons of destruction:

> Christian mercy must discover, in faith, in the Spirit, a power strong enough to initiate the transformation of the world into a realm of understanding, unity, and relative peace, where men, nations, and societies are willing to make the enormous sacrifices required if they are to communicate intelligibly with one another, understand one another, cooperate with one another in feeding the hungry millions and in building a world of peace.
>
> Such is the eschatological climate of the new creation, in which pardon replaces sacrifice (Osee 6:6; Matt 9:13) and the whole world is filled with the mercy of God as the waters cover the sea.[55]

In these reflections I have suggested that the way out of the crisis of dehumanization and into a future of hope and joy lies in adopting the *habitus* of charity. At first glance, this account of charity and the life which flows from it may sound appealing but utopian, too far removed from life as we know it to be within our reach. But we should take another look.

52. Thomas Merton, "The Climate of Mercy," *Love and Living*, 189–190.
53. Ibid., 195.
54. Ibid., 196–197.
55. Ibid., 197.

The life of charity is the only truly human way out because in its commitment to mercy, justice, peace, and forgiveness, charity means, as both Aquinas and Merton testified, that the reign of God need not be completely postponed. Its fullness may be in the future, but its beginnings are now with those who make the life of charity their own. If we are courageous and hopeful enough to embrace the life of charity and all the evangelical practices which flow from it, we will provide an urgent service to our world. We may be a sign of contradiction, but we will also be a beautiful sign of hope because our lives will confirm that God's dream for the world is not some farfetched fantasy, but is the deep down truth of things.

The Virtuous Teacher:
Thomas Merton's Contribution to a
Spirituality of Higher Education

Roy D. Fuller

In perhaps what is his most extended statement on higher education, "Learning to Live," Thomas Merton draws a comparison between the university and the monastery. Merton declares that the university, "is at once a microcosm and a paradise."[1] Noting that throughout the Middle Ages speculation abounded concerning the location of the earthly paradise, Merton, ever following the example of the early Fathers, defines paradise as "simply the person, the self, but the radical self in its uninhibited freedom. The self no longer with an ego."[2] Having located paradise within, Merton further observes that only with the activation of that innermost "spark" or self may one realize the "fruit of education."[3] And not infrequently is this work done outside of the classroom, even away from the campus, where Merton encountered "small bursts of light that pointed out my way in the dark of my own identity."[4]

---

1. Thomas Merton, "Learning to Live," *Love and Living*, eds. Naomi Burton Stone and Patrick Hart (New York: Farrar, Straus, Giroux, 1979) 7. This essay was originally titled "Learning to Learn," as Lawrence Cunningham has noted in his introduction to this essay in *Thomas Merton: Spiritual Master* (New York: Paulist, 1992) 357.
2. Merton, "Learning to Live," 8.
3. Ibid., 9.
4. Ibid., 13. See Thomas Del Prete, *Thomas Merton and the Education of the Whole Person* (Birmingham: Religious Education Press, 1990) 13. Concerning this essay by Merton, Del Prete observed, "Though unfortunately brief, his statement was the fruit of many years of written reflection and meditation on the meaning of the "self" and "person." It captured as well his own commitment and experience

Thomas Merton's writings specifically pertaining to education are limited, and this essay will restrict itself to these particular works.[5] The structure of this examination is twofold. First, contemporary critics of higher education in America will be engaged in dialogue with Merton's reflections on education. The second part of the paper will focus on what insights Merton's writings hold for the current discussion of academic virtues.

Merton and Contemporary Higher Education

There would seem to be little debate concerning the existence of a "spiritual void" within much of what passes for higher education. Parker Palmer observes "a tremendous deep spiritual hunger" within the realms of higher education.[6] One need look no further than the best-sellers list of the past few years to see the increasing number of authors/scholars who have critiqued and suggested improvements of the American system of higher education. E. D. Hirsch, Jr., in *Cultural Literacy,* submits that the cure for what ails education is the learning of "large amounts of specific information" which would equip humans to "thrive in the modern world," a phrase by which he means the advancement of one's vocation as well as the individual's level of

---

in personal growth." Del Prete's work stands as the only monograph exclusively devoted to Merton's views on education.

5. The limits of Merton's writings on education were observed by both Del Prete and William Shannon. In his review of Del Prete's work, Shannon observed that Merton, "wrote very little explicitly about education" (back cover, Del Prete). Del Prete himself explored Merton's ideas about how education should involve "the formation of the whole person." Del Prete did not deal with Merton's educational methodology by design, though research should be done in this area. The wealth of tapes (over 600) at the Thomas Merton Center at Bellarmine College would offer much for an analysis of Merton's educational methodology, as would further analysis of his letters. Both areas were outside the specific intent of this paper.

For a perspective from those who sat under Merton as students, see "Merton as Novice Master," *Up and Down Merton's Mountains: A Contemporary Spiritual Journey,* ed. Gerald Groves (St. Louis: CBP Press, 1988).

6. Parker Palmer, "The Violence of Our Knowledge: Toward a Spirituality of Higher Education," presented as the H. I. Hester Lecture given at the Association of Southern Baptist Colleges and Schools, Riverside, California, June 1993. Reprinted in *The Southern Baptist Educator,* vol. 57, no. 9 (August 1993) 7.

self-actualization.[7] Merton maintains that one of the goals of education is to prepare persons "to lead a productive and happy life," and
this must include knowledge of "the ultimate spiritual values that men
have to live by."[8] Merton would certainly have agreed with Hirsch
in regard to the necessity of education to impart a love of reading.[9]

Whereas Hirsch analyzes the failure of education at the primary
levels, Allan Bloom in his book, *The Closing of the American Mind*, reveals a world of higher education where the character of students is
so deformed as to defy all efforts to instill new habits and values within
them.[10] The popularity of Bloom's book seemed to be found in his tendency to blame the impoverished student for the problems of higher
education. While primarily writing to those interested in monastic education, Merton makes a similar point:

> The monastic life as it exists today often presupposes too much
> in the young postulant who seeks admission. It presupposes that
> he knows his own mind, that he is capable of making a mature
> decision, that he has grown up, that he has received a liberal
> education. It is often discovered too late that such things cannot
> be taken for granted. Before the average youth of today is ready
> for monastic life, his senses, feelings and imagination need to be
> reformed and educated along normal natural lines.[11]

7. E. D. Hirsch, Jr. *Cultural Literacy: What Every American Needs to Know* (Boston: Houghton Mifflin Co., 1987) xiii, xv.

8. *Witness to Freedom: The Letters of Thomas Merton in Times of Crisis*, ed. William
H. Shannon (New York: Farrar, Straus, Giroux, 1994) 155.

9. Conference Tape #43, "Liberal Arts: Good or Bad?" January 14, 1962
(Thomas Merton Studies Center collection, Bellarmine College). Merton's observation is as follows: "The major shortcoming of seminary is the inability to impart
a love of reading."

10. Allan Bloom, *The Closing of the American Mind* (New York: Simon and
Schuster, 1987) Part One. "Students," 47–137.

11. "The Inner Experience," 269. In this same article, Merton fretted over
the influence of the university model upon the monastic environment, especially
as he noted: "Yet inevitably the monastic library tends to imitate the library of
a university, and some of the monks become graduate students doing research. . . .
The Bible is read, but it is full of mysteries which remain to be unveiled by an
expert with a degree and he, too often, is interested only in details of archeology
and linguistics" 274. Merton was always concerned with education which produced
specialists who had lost the ability to find wholeness.

If one substitutes "higher education" for "monastic life" here, Merton may be seen as an early prophet of what ails contemporary education.

While Hirsch and Bloom raise questions worthy of continued discussion within academia (and society at large), their analyses and solutions proffered seem reductionistic. In both cases, students are improved by enhancing their curriculum (i.e., more classics and other knowledge which amounts to "cultural literacy"). Thus, when we have better students, higher education will, seemingly automatically, be improved and able to complete its task. A more accurate description of what ails higher education is the analysis offered by Page Smith in *Killing the Spirit*. Smith identifies several maladies of higher education: "presentism," a tireless lust for the new; specialization, at the loss of capacity for generalization or any awareness of unity; knowledge for its own sake; relativism, which denies any moral structure in the world; and "academic fundamentalism," which omits half or more of the human experience.[12] Thomas Merton offers a similar critique, in the form of describing the "products" of the modern education process:

> Those who claim to be educated are in reality not formed: they are formless bundles of unrelated factual knowledge, disoriented and passive, superficially acquainted with names, dates, facts and with the "how" of various material processes. But they have no way of using what they "know." Consequently, since their "knowledge" is not integrated into their lives, they cannot really be said to possess it. It has not entered their being. It has not really become a part of them. . . . He may be in some sense educated, but his education has little to do with real life, since real life is not something with which modern man is really concerned at all.[13]

Smith's most significant contribution to the debate centers on the vocation of teaching. While the importance of teaching students to think clearly should not be diminished, Smith quotes Sir Richard Livingstone, who stated, "to teach people to see and feel is more important still."[14] Smith also quotes William Lyon Phelps, who wrote, "If a teacher wishes success with pupils, he must inflame their imagi-

---

12. Page Smith, *Killing the Spirit: Higher Education In America* (New York: Viking, 1990) 294.

13. "The Inner Experience: Problems of the Contemplative Life (VII)" *Cistercian Studies* 19 (1984) 270, 271.

14. Ibid., 200.

nation.''[15] This is similar to Merton's comment concerning ''the activation of that innermost spark.'' Smith observed that ''true education,
one designed to produce a true person, must include instruction in
courage.''[16] Talk of courage implies taking positions, subjective emotions, and trust, three ingredients which currently seem in short sup-
ply within the halls of academia.

While *Killing the Spirit* deals with the history of higher education in America in an effort to understand how it has sunk so low,
Smith's emphasis upon the crucial function of the teacher brings us
to an area where another critic of higher education has raised significant questions concerning the vocation of teaching in America. Parker
Palmer asserts that the transformation of teaching must begin with the
transforming of teachers.[17] He further states:

> Only in the heart searched and transformed by truth will new
> teaching techniques and strategies for institutional change find sure
> grounding. Only in such a heart will teachers find the courage to
> resist the conditions of academic life while we work and wait for
> institutional transformation.[18]

Palmer goes on to demonstrate how classical spiritual virtues can contribute to the transformation of both teachers and learners. Specifically,
he identified the following virtues or ''fruits of spiritual practice'' as
necessary for the practice of teaching: humility and faith, reverence
without idolatry, love and openness to grace.[19]

Such virtues have been pushed aside at many American colleges
and universities, as has been clearly shown by George Marsden's analysis in *The Soul of the American University*. Marsden documents the move
away from the religious values and virtues which long stood as the

---

15. William Lyon Phelps, quoted by Smith, 213.
16. Ibid., 204. Such courage must not only be talked about but ''demonstrated.'' This requires what Smith identified as ''the essence of teaching—taking
chances,'' 216.
17. Parker Palmer, *To Know as We Are Known* (San Francisco: Harper & Row,
1983) 107.
18. Ibid., 107–108.
19. Ibid., 108. Palmer holds that in addition to being spiritual virtues, these
fruits are epistemological virtues as well, ''the degree to which they are present
in us has much to do with our capacity to know and be known in truth,'' 108.

foundational principles of American educational philosophy.[20] This paradigm shift has tremendous significance, as Marsden observes:

> While American universities today allow individuals free exercise of religion in parts of their lives that do not touch the heart of the university, they tend to exclude or discriminate against relating explicit religious perspectives to intellectual life. In other words, the free exercise of religion does not extend to the dominant intellectual centers of our culture.[21]

If this is the reality of a university education, how can such institutions be expected to fulfill Merton's purpose of education, that being "the formation of the whole person." Consistent with this focus, Merton claims that "The function of a university is, then, first of all to help the student to discover himself: to recognize himself, and to identify who it is that chooses."[22] Whether universities will recover this perspective remains an open question.

In *Exiles From Eden*, Mark R. Schwehn offers a trenchant analysis of what ails higher education in America. Schwehn goes beyond the obvious (and often only symptomatic) maladies which plague education, and focuses on why teaching has come to view itself as it does, and how this flawed vision might be corrected. Like Palmer, Schwehn pursues the connection between spiritual virtues and the practice of teaching and it is in this area where Schwehn makes his most valuable contribution. He suggests that "every teacher is teaching at least two things in every classroom: his or her subject and the manners of learning."[23] Schwehn defines "manners" as embodying both methods and virtues. The question of the virtues necessary for both learning and teaching is one which provides an opening for Thomas Merton's contribution to a spirituality for higher education.

---

20. George Marsden, *The Soul of the American University: From Protestant Establishment to Established Nonbelief* (New York: Oxford University, 1994). While Marsden focused on colleges and universities that are Protestant in origin, his framework would hold true for Catholic institutions as well.

21. Ibid., 6.

22. "Learning to Live," 4.

23. Mark R. Schwehn, *Exiles From Eden: Religion and the Academic Vocation in America* (Oxford University, 1993) 34.

Merton's "Ethos of Inquiry"

Schwehn offers four "spiritual virtues" which he suggests are indispensable to learning and teaching: faith, humility, self-denial, and charity.[24] Why the virtues? As Schwehn observes:

> Academies, if they are to flourish over the long run, must therefore cultivate and sustain in their members those virtues that are required for the kind of learning they hope to promote. Taken together, these virtues constitute the ethos of inquiry.[25]

Does Thomas Merton speak to us on this question of the virtues necessary for teaching and learning? Using Schwehn's virtues as a guideline, we will proceed with an investigation of Merton's "ethos of inquiry."

Thomas Merton did not devote much writing to the specific issue of higher education. (One may be tempted to say "secular" higher education, but as has already been suggested, the idea itself may be a misnomer.) In his essay "Learning to Live," Merton defines the purpose of education as being "to show a person how to define himself authentically and spontaneously in relation to his world."[26] In a letter to Mary Declan Martin, who had written him concerning his views of education, Merton responds, "I believe education means more than just imparting 'knowledge.' It means the formation of the whole person."[27] Merton seems to echo Bernard of Clairvaux who wrote:

> Some seek knowledge for the sake of knowledge; that is curiosity.
> Others seek knowledge that they may themselves be known; that
> is vanity. But there are some who seek knowledge in order to serve
> and edify others. And that is charity.[28]

24. Ibid., 48–57. Schwehn mentions additional virtues, namely loyalty and hospitality, but these were not developed as were the aforementioned virtues.
25. Ibid., 44.
26. "Learning to Live," 3.
27. *The Road To Joy: Letters of Thomas Merton to New and Old Friends*, ed. Robert E. Daggy (New York: Farrar, Straus, Giroux, 1989) 364. See also Del Prete, *Thomas Merton and the Education of the Whole Person*, chapter 2.
28. Bernard of Clairvaux, quoted by Josef Pieper, *Scholasticism* (New York: Pantheon, 1960) 155.

This seems to be precisely Merton's view of the function of knowledge in education, "to serve and edify others."

Whereas modern higher educational institutions have made the production and distribution of knowledge as their ongoing goal, Merton maintains that this is the very danger of education, it "confuses means with ends."[29] Rather than an "end," Merton suggests that the purpose of education may be seen in the etymology of the word itself. In his introductory essay on the letters of Adam of Perseigne, Merton observes that to educate a monk (in monastic terms, to "form"), one must "draw out" or "bring out" the true self.[30] To educate, whether in the context of monastery or university, is an activity of "leading out." Too often the task is viewed as one of "putting in" as in pouring knowledge into students. Endless debates on curriculum reform and what constitutes the "core" would take on a different tone if institutions became more concerned about "leading out" than "putting in."

When education is viewed in its original intent as a leading or bringing out of the inner or true spiritual self, the role of the educator is likewise restored. Merton has much to say concerning the role and characteristics of the educator. His role as educator consumed a large portion of his efforts, having been Master of Scholastics for four years (1951–1955) and Master of Novices for ten years (1955–1965). In most of his work on education, Merton is naturally discussing the education or formation of monks. In this context the educator may be understood as spiritual director. Here I would begin to make the case for understanding Merton as "guru" or "virtuous teacher." But first, a brief overview of the meaning and function of "guru" as the term is used in its Eastern context.

In Sanskrit, the word "guru" literally means heavy or weighty. In popular Eastern usage, a guru is a person who is acknowledged to be in close communion with deity.[31] Huston Smith notes that the Sikh tradition regards the guru as (1) a dispeller of ignorance or darkness (*gu*) and (2) a bringer of enlightenment (*ru*).[32] The idea of enlighten-

29. "Learning to Live," 11.

30. "The Feast of Freedom," in *The Letters of Adam of Perseigne* (Kalamazoo: Cistercian Publications, 1976) 9.

31. C.S.J. White, "Guru," *Abingdon Dictionary of Living Religions*, ed. Keith Crim (Nashville: Abingdon, 1981) 287.

32. Huston Smith, *The World's Religions* (New York: HarperCollins, 1991) 75.

ment is captured by Merton in "The Feast of Freedom," where in discussing monastic formation he observes that as part of this formation the desire is "to encourage the growth of life and the radiation of light within his soul."[33] Within the context of Hinduism the meaning of guru is not different, only expanded. As Swami Prabhavananda defines the term, guru is "an illumined teacher" and "one who is competent and holy, who has demonstrated the truths of religion in his own life."[34] Speaking about the infinite variety of methods between masters and students, Prabhavananda remarks:

> The guru has perhaps no more important duty than to study carefully the personality and temperament of the pupils committed to his charge, and to prescribe to each, according to his nature, an appropriate method of meditation.[35]

Merton's own thoughts on the characteristics of a spiritual director reveal a similar understanding. Merton notes that the director must be a "master who teaches the spiritual life both by *discipline* and by *instruction*."[36] Merton understands the spiritual director as "a *guide* and a *friend* even more than a teacher . . . he must be adept at *listening*."[37] As M. Basil Pennington explains, "The listening of the spiritual father is not a passive thing, it is very active."[38] In Merton's own words, "I have looked into their hearts . . ."[39] Pennington's comment in the footnote is worth repeating: "One of the monk-priests who was a scholastic at that time attests that he (Merton) was certainly highly gifted for active listening and made one feel listened to."[40] Merton possessed the necessary skills to function within the community as a director or master.

33. "The Feast of Freedom," 9.

34. Swami Prabhavananda, *The Spiritual Heritage of India* (Hollywood: Vedanta, 1973) 20, 147.

35. Ibid., 67.

36. "Spiritual Direction," *Merton: Collected Essays*, vol. 13, 206. (The Thomas Merton Study Center, Bellarmine College). Though never published, this essay was apparently written for the *New Catholic Encyclopedia*.

37. Ibid.

38. M. Basil Pennington, "The Spiritual Father: Father Louis' Theory and Practice," *Toward An Integrated Humanity: Thomas Merton's Journey*, ed. M. Basil Pennington (Kalamazoo: Cistercian Publications, 1988) 34.

39. *The Sign of Jonas* (New York: Harcourt, Brace and Co., 1953) 330.

40. Pennington, "The Spiritual Father," 50.

The natural inclination to attribute "guruness" to Merton is understandable, and perhaps accurate. Would Merton have agreed? In *The Ascent To Truth*, in the context of discussing the necessity of submission to a teaching authority, Merton turned to the guru/disciple relationship for purposes of comparison. The comparison is not favorable to Hinduism and in context should be seen as representative of an apologetic Merton, advocating Catholicism as less severe in its demands than other religious traditions. Merton points out that the Hindu aspirant is expected to see the guru as not only a representative of God, "he must see the Divinity itself living and acting in him."[41] To demonstrate his point Merton quotes Ramakrishna who stated that as the Hindu disciple progresses "the disciple will realize that the Guru and God are one and the same."[42] Certainly Merton would have rejected this incarnational aspect of the guru. However, Merton would agree with the title of spiritual father, even while admitting that in his own role as spiritual father "on many days we have gone around in circles and fallen into ditches because the blind was leading the blind."[43] Perhaps the most applicable correlation of Merton with the concept of guru would be the popular definition of someone who is in close communion with deity. This, after all is said and done, was Merton's own goal.

Merton's "Manners" of Learning

To further elucidate Thomas Merton's "ethos of inquiry" we must look at what Schwehn identifies as the "manners" of learning. Schwehn distinguishes four virtues essential for teaching and learning: humility, faith, self-denial, and charity. By examining Merton's understanding of these virtues, and how he exemplified them in his own work as educator and author, light will be shed not only on him, but upon the institution of teaching as it could exist within higher education.

Humility. Schwehn defines humility in the context of learning as "the *presumption* of wisdom and authority *in the author.*"[44] Merton understood and embodied this understanding of humility. In "The

41. *The Ascent To Truth* (New York: Harcourt, Brace and Co., 1951) 147.
42. Ibid., 148.
43. *The Sign of Jonas*, 333.
44. Schwehn, *Exiles From Eden*, 48.

Feast of Freedom," in a commentary on Adam of Perseigne's eigh-
teenth letter, Merton writes: "Humility is indeed the close friend of
wisdom and of all the virtues . . . if we do not have humility, we
cannot learn any of them."[45] In both learning and teaching, humility
is to be our constant companion, for without it, errors are unavoidable. In an unpublished essay on spiritual direction Merton wrote:
"A humble person is protected by his humility itself from many delu-
sions and mistakes."[46] All learners (students and teachers) benefit
when we begin by examining our own intentions whenever the subject seems obscure or inconsistent. As Schwehn points out, "this does
not mean uncritical acceptance" but rather that the problem could very
well be within ourselves.[47] Thus the "presumption" that the author
has both wisdom and authority is a fruit of humility.

A further benefit of humility for the academic is the attitude it
fosters concerning the role of knowledge in our lives. The debate in
education which centers around knowledge as either means or ends
is misguided. In one of his final addresses, while in Thailand, Merton
spoke of his hopes for his Asian journey. He writes:

> I have left my monastery to come here not just as a research scholar
> or even as an author (which I also happen to be). I come as a pil-
> grim who is anxious to obtain not just information, not just "facts"
> about other monastic traditions, but to drink from ancient sources
> of monastic vision and experience. I seek not only to learn more
> (quantitatively) about religion and about monastic life, but to be-
> come a better and more enlightened monk (qualitatively) myself.[48]

This passage touches on several themes related to the virtue of humility. First, the recognition of one's own position. Merton identifies
himself, in spite all other accomplishments, as a pilgrim. This is humility in its popular usage as a modest sense of one's own importance.
Merton also indicates his purpose as "to drink" from the other religious traditions. This is humility as a virtue, essential to establishing

45. "The Feast of Freedom," 26.
46. "Spiritual Direction," *Merton: Collected Essays*, vol. 13, 206. For Merton's
thoughts on the concept of "Mertonism," see *The School of Charity: The Letters of
Thomas Merton on Religious Renewal and Spiritual Direction*, ed. Patrick Hart (New
York: Farrar, Straus, Giroux, 1990) 186.
47. Schwehn, *Exiles From Eden*, 48.
48. *The Asian Journal* (New York: New Directions, 1973) 312–313.

a context for learning. Finally, this passage reveals a Merton seeking knowledge not only as an end (to learn more facts) but also knowledge as a means (to become a better human being). The dichotomy of knowledge as either an end or a means is false. On this final journey Merton's focus was on both the quantitative and qualitative.

Faith. Schwehn quotes James Gustafson who observed "that all our knowing involves 'faith,' human confidence in what we have received."[49] As a virtue for learning and teaching, this faith is not so much synonymous with "belief" but rather should be viewed as "trust." We all rely and build on the work and thoughts of others. Merton understood this in terms of his relationship with tradition, specifically the Catholic tradition. This relationship has best been traced by William H. Shannon in *Silent Lamp,* particularly chapter 9, "Gethsemani: The Gift of Faith." Shannon's work will not be rehearsed here, except to point out two passages where Merton's comments reveal the virtue of faith as necessary for an "ethos of inquiry." In a discussion of monastic tradition in *No Man Is an Island,* Shannon quotes Merton, who writes:

> Tradition is living and active . . . [It] does not form us automatically: we have to work to understand it . . . [It] teaches us how to live and shows us how to take responsibility for our own lives. Tradition, which is always old, is at the same time ever new because it is always reviving—born again in each generation, to be lived and applied in a new and particular way . . . Tradition is creative. Always original, it always opens out new horizons for an old journey . . . Tradition teaches us how to live, because it develops and expands our powers and shows us how to give ourselves completely to the world in which we live.[50]

Such a statement cannot be made without a faith or trust in what one has received. As was the case with humility, faith is not an uncritical acceptance, rather it seeks to return continually to that knowledge (revelation) which must be applied anew by each generation. Or as Merton put it as he was identifying himself as "a progressive," faith seeks "continuity with the past" and yet is "completely open to the

---

49. James Gustafson, "Human Confidence and Rational Activity," in *Cresset* (September 1988) 17. Quoted by Schwehn, *Exiles from Eden,* 49.

50. *No Man Is An Island,* 150–151, as quoted by William Shannon in *Silent Lamp* (New York: Crossroad, 1992) 166.

modern world.''[51] The ethos of inquiry can only be improved with the addition of a virtue so described.

Self-Denial. As defined by Schwehn, this virtue includes "the capacity first to risk and then to give ourselves up if necessary for the sake of the truth."[52] For Schwehn, this involves not only a process of testing our opinions but awareness that while so doing, we literally "risk ourselves."[53] Merton would seemingly be paradigmatic with regard to this virtue. Monastic discipline itself is this process of "risking" oneself, in this case for the sake of the gospel. Ultimately, monastic formation "means the transformation of the monk himself."[54] In the academic setting, such "risking" would be characterized by a willingness to give up what we think we know for what we find to be true.

The search for truth increasingly led Merton to the Eastern religious traditions, a step which was seen as controversial, especially in the days prior to Vatican II. Since Merton's encounter with Asian traditions has been covered in other places, I wish to make only one or two observations.[55] The idea of risking oneself for the sake of truth seems best captured in the following observation by Merton in *Conjectures of a Guilty Bystander:*

> If I affirm myself as a Catholic merely by denying all that is Muslim, Jewish, Protestant, Hindu, Buddhist, etc., in the end I will find that there is not much left for me to affirm as a Catholic; and certainly no breath of the Spirit with which to affirm it.[56]

Such risking of our self in the pursuit of truth must go beyond any sort of detached objectivism. Merton warns of this possibility in an article for *The Catholic World:*

51. *Conjectures of a Guilty Bystander,* 312.
52. Schwehn, *Exiles From Eden,* 49.
53. Ibid.
54. "The Feast of Freedom," 10.
55. See Alexander Lipski, *Thomas Merton and Asia: His Quest for Utopia* (Kalamazoo: Cistercian Publications, 1983); Lawrence S. Cunningham, "Crossing Over in the Late Writings of Thomas Merton," *Toward An Integrated Humanity: Thomas Merton's Journey,* ed. Basil Pennington (Kalamazoo: Cistercian Publications, 1988) 192–201; and Deba P. Patnaik, "Syllables of the Great Song: Merton and Asian Religious Thought," *The Message of Thomas Merton,* ed. Patrick Hart (Kalamazoo: Cistercian Publications, 1981) 72–90.
56. *Conjectures of a Guilty Bystander,* 129.

> Can we be content to leave the rich Asian heritage of wisdom at the level of "comparative religion," and subject it to superficial and passing consideration, checking off concepts like 'Tao' and 'Dharma' and 'Dhyana' as a bored tourist might saunter through the Louvre vaguely registering the famous masterpieces as he walked by them?[57]

The academic virtue of self-denial or risking oneself would seem to be the necessary corrective to the "bored tourist" syndrome endemic within contemporary higher education. Parker Palmer claims that the discipline of studying outside of one's field involves a "risking oneself."[58] Thomas Merton's wide-ranging interests contributed in no small part to his teaching ability and serve as an example to academics on the dangers of overspecialization.[59]

  Charity. Schwehn identified charity or love as the greatest of the virtues, and sought to define it through examples. As a historian Schwehn wondered if the exercise of charity (tempered with justice) toward historical subjects increased the quality of his thinking. He declares that such an exercise

> is bound to make me a better historian: more cautious in appraisal, more sympathetic with human failings, less prone to stereotype and caricature. And insofar as this is so, the manner of teaching others to think historically ought to cultivate, at least through force of example, the virtue of charity.[60]

Many examples of this in Merton's writings offer themselves as evidence of this understanding of charity as an academic virtue.

  In his essay on "Vocation and Modern Thought," Merton offers a charitable (though brief) rereading of many of the great thinkers who had been dismissed on ideological grounds. Why charity towards Marx, Freud, Nietzsche, Lenin, and others? Merton answers the question:

57. "Christian Culture Needs Oriental Wisdom," *The Catholic World* (May 1962) 182.

58. Parker Palmer, *To Know as We Are Known*, 114.

59. See Lawrence S. Cunningham, "The Life of Thomas Merton as Paradigm: The View of Academe," *The Message of Thomas Merton*, ed. Patrick Hart (Kalamazoo: Cistercian Publications, 1981) 154–165.

60. Schwehn, *Exiles from Eden*, 51.

But we must frankly recognize the importance of these thinkers: they have all in one way or another concerned themselves very deeply with the predicament of modern man; with his special needs, his peculiar hopes, his chances of attaining these hopes. This concern in itself is by no means incompatible with a Christian outlook.[61]

Merton is able to find much of value in these very different thinkers, though he certainly is not blind to their faults.[62] In this passage, Merton embodies an observation made by Schwehn, who noted: "A reviewer who tempers justice with charity just will be to that extent a better reviewer than one who is uncharitable or unjust."[63]

When we turn from major post-enlightenment thinkers to the study of monasticism, the expectation of Merton's charity would seem obvious and hardly worthy of note. Yet, in these works we see the other side of "academic" charity, one which must be tempered with justice. In the introductory essay to *The Wisdom of the Desert*, Merton again strikes what seems to be the appropriate balance between charity and justice. While noting the "strange reputation," "lack of conventionality," and "fanaticism" of the Desert Fathers, Merton sets them in their context, continually finding ongoing relevance for their message and method.[64] The same may be said of Merton's essay, "Herakleitos: A Study," which details the life and work of a philosopher of the fifth century B.C.[65] An examination of the literary essays would find the same charity much in evidence.[66]

Humility, faith, self-denial, and charity. Spiritual virtues which are found in some form in many, if not all, religious traditions. Merton saw them embodied in his own mentors and they are embodied

61. *Contemplation in a World of Action* (Garden City, NY: Doubleday, 1971) 51.

62. Ibid., 53–57. Here Merton evaluates Marx, Freud, Kierkegaard, Nietzsche, Sartre, Heidegger, T. S. Eliot, Darwin, and de Chardin. Only de Chardin was singled out by Merton as being immensely popular within Catholic seminaries of the period.

63. Schwehn, *Exiles From Eden*, 69.

64. "The Wisdom of the Desert," *Thomas Merton: Spiritual Master*, ed. Lawrence Cunningham (New York: Paulist, 1992) 265–279.

65. "Herakleitos the Obscure" first appeared in *Jubilee* magazine in September 1960. Reprinted in *The Behavior of Titans* (1961). It also appears in Lawrence Cunningham's *Thomas Merton: Spiritual Master* (New York: Paulist, 1992) 280–293.

66. *The Literary Essays of Thomas Merton*, ed. Patrick Hart (New York: New Directions, 1981).

in Thomas Merton, along with many others of importance in education: loyalty, hospitality, and friendship.[67] These virtues offer more
than a moral challenge, they have cognitive dimensions.[68] Their place
in our lives will not only improve our character, but will improve our
learning and teaching. As Thomas Del Prete notes, perhaps Merton's
description of scholar Ananda K. Coomaraswamy, can serve as a tribute to Merton himself:

> [He] was a voice bearing witness to the truth, and he wanted noth-
> ing but for others to receive that truth in their own way, in agree-
> ment with their own mental and spiritual context. As if there was
> any other way of accepting it.[69]

Only by embodying these types of academic virtues can teachers hope
to transform themselves and their students. It begins (and ends) with
the teacher. Again Merton: "Merely reading books and following the
written instructions of past masters is no substitute for direct contact
with a living teacher."[70]

67. For an analysis of Merton's mentors and models, see Thomas Del Prete,
Thomas Merton and the Education of the Whole Person, 148–155. Most prominent among
Merton's mentors was Mark Van Doren, who both embodied many of the aca-
demic virtues and who elicited them from his students.

68. Schwehn, *Exiles From Eden*, 50.

69. *The Hidden Ground of Love*, ed. William H. Shannon (New York: Farrar,
Straus, Giroux, 1985) 129.

70. *Contemplation in a World of Action*, 299. Additional research could compare the idea of the wisdom teacher within Western monasticism to that of the
Eastern wisdom traditions, particularly the master/disciple relationship. Merton's
life and work would appear to provide a framework for such a project.

Humanizing the University:
Adding the Contemplative Dimension

Julia Ann Upton, R.S.M.

"The purpose of education," Thomas Merton wrote, "is to show a person how to define himself authentically and spontaneously in relation to his world—not to impose a prefabricated definition of the world, still less an arbitrary definition of the individual himself."[1] Later in the same essay he reflected on the purpose of higher education "in more outrageous terms," as he put it. "The function of the university is to help men and women save their souls and, in so doing, to save their society . . . from the hell of meaninglessness, of obsession, of complex artifice, of systematic lying, of criminal evasions and neglects, of self-destructive futilities."[2]

Higher education has come under intense scrutiny recently for a number of interrelated reasons. Both public and private institutions are perceived as failing to prepare students for their roles in a changing society. People are calling for more accountability. In effect, they want a guarantee on their investment. So there is a flurry of activity in developing adequate assessment tools. Still an essential ingredient is missing. I propose that before we can adequately prepare students to assume their role in society, we need to restore to all of our educational institutions the contemplative dimension.

One of the most impressionable pieces of information I recall learning in high school world history class concerned the four cradles

1. Thomas Merton, "Learning to Live," in *Love and Living*, edited by Naomi Burton Stone and Brother Patrick Hart (New York: Harcourt, Brace, 1985) 3.
    2. Ibid., 4.

of civilization: the valleys of the Nile, the Tigris and Euphrates, the Indus, and the Yellow Rivers. The change to the so-called "civilized" ways of living took place in these great river valleys first, where the land was fertile and the inhabitants, freed from the intense struggle for survival and always on the move looking for new gaming and fishing sites, learned to meet their basic needs through agriculture. The time and stability this brought, we were taught, became catalysts for the growth of civilization. People sought ways to improve and decorate their essentials: tools, clothing, and shelter, for example. Thus humankind was set on the trajectory called civilization, leading eventually to exploration, invention, industrialization, automation, and technologization. Neil Postman, in his most recent book, has gone so far as to say that we have now actually become a "technopoly" in which technology has become our God.[3]

Thomas Merton wrote one essay, "Learning to Live," concerned specifically with higher education. The first draft of this essay, originally entitled "Learning to Learn," was written in July 1967 for a volume of essays by distinguished alumni of Columbia University, published under the title *University on the Heights.*[4] The essay also appears in the collection *Love and Living.*[5] Perhaps because Merton was writing this essay in the same season I was graduating from a college not too far from Gethsemani, I have found myself mulling over Merton's ideas in relation to my own life within and outside the university, and as they apply to society at large.

In his essay "Learning to Live" Merton states that the goal of life is "learning who one is . . . what one has to offer to the contemporary world, and then learning how to make that offering valid."[6] As was stated earlier, in Merton's point of view the purpose of education is "to show students how to define themselves authentically and spontaneously in relation to their world." Notice that his focus is on the student; not a collection of courses or accumulation of credits. A principal function of colleges and universities, he concludes, should

---

3. See Neil Postman, *Technopoly: The Surrender of Culture to Technology* (New York: Random House, 1992) 40–55.

4. Wesley First, ed., *University on the Heights* (Garden City, N.Y.: Doubleday, 1969) 187–199.

5. Thomas Merton, *Love and Living*, 3–14.

6. Merton, "Learning to Live," 3.

therefore be "to help students discover themselves—to help men and women to save their souls, and in so doing, to save society."[7]

Saving one's soul is not an antiquated concept. In fact, it is enjoying quite a popular renaissance today. Having moved beyond our churches, concern for and care of the soul has currently taken up residence on the best-seller lists and talk-show circuit. "Becoming the most that we can be is also the definition of *salvation*," Scott Peck points out in language that is congruent with Merton's own. "The term literally means 'healing.' As we apply 'salve' to our skin to heal it, so we can learn to apply the principles of mental health to our lives to heal, to make us whole, to save our souls, individually and collectively."[8]

Among other things, Merton saw society needing to be saved from "the hell of meaninglessness, of obsession, of systematic lying, of criminal evasions and neglect, and of self-destructive futilities."[9] A generation later, however, we find our culture in that very "hell of meaninglessness," where we market Obsession (using advertisements that in another context we would certainly label "pornographic"), where we not only condone, but actually celebrate lying, where we witness criminal evasions and neglect by the highest authorities of church and state, and where self-destructive futilities are played out in television news broadcasts night after night.

Still speaking of higher education, Merton recognized that the "danger" of education is that "it so easily confuses means with ends," or worse, that "it . . . forgets both and devotes itself merely to the mass production of uneducated graduates.[10] In his best-selling book *The Care of the Soul*, Thomas Moore sees that this has already happened. "Soul" has been extracted from education because we conceive education to be about skills and information, not about depth of feeling and imagination.[11]

In a recent address, Frank Wong, the provost and vice-president for academic affairs at the University of Redlands, said of higher education: "It may be that we are losing the public trust because at some

---

7. Ibid., 3–4.

8. M. Scott Peck, M.D., *A World Waiting To Be Born: Civility Rediscovered* (New York: Bantam 1993) 12.

9. Merton, "Learning to Live," 4.

10. Ibid., 11.

11. Thomas Moore, *Care of the Soul: A Guide for Cultivating Depth and Sacredness in Everyday Life* (San Francisco: HarperCollins, 1992) 208.

deeper level we are not providing what the public needs." Developing this idea, he further observed:

> It may be that we are not so much responding to the accelerated sense of disconnection in our time but that we are reflecting it— perhaps even exacerbating it. It may be that we have unintentionally promoted a fragmented, disconnected, incoherent view of life because we have become so narrowly specialized in our separate, private visions of knowledge and the world.[12]

Carpe Diem

There is no denying that we are in a time of crisis, but I prefer the Native American approach which sees crises as opportunities to be seized rather than occasions to abandon ship. We have before us one of those rare opportunities to look at our culture and our lives woven into it, and to decide how we want to live our lives and what impact we want to have on the next generation.

In addressing the national convention of the National Education Association in 1990, Norman Lear, the celebrated writer/producer of prime-time television entertainment, conveyed deep concern about what he regards as our "unhealthy reticence . . . to discuss what may be our most distinctive trait . . . our mysterious inner life, the fertile invisible realm that is the wellspring for our species' creativity and morality."[13]

As was stated earlier, my thesis is that one antidote to our present situation is restoring the "contemplative dimension" to university life. I use the verb "restore" very deliberately, because once upon a time universities, like monasteries, were seen to offer people a way of life, not simply a career path. As Marvin Bell reflects:

> A career means you solicit the powerful and the famous. A way of life means you live where you are with the people around you. A career means you become an authority. A way of life means you stay a student, even if you teach for a living. A career means your life increasingly comes from your art. A way of life means your

12. Frank F. Wong, "Integrated Vision and Disconnected Education: Do We Need a New American College Model?" Address dated February 3, 1993.

13. Norman Lear, "Education for the Human Spirit," an address delivered to the national convention of the National Education Association [NEA], July 7, 1990.

art continues to arise from your life. Careerism feeds off the theo-
retical, the fancified, the complicated, the coded, and the over-
wrought. . . . A way of life is nourished by the practical, the
unadorned, the complex, and a direct approach to the mysterious.[14]

Using Joan Chittister's definition of contemplation as "the ability to see through, and to see into, and to see despite, and to see without blinders," I will examine four aspects of the contemplative
dimension which we have lost from university life, and consequently
from the culture: silence, solitude, sabbath and stability. I agree with
Chittister when she writes that "in America today, perhaps as never
before, there is a great need for seeing hearts, for contemplative awareness of the kind of world we are creating for tomorrow."[15] Adding
these four aspects of contemplation to university life, even in the slightest degree, I believe, will remove the blinders and give us "seeing
hearts."

The Sounds of Silence

Whatever happened to the "sounds of silence" about which we
were singing around the same time Merton was writing "Learning to
Live"? Now we live with noise pollution, and many people find silence a great burden—a possibility too frightening to even consider.
As a result muzak fills our elevators, and televisions blare from every
room in the house from morning until night. We have the expression,
"I don't have time to think," but the reality is that we no longer have
the quiet to think.[16]

In a recent *Time* essay, Pico Iyer observed that first we have to
earn silence, and then work for it—that is, work "to make it not an
absence but a presence; not emptiness but repletion." Whereas some

14. Marvin Bell, "Poetry Is A Way of Life, Not a Career," *The Chronicle of
Higher Education* (Febuary 16, 1994) B5. From the author's essay "Homage to the
Runner: Bloody Brain Work" in *The Pushcart Prize XVIII: Best of the Small Presses*
(Pushcart Press, 1993).

15. Joan Chittister, "Of Moses' Mother and Pharaoh's Daughter: A Model
of Contemporary Contemplation," *The Merton Annual* 3 (1990) 62. Originally delivered at the Merton Center at Columbia University, New York, on November
12, 1987.

16. Joan Chittister, *The Rule of Benedict: Insights for the Ages* (New York: Crossroad, 1992) 124.

might see silence as a pause, Iyer sees it as "that enchanted place where space is cleared and time is stayed and the horizon itself expands." "In silence," he continues, "we often say, we can hear ourselves think; but what is truer to say is that in silence we can hear ourselves not think, and so sink below our selves into a place far deeper than mere thought allows. In silence, we might better say, we can hear someone else think."[17]

Why such fear of silence? I think the real fear is of emptiness. Because we are so culturally adapted to having someone else fill in all our silent spaces, university students, along with others, either plug themselves in to someone else's thoughts and values, via car radio or CD player, or they fill in the silent spaces with their own inner chatter—"monkey mind," as one author calls it. The fullness we all seek is speaking in the silence within us, but we block it out with "the static of nonsense day in and day out, relinquishing the spirit of silence, numbing our hearts in a noise-polluted world."[18]

Flight from Solitude

"Never be alone, never be lonely" is the message pounded into people unconsciously by the entertainment industry. The image that flashes across television and movie screens is that happiness and popularity are to be found only in an endless round of the social swirl. Our cultural dualism, Parker Palmer points out, leads us to think of solitude and community as polar opposites.[19] The irony is that instead of finding community at the other pole, one finds loneliness, and what has been lost in the mad dash away from even the possibility of solitude is one's self and the heart of the world. "The price for this evasion," Rollo May writes, "is a deep loneliness and sense of isolation. With these go depression and the conviction that we have never really lived, that we have been exiled from life."[20]

In solitude, with which and for which he struggled, Thomas Merton not only came to know himself, he came to know the world.

17. Pico Iyer, "The Eloquent Sounds of Silence," *TIME* (January 25, 1993) 74.
18. Chittister, *Rule*, 61.
19. Parker Palmer, *The Company of Strangers: Christians and the Renewal of America's Public Life* (New York: Crossroad, 1991) 57.
20. Rollo May, *The Cry for Myth* (New York: Norton, 1991) 106.

Although in the passage below Merton is referring specifically to his relationship with Pasternak, it is clear (later in the passage) that he considers it possible to develop a relationship with others beyond the limits of individuality. Reflecting on this in a letter to Boris Pasternak, dated August 22, 1958, Merton wrote:

> It is as if we met on a deeper level life on which individuals are not separate beings . . . known to one another in God. This is a very simple . . . obvious expression for something quite normal and ordinary. . . . each person is destined to reach with others an understanding and a unity which transcends individuality, and Russian tradition describes this with a concept we do not fully possess in the West—*sobornost*.[21]

Thomas Del Prete, who probably knows more about what Merton thought about education than even Merton knew, concludes that "Merton's fundamental social concern was for the modern, particularly Western, world's loss of a sense of interiority and therefore its disconnection from a true sense of reality and spiritual identity.[22] If Merton had such concern three decades ago, what would he ever say to us today?

In the preface to *Disputed Questions*, Merton wrote, "mass society is constructed out of disconnected individuals—out of empty and alienated human beings who have lost their center and extinguished their own inner light in order to depend in abject passivity upon the mass in which they cohere without affectivity or intelligent purpose.[23]

To use Parker Palmer's image, we must "catch a vision of community which supports the solitude that makes authentic inwardness possible."[24] Institutions of higher learning are ideal places for "catching" just such a vision and, fortunately, renewed attention is being given recently to seeing colleges and universities as "learning communities."[25]

21. Thomas Merton, *The Courage for Truth: Letters to Writers* [CT], edited by Christine M. Bochen (New York: Farrar, Straus, Giroux, 1993) 88.

22. Thomas Del Prete, *Thomas Merton and the Education of the Whole Person* (Birmingham: Religious Education Press, 1990) 6.

23. Thomas Merton, *Disputed Questions* (New York: Harcourt, Brace, Jovanovich, [1960] 1985) x.

24. Palmer, 156–157.

25. See Barbara Leigh Smith, "The Learning Community Model," *Liberal Education* 77/2 (March–April 1991) 32–39.

In a letter to Helen Wolff, Boris Pasternak's publisher, dated November 2, 1967, Merton wrote:

> I think it is terribly important today that we keep alive the sense and possibility of a strong communion of seemingly isolated individuals in various places and cultures; eventually the foundation of true human community is there and not in the big states or institutions.[26]

I agree, although I think that even a large academic institution might be the foundation of true human community. "One of the constant characteristics of mystics of all cultures and all religions in all ages," Scott Peck writes, "has been their ever-present consciousness of an invisible interconnectedness beneath the surface of things."[27] Wouldn't it be wonderful if that could be said of academicians as well?

Our Lost Sabbaths

In *The Silent Pulse: A Search for the Perfect Rhythm That Exists in Each of Us*, biologist George Leonard develops the thesis that the entire universe has a single pulse, sharing the same heartbeat. We experience this phenomenon periodically, label it "synchrony," and regard it with surprise. Leonard has studied the phenomenon with the discipline of a scientist and sees it as the right order of things, the "silent pulse of perfect rhythm."[28]

Do you remember the days when our culture kept Sunday holy unto the Lord? Stores, even pharmacies, were closed. We wore Sunday clothes, indulged in the Sunday pleasures of visiting, family dinners, and relaxation. What has happened to all our lost sabbaths?

"Time," the historian Edward Thompson observes, "has become a currency which we "spend" instead of "pass."[29] We are all so busy that we no longer have time to relax—to sabbath. And what are we so busy doing? Studies across the country have shown that Americans spend more time shopping than anyone else. Not only do they

26. Merton, CT, 107–108.
27. Peck, 20.
28. George Leonard, *The Silent Pulse: A Search for the Perfect Rhythm That Exists in Each of Us* (New York: Dutton, 1978) 132.
29. E. P. Thompson, "Time, Work-Discipline and Industrial Capitalism," *Past and Present* 38 (December 1967) 61.

spend a higher fraction of the money they earn, but with the explosion of consumer debt, they are now spending what they haven't earned.[30]

The ideology of modern economics would have us believe that material progress has resulted in greater satisfaction and a sense of well-being. The reality, Juliet Schor points out in her study of the "overworked American," is that the rising workload has contributed significantly to a variety of social problems: an alarming increase in stress-related diseases, particularly among women; a "sleep deficit" among Americans, with the average person getting 60–90 minutes less a night than they should for optimum health and performance; and most alarming of all is our neglect of the children, up to one-third of whom care for themselves.[31] The economist Sylvia Hewlett links this "parenting deficit" to a number of problems plaguing the country's youth: poor performance in school, psychological problems, drug and alcohol use, and teen suicide. Children are being "cheated" out of childhood, and there is a profound sense among the children that adults just don't care about them.[32]

College students are caught up in this as well, and many today hold full-time jobs while carrying a full load of classes. A generation ago that was just not possible, but with so many businesses now operating twenty-four hours a day, possibilities abound.[33] I have several students who come to early morning classes, having just put in an eight-hour night on the job. Although it would be more conducive to education if their jobs were related to their studies and functioned more as internships, it is not surprising that money is more often the determining factor.

We are now a nation locked into a work-spend cycle with leisure—sabbathing—left out of the loop. This maniacal life-style, reflected in the university as well as in the larger society, is now seen to be a kind of drug. First you like it, then you get used to it, then you need it. Psychologists and sociologists are drawing our attention

30. Juliet B. Schor, *The Overworked American: The Unexpected Decline of Leisure* (New York: Basic Books, 1991) 3.

31. Schor, 11–12.

32. See Sylvia Hewlett, *When the Bough Breaks: The Cost of Neglecting Our Children* (New York: Basic Books, 1991).

33. See Martin Moore-Ede, *The Twenty-Four Hour Society: Understanding Human Limits in a World That Never Stops* (Reading, Mass.: Addison-Wesley, 1993).

now to this madness that has us "psyched up" at all hours—dealing with things, organizing bits of information, making schedules, grinding out publications. As Carol Orsborn notes, with apologies to Descartes, "I do, therefore I am."[34]

In "Making Sense of Soul and Sabbath; Brain Processes and the Making of Meaning," James B. Ashbrook advances two interconnected speculations: that sabbathing is found in the brain's biorhythms; and that the essential structure of our unique individuality requires sabbathing for its coherent vitality. "Because our essence as human beings involves the making of meaning, the biorhythms of sabbathing and remembering are the means by which soul makes its story viable.[35]

Memory consolidation takes time, specifically a period of one to three years. To be retained, memories must be dreamed, and dreaming involves intense emotional appraisal over time.[36] Without working memory, nothing is personally meaningful. We have no unique identity, no sense of continuity, we lack a sense of self.[37] In truth we lose our soul—that basic structuring of our unique self-world interaction.[38]

Ashbrook recounts a wonderful anecdote which reportedly took place in Africa during the last century. He tells of a caravan of traders that had been pushing their porters hard. Eventually, the porters stopped, and nothing would get them going again. When the traders demanded to know what was wrong, the Africans explained: "We have been traveling so long and so fast that we need to wait for our souls to catch up with our bodies." While Ashbrook calls jet lag "an empirical equivalent" of "waiting for our souls to catch up with our bodies,"[39] I think our souls are still on the losing end.

34. Carol Orsborn, *Enough is Enough: Simple Solutions for Complex People* (San Rafael: New World Library, 1992) 70.

35. James B. Ashbrook, "Making Sense of Soul and Sabbath; Brain Processes and the Making of Meaning," *Zygon: Journal of Religion and Science* 27/1 (March 1992) 32–33.

36. Robin Fox, "The Passionate Mind: Brain, Dreams, Memory, and Social Categories," *Zygon: Journal of Religion and Science* 21 (March 1986) 35–38.

37. Eugene Winograd, "Continuities between Ecological and Laboratory Approaches to Memory," in *Remembering Reconsidered*, ed. Alric Neisser and Eugene Winograd. Emory Symposia in Cognition Series, no. 2. (Cambridge: University Press, 1988) 17.

38. Ashbrook, 36.

39. Ashbrook, 32.

Talmud scholars teach that the Sabbath is important for three reasons:

> It equalizes the rich and the poor, so that for at least one day a week everyone is the same—equally free.
>
> It gives us time to evaluate our work, just as God evaluated the work of creation on the Sabbath.
>
> It gives us time to contemplate the meaning of life.[40]

In nature God offers all of us a chance to enter the crystalline state. Sabbathing is not impossible, does not require great wealth or a monumental time commitment. "To leave the disrhythmnic city streets for some deserted wood or meadow or seashore is often enough in itself to trigger a period of perfect rhythm"[41] and allow our souls time to catch up with our minds and bodies.

Finding Stability in an Increasingly Unstable World

"Stability," not only sounds antiquated, it sounds downright un-American. After all, we are the "westward ho!" nation that prides itself on progress—or at least on the illusion of progress. In *aikido*, you are taught to become fully aware of and take responsibility for your own center. Then your center becomes one with the center of the universe.[42] But then that would require standing still, mindfulness, commitment—concepts that have become antithetical to this technopoly. Instead of being captivated by the holy, we are seduced by the new. "We not only believe in change," Rollo May observes, "we worship it."[43]

Always on the move, we are unable to put down roots, we no longer have a sense of place. The increasing incidence of homelessness in American cities and towns is a metaphor for homelessness in our hearts. "Homeless people embody a deprivation of soul which we all experience to the extent that we live in an inanimate world without the sense of a world soul to connect us to things."[44] In Europe a com-

40. Ingrid Trobisch, *The Confident Woman: Finding Quiet Strength in a Turbulent World* (San Francisco: Harper, 1993) 149–150.
41. Leonard, 122–123.
42. Leonard, 113.
43. May, 102.
44. Moore, 271.

munity's "home" is the village church. In New England villages, May points out, we probably see the last vestige of this in the "common." What has replaced common ground for the rest of us? The Mall—our "new cathedrals."

In 1992 the African nation Ivory Coast, although not without controversy and dissention, completed the largest basilica in the world. In the same year The Mall of America near Minneapolis was completed—"a retail/entertainment complex of unparalleled proportions." Is that what the world needs—yet another retail paradise?

In a presentation James Appleberry made at California State University in 1992, he observed that "the sum total of humankind's knowledge doubled from 1750 to 1900 (or 150 years). It doubled again from 1900 to 1950 (50 years), [and] again from 1960 to 1965 (5 years). It has been estimated that the sum total of humankind's knowledge has doubled at least once every five years since then. . . . It has been further projected that by the year 2020 knowledge will double every 73 days!"[45]

I wonder how I will be able to cope with such relentless change. And then I remember an experience I had standing on the beach at Paradise Island in the Bahamas one day. An avid swimmer accustomed to the wild Atlantic, even I knew the surf and the undertoe were too dangerous that day. So I stood ankle-deep and admired the raging power of the usually calm Caribbean. As I did, I realized that in order to remain upright, I had to dig my feet into the sand, because the sea was stealing the ground from beneath me. "How like life!" I observed. In the turbulent times one needs to dig in deep. That's one way of practicing stability.

By Way of Conclusion

In *The Unsettling of America* Wendell Berry uses two images to illustrate these opposite approaches to life: a strip-miner and the old-fashioned idea or ideal of a farmer.[46] The first is exploitative; the second nurturing. "The first principle of the exploitative mind is to di-

45. Quoted in President James J. Whalen, "Humanity and the Knowledge Explosion: Preserving the Delicate Thread That Binds Us," Ithaca College Convocation, August 23, 1993.

46. Wendell Berry, *The Unsettling of America: Culture and Agriculture* (San Francisco, Sierra Club 1977) 7.

vide and conquer. And surely there has never been a people more ominously and painfully divided than we are—both against each other and within ourselves."[47] What we lack in our day is a sense of peace— quiet, deep, relaxed peace.

Berry looks to the Amish as model nurturers—a community in the full sense of the word. They are able to survive because at their center is God, and they seek to live in harmony with all creation. They have not sold their souls to institutions, and so are not victimized by them. Berry calls the Amish "the truest geniuses of technology" because they understand the necessity of limiting it, and they know how to limit it, because the health of the community is their standard.[48]

What Rollo May refers to as "the seduction of the new,"[49] and Neil Postman calls "our boundless lust for what is new,"[50] is basically consumerism, the addiction to consumption. People who are addicted in this way are not able to become rooted and find repetition itself boring. They have no felt connection to things, no appreciation for symbols or rituals. To be addicted is to have sold your soul. "To elevate one god," Neil Postman writes in *Technopoly*, "requires the demotion of another. 'Thou shalt have no other gods before me' applies as well to a technological divinity as any other."[51] When one renders to Caesar the things that are God's, one can't then render them to God.

I began my college education as a chemistry major, and I recall making various types of solutions. In a super-saturated solution, there is too much solid to be absorbed by the solution, and consequently some of the solid material is lost from the solution, and settles at the bottom of the beaker. Ours is a super-saturated society. We have too much of almost everything—noise, information, consumer goods. My concern, both as a theologian and as an educator, is that what will be lost is what we need most to survive as a people—the essence of our humanity, our soul.

47. Berry, 11.

48. Berry, 210–211.

49. Rollo May, *The Cry for Myth* (New York: Norton, 1991) 101.

50. Neil Postman, *Technopoly: The Surrender of Culture to Technology* (New York: Random House, 1992) 11.

51. Postman, *Technopoly*, 165.

Learning to Live:
Merton's Students Remember His Teaching

Gloria Kitto Lewis

Merton once said that the great thing in his life was his love of truth, by which he meant wisdom as opposed merely to knowledge. He maintained that nothing was more precious than "communicating and sharing the truth."[1] It is not surprising, therefore, that he felt his vocation was to be not only that of a hermit and writer, but equally important, to be a teacher. Indeed, when we look at his life, we immediately see the centrality of the latter. Most of his life was devoted to teaching, first in colleges (Columbia, 1940–1941, and St. Bonaventure, 1941) and in the monastery where, from 1951 through 1965, he was Master of Students and later Novice Master. Currently, there is notable interest in Merton as teacher. In some measure this interest is traceable to the research being published on holistic education and the place of the intuitive, the spiritual and the ethical in liberal arts study. Merton himself as a person, is, to be sure, our primary source if we wish to investigate his spirituality of education and pedagogical strategies. In unpublished material (his orientation notes for lectures, conference tapes and the like) as well as in published works (*Love and Living*, *The Inner Experience*, and *The Seven Storey Mountain*), we find comments about his educational background, philosophy of learning, students, and the two teachers who played a decisive role in his own formation: Mark Van Doren and Dan Walsh. But any real understanding of Merton as teacher must also turn to the practical effects of his instruction on students. And yet, understandable as it may be, it is

1. Thomas Del Prete, *Thomas Merton and the Education of the Whole Person* (Birmingham: Religious Education Press, 1990) 165.

still astonishing that, with the notable exception of Thomas Del Prete and Victor A. Kramer, scholars have paid little attention to this side of Merton's teaching.[2]

In an effort to learn more about the responses of Merton's students to his abilities as teacher, I asked Brother Patrick Hart for permission to conduct one-hour taped conferences with seven of Merton's students at the Abbey of Gethsemani. Brother Patrick granted my request and on May 9–10, 1992, I engaged in interviews with Brothers Paul Quenon, Harold Thibodeau, Columban Weber, Fathers James Conner, Michael Casagram, and Matthew Kelty; as well as Abbot Timothy Kelly. Brother Patrick served as my host, and I had ample opportunity to talk informally with him also. Because all these monks had come to the monastery in the 1950s and 1960s, they attended Merton's conferences.[3] The subjects they studied under Merton were many: the thought of St. Bernard and the Desert Fathers; the monastic vows; spiritual direction; and mystical theology. Though all of those interviewed attended Merton's conferences on monastic and theological subjects, only some had regularly attended Merton's Sunday conferences. These Sunday afternoon lectures, presented during 1965–1968 while Merton was living in the hermitage, were frequently on literary figures: Rilke, Hopkins, Blake, T.S. Eliot, Camus, and Faulkner.

Preparing students for life in the monastery was challenging for Merton because their backgrounds were so diverse. Matthew Kelty described the novice group in the 1960s, for example, as a frustrating

2. Del Prete, 169–170; Matthew Kelty, "Looking Back to Merton/Memories and Impressions: An Interview," interviewer, Victor A. Kramer; ed. Dewey Weiss Kramer, *The Merton Annual*, vol. 1, eds. Robert Daggy, Patrick Hart, Dewey Weiss Kramer, and Victor A. Kramer (New York: AMS Press, 1988) 55–78; Flavian Burns, "Merton's Contributions as Teacher, Writer, and Community Member: An Interview," interviewer, Victor A. Kramer; ed. Dewey Weiss Kramer, *The Merton Annual*, vol. 2, eds. Robert Daggy, Patrick Hart, Dewey Weiss Kramer, and Victor A. Kramer (New York: AMS Press, 1989) 71–92.

3. Brothers Columban and Paul and Father Timothy attended conferences as novices under Merton. Fathers James and Michael attended these conferences as junior professed. Father Michael came to the Abbey of Gethsemani in 1964 from another monastery and, along with other juniors, was allowed to sit in on the novices' sessions. Father Matthew also attended the sessions; however, he was already a priest. Brother Patrick was not actually a student of Merton's, but he did attend Merton's conferences on occasion and did listen to the talks Merton had given the day before to the novices as he, along with the other brothers, prepared vegetables in their workroom.

mixture of young high school boys, college graduates, businessmen, and priests.[4] Brother Paul entered the monastery in 1958, just out of high school, while Father Matthew came to the Abbey of Gethsemani in 1960, at the age of forty-five, as an ordained priest. Few had had Merton's rich and rigorous liberal education which helped him to develop a certain self-reflective stance toward his intellect, his senses, his feelings and spirit.

By drawing upon his deep spiritual and intellectual strengths, Merton found himself able to teach this widely divergent group of students. With commitment and passion, he sought to enable these students to discover their true selves in their religious study, believing that the general goal of education was to discover "in the ground of one's being, a 'self' which [was] ultimate and indestructible."[5] Patiently, carefully, reverently, he instructed them in monasticism; and because he valued a humanistic education, he also chose to introduce them to literature, music, and fine art, particularly in the later Sunday conferences. Through these encounters with philosophers, theologians, and artists, Merton believed that students could discover their inner or real selves. In using their imagination, intuition, and senses in these studies, they could begin to approach wisdom, a wordless perception of the unity of self, nature, and God. In this kind of experiential, participatory study involving intellectual rigor and, more importantly, meditation, prayer, and contemplation, students could come not only to acquire surface understandings but to understand deep and abiding truth. Merton served his students not merely as a sage and task master, but as a guide, a fellow student, a monk sharing a spiritual journey with his brothers. Kindly and gently, he suggested a cognitive and, ultimately, an affective path to active and profound learning about self.

In my series of interviews with the monks, they related experiences with their teacher and fellow sojourner. I listened quietly as these monks revealed what the tapes of the conferences cannot fully reveal, namely, how students interacted with Merton in class and in private conference; how they learned best in his conferences; what they remembered and why; and how they applied what they learned in their

    4. Kelty interview with Victor A. Kramer, 57.
    5. Thomas Merton, "Learning to Live," *Love and Living.* eds. Naomi Burton Stone and Patrick Hart (New York: Bantam, 1979) 3–14.

lives as monks. Clearly, in formal conferences and informal private sessions, they learned not only from what he said, but so often from how he said it. Conscious of the tone he used, watchful of his gestures, and aware of his asides, his jokes, and his repetitions, they formed strong impressions about their mentor and friend. Together they told their invaluable story about Merton and the deep spiritual source of his teaching. Thus this commentary on Merton is *their* commentary. They talked and taught; I listened and learned.

I.

All the monks stressed that Merton established a clear and appropriate goal in his conferences that he shared with his students at the outset and adhered to through the course of study. This goal, as Brother Patrick noted, was to enable the students to move through the four classic stages: from *lectio* (reading) to *meditatio* (meditation), to *oratio* (prayer) and, finally, to *contemplatio* (contemplation). Brother Paul elaborated about Merton's purpose in the conferences:

> Father Louis was in pursuit of wisdom. His teaching was not a matter of imparting knowledge, but was aimed at the formation of the whole person, a mature monk. Thus, it did not have an academic style, but was basically monastic and sapiential. Wisdom, *sapientia* in Latin, has the same root as "to taste," *sapere*. The purpose of education is to get a taste for truth and to taste it continuously, which in fact is meditation.
>
> You know the four steps of spirituality in medieval monasticism are reading, meditation, prayer and contemplation. One leads to the other, and monastic education is a leading upward on that path. Conferences have a limited value, limited mainly in moving us into reading, and from reading to thought and understanding. Understanding in this case is mainly through experience. Father Louis kept this goal in mind: to start with the Word of God and go on to understanding it through experience. Ultimately, the goal is something only God can impart, and formal education is only the beginning.

In addition to being clear about objectives, Merton was also clear and precise about the structure of his lectures. As Father Timothy noted: "As a teacher, he was always well prepared, a capable person, well organized. He knew exactly where he was going and how he was

going to get there. . . . As novices we had to learn a certain amount
of nuts and bolts and some specifics relative to the obligations for vows.
He was very exacting in those areas, very precise. Yet, he could make
the dry text come alive. He taught with a lot of respect—always."

It was essential for Merton to present material in a tight, clear,
and organized manner. The conference periods were short—a half
hour for the conferences on monasticism and an hour for the Sunday
conferences on literature or subjects of contemporary interest. Also,
students were not expected to take notes or write papers or take ex-
aminations. Most learned by listening, as the monastic style of teaching was based on the oral repetition of main points. Though they spent
time reading in their cells and in the library, they did not have assigned
texts, nor even required or recommended reading lists. (Today, in contrast, the novices do have a specific reading list, an addition to their
course of study for which Merton is to receive credit.)

In stating that Merton's teaching style was both structured and
organic, Father Timothy emphasized Merton's flexibility, his ability to
improvise and move inductively. He found that in Merton's many well-
organized yet creatively extemporaneous presentations, there was new
and liberating space for student and teacher to explore and question.
In the end what impressed Father Timothy the most was Merton's ability to experiment and, subsequently, to initiate a new style of teaching in the abbey:

> I would say that his basic presentation on the spiritual life
> and the spiritual journey was a kind of whole new approach, a
> much healthier, broader approach. In the older traditions, the monk
> was a penitent, making reconciliation to the Lord so that the sins
> of humankind and his own sins would be forgiven. So there was
> a whole mentality that created an environment that was somewhat
> lugubrious, to say the least. Merton was anything but that. Com-
> ing with a real respect for the whole life of discipline and asceti-
> cism, he taught from the aspect of a way to freedom. He was a
> joyous, delightful person.

Along with Father Timothy, Father James appreciated Merton's
ability to be "flexible and open," to change an agenda and even his
opinions quite spontaneously. Yet, as Father Matthew observed, that
spontaneous playing with ideas bothered some:

> He could say one thing today and tomorrow he would con-
> tradict it. Not that he would say the opposite, but he would look

at it from the other side of the street. . . . It used to rattle people a little, but you needed to know that he was not to be taken literally, that you had to interpret what he had to say.

Brother Paul noted that sometimes he would change his topic simply because he saw that his students were not motivated to listen. If students stopped listening because they were seemingly uninterested in the topic for the session, Merton would simply scrap that class topic and go on to a new one. As Brother Paul recalled:

> He knew how to diversify, how to keep it lively, perhaps how to change pace. I remember his stopping and saying after two conferences on Blessed Guerric of Igny, one of our twelfth-century Cistercian Fathers, "You guys do not seem too interested in Guerric." I do not think he went on with that. He shut that off and went on to something else.

Merton's classes were lively in part because there was necessary change of pace and even of topic, and also because there was a good deal of laughter. The monks found Merton to be genuinely humorous, as the tapes of his conferences reveal. Brother Columban mentioned the good humor in the conferences:

> Father Louis once asked me how things were going—class-wise—and I responded that I was enjoying them very much. I commented that his sense of humor surprised me and he said, "If you have a sense of humor, you should use it." He would often poke fun at various things we did around the monastery in a way that we could see the wisdom of it. Someone should do a study of Merton's sense of humor.

Yet Merton's humor occasionally revealed a darker side. For example, though Father Matthew agreed that Merton was witty, he pointed out that occasionally Merton's wit could be caustic. He observed, "He had the British gift . . ., to—what do you call it—put someone down with wit, to make an understatement. You do not lose your cool—oh, no—but in elegant language you make the guy look bad. You would not do that often. That would catch up with you." He also pointed out that Merton liked to add humor, but was less receptive to students doing so. To illustrate, he told a story that reveals a part of Merton that was rather controlling and close-minded:

One time we were studying the Beguines, and this wit from
Detroit raised his hand and in seeming innocence asked, "When
did these Beguines begin?" There was a lot of laughter. Merton
didn't think it was funny because that was referring to a popular
song, "Begin the Beguine." That was typical of him. If he didn't
initiate the joke, if he wasn't in charge of the thing, it would rattle
him a little.

In his carefully conceived conferences, filled often with spontaneity and surprise, it is clear that Merton succeeded in allowing a
healthy kind of organic flow of ideas. He was able to infuse life into
the conferences in part because he engaged students in Socratic dialogue. He was skillful in asking thought-provoking questions and in
encouraging students to discover their own answers to those questions.
No doubt, he had learned a great deal from Mark Van Doren about
leading discussions while attending Van Doren's course in English
literature at Columbia University in 1935. In recalling that class in
eighteenth-century English literature, Merton concluded that Van
Doren's "questions were very good, and if you tried to answer them
intelligently, you found yourself saying excellent things that you did
not know you knew, and that you had not, in fact, known before. He
had 'educed' them from you by his question."[6]
On balance, the monks found that Merton carried on useful discussions, even though some of these oral exchanges were quite short
and were abruptly terminated. They talked, in particular, about his
effective use of questions. Their responses to this verbal interaction
through questions are significant. After all, as they were the recipients
of his queries, they are the only ones who could attest to the effective-
ness of these questions. Yet their reactions were rather surprising.
In listening to the tapes of his conferences, I felt that Merton often
rushed through a host of questions and bombarded his students with
too many questions. However, the monks, Brother Harold for one, did
not remember feeling frustrated when Merton attempted to get them
involved by throwing questions at them. In recalling Merton's presentations, he observed:

It was not a dry lecture. He was aware of his audience. If
you were falling asleep or not paying attention, he would say,

6. Thomas Merton, *The Seven Storey Mountain*, (New York: Harcourt, Brace
and Co., 1948) 139.

"Well, what do you think of that, Brother so-and-so?" If you gave
the wrong answer and everyone would laugh, he would say, "Do
you really think that?" And then he would like to interrogate for
a while. Often if you might say something that was not really on
target, he would weave it into his next theme and make it sound
all right. If it was not far off, [but] not complete enough, he would
even fill it out for you.

Brother Paul agreed, adding that Merton often used rhetorical questions effectively:

He was good at asking questions. He got us thinking. He
would sort of probe us to get some kind of response, to get our
minds in gear, and then he would go on developing it. He would
ask questions as a preparation, and then at the end, we would be
asking the questions.

However, the monks were quick to point out that Merton was
always intent on getting through a substantial amount of material and
often did not really encourage a lot of questions from them. As Father
Timothy remembers:

He could be very curt. He would answer your question very
specifically and was clear in his body language that he wanted no
more, that is, time's up. Of course, our style was not open to much
dialogue and questioning, so he really did not open classes up to
questions. It was also foreign to his style. He sometimes asked
questions to get the answers he wanted.

Brother Columban also found Merton short and sharp and noted:

I often got the impression that if he liked a particular person . . . then this student's question was okay. Merton would
even maneuver the issue to the student's advantage. But if he
didn't like the guy, he could shoot him down pretty fast, and
often did. Merton, like all teachers, had his fair-haired boys—those
who were heavily into the monastic fathers or were writing in the
French monastic journals, etc. [Most] of them are not around today!

Merton could be especially abrupt if he did not like a question
or comment. Father Timothy recalled a class on the Book of Jonah:

I remember on this day he gave this very beautiful conference on Jonah, a favorite of his, and there was this young monk

who kept raising his hand while he talked and Merton finally accepted his question. At the same time, we had a Scripture professor coming once a month, and it was just at this time when a lot of scriptural scholarship was changing, and this professor had given us a conference a month or so before on Jonah as a midrash. He said that Jonah was more of a symbolic figure. He was not a true person. Well, Merton had just given this conference on personifying Jonah as a type of spiritual person, and this guy raised his hand all the time and said that this professor had characterized Jonah completely differently, which, of course, was a poor understanding of what the professor had said and what Merton had said. Well, Merton closed his book and did not give us another talk on Scripture for another year.

Though interchanges in class were sometimes controlled, abrupt, even aborted, on balance it is fair to say that the monks agreed that Merton wanted all his students to question, to challenge, to probe— sometimes in class, always in their private study and meditation. He wished for his students to be independent not derivative thinkers. As Father Timothy said: "He gave me the impression that he really did not want disciples. If novices became interested in quoting Merton to Merton, he was very quick to cut them off and to distance himself from them." It would have been very easy for Merton, a strong-willed, fluent thinker, placed in a position of some authority, to have persuaded his students to think and feel as he did.

Though class discussions were sometimes strained, Merton's students knew that he had an ability to engage in genuine dialogue. It was in his private conferences with his students that Merton was able to establish a more equal and intimate exchange. In these one-on-one meetings, Merton revealed his well-developed listening and interpersonal skills. This ability to relate perceptively to individual students is invaluable to a teacher. Merton knew that it is in quiet discussions outside the classroom where the best teaching often occurs— for both teacher and student. The monks frequently talked about their private conferences with him, in which they had their most productive and memorable exchanges. Though it is clear that Merton was certainly a persuasive, eloquent lecturer, it was in his private encounters that he was probably the most charismatic.

Because Merton was Novice Master, novices also had special opportunities for such private conferences. Brothers Columban and

Harold remembered some of their conversations well. Brother Columban recalled:

> On a one-to-one he was marvelous. He reminds me a lot of the great communicators of our time—John Paul II, Mother Teresa of Calcutta, Matthew Fox, etc. These people are great actors, and are able to attune themselves to the particular audience at hand. You feel as if you are the only person in the world and that for them, you are. Merton fit right into this.

Brother Harold spoke about one conference in particular:

> One day I was not saying much—and this is what was amazing. Suddenly the bell rang for Compline, and I went toward the door and Merton said, "Well sooner or later you will have to stand on your own two feet." Well, that hit me like a bomb. I didn't know where that came from, because we were not even talking about me. Only later did I realize that I was really very dependent upon him and I needed to be standing on my own two feet.
>
> Ironically, in his talk in Bangkok before he died, he read this story about a Tibetan monk who was exiled, and Merton asked what you do when you get booted out of your monastery. The Tibetan monk answered that you move on. He said, "Well, you have to cross the river and stand on your own two feet." I remembered that when I read the paper later, and I remembered how true that would be because now Merton would not be coming back. I felt it more deeply then. The truth has never left me. That gives you a certain sense of your own freedom when you make your own decisions. It is still a big help to me and I tell it to people.

Because of his ability to relate to the monks on an informal basis, it is not surprising that a goodly number of the monks vividly remembered the first time they met Merton. Father Timothy's experience was typical:

> My first encounter with Merton was at the guest house. I did not know Merton was the Novice Master, and so I was just told I would meet the Novice Master in my room. And so the Novice Master came in and asked the usual questions. I introduced myself, and in conversation he asked what I knew about the monastic life, and where I had obtained my information. I said I really had read all of Merton. He asked, "What did you think?"

> I said I thought he was very romantic. He said, ''Yes, you have
> to be awfully careful of what you read.'' Together we laughed.

The students found Merton in those first meetings to be very
unassuming. That view of Merton was underscored in Merton's manner in the classroom. As Father James said, ''He was just such a totally human person, so alive and so down-to-earth and not artificial.
This was not always the case with some of the people I was exposed
to in my early years. I was never really in awe of him.'' As one of those
young men who had come to the monastery at age sixteen, and who
by his own admission was not very sophisticated, this assessment is
especially noteworthy.

That Merton was so approachable and unassuming in manner
is particularly impressive given the fact that he was a well-known literary figure. Father Matthew had an intriguing insight about Merton and
his handling of his notoriety:

> Merton had a sense of his importance. He was extremely
> aware that he was a servant for the cause and all that, and yet he
> was detached from it. I always compare it to a woman who is a
> model. She is expected to be beautiful—shockingly beautiful—and
> yet she has to convey the impression she does not know [this].
> Or it is like a child who is very pretty. When she is unconsciously
> beautiful, it is charming. Well, he was like that. He had an amaz-
> ing capacity to lose himself in whatever he was doing and pull it
> off, and that is not very common. It is hard to do. I would put
> that pretty close to holiness.

Merton was able to engage his students in lively conversations
about the conference material in large measure because he was able
to convey his love of learning in general and his fascination and respect for his subject matter in particular. Perhaps this was his greatest
gift. If a teacher communicates a fascination and delight in the study
at hand, it is quite likely that the students will also have a positive mind-
set toward the subject matter for the rest of their lives. Fortunately,
for him and his students, Merton had the opportunity to teach what
he passionately cared about. The monks talked in poignant detail about
Merton's love for monastic and literary study. As a preface to a couple
of anecdotes, Father Michael talked about Merton's love for literature:

> The Sunday conferences reflected his love for the literary
> world. He encouraged us to read novels. He said, ''you are going

to learn things in novels you are not going to get out of a spiritual book. You are going to learn a dimension of your own humanity. . . ." The other thing I would add is that I felt that what Merton said in the conferences and what made him so effective as a teacher was that he experienced the things he talked about in his own heart, in his own life. He loved literature. He loved the mystery of our humanity.

When Father Michael went to the Taizé community, he met a monk named Mark, a potter, who asked to speak with him because he read Merton's work. Father Michael asked him what fascinated him about Merton and he said: "There is no part of our humanity that he didn't explore and didn't face. He was just so honest about his own human experience." Father Michael agreed, adding that in a way Mark's comment summed up the students' lives with Merton:

> He was just so honest and unafraid to talk about his own deep human experiences, and I think what helped him to do that was his familiarity with the literary world. That opened the world to him. A basic dimension of his philosophy was that if you go deep enough to human experience you will find God. He speaks of God as the ground of our being. I think he sensed that if you really face your own humanity, then you are going to find God. So in those conferences, what they said to me is that he tried to communicate experience. I mean he read poetry and would pick out some idea and talk about it, and you left the conference with the sense that this was really good stuff, not something you put in a package and just carried around with you. It addressed your life . . . and you knew what he told you was something that he had already experienced within himself to some degree. He tried to make you aware of your own human experience so that it might be a channel for self-knowledge and a way of opening to the life of the Spirit.

Merton saw similar spiritual possibilities in all the arts. On occasion, he brought the arts into discussions in the conferences, dedicated as he was to interdisciplinary study in the humanities. Father James pointed out that Merton "felt that the novitiate and the community needed a more well-rounded background to guard against their becoming too enclosed in the pejorative sense." He remembered, in particular, Merton's love for music:

Once in a while on a Sunday afternoon, he would bring his little phonograph player out which was completely unheard of in the monasteries in those days. Not only was he very emotive about music—he may talk about that in the journal—he got very excited about Bob Dylan and had a whole series of his records. Joan Baez, of course, came to visit him. Though he did not talk a lot about music, he had a real appreciation for classical music and also for Gregorian chant. He was somewhat subdued on that because he thought, well, he was just more likely to step on somebody's toes.

Father Matthew also noted Merton's interest in good music, particularly jazz.

Merton admired artistic persons as well as their works. Brother Harold recalled something Merton said in a class that stayed with him, "Truth often comes on the wings of beauty." Then he shared his story:

Being a florist I was always decorating the novitiate with things. Well I thought the place needed sprucing up for the Feast of the Little Flower. So in the Fall I brought in some bittersweet and put it around the statue. It was a wooden statue that came from South America. So Merton said, "Why did you do that?" Well, no one ever asked me why I did that. I said, "Well it represents the fruit of virginity." He did not ask me any more questions after that. Then one day he said, "You really should ask for permission before you start putting things around." I said, "O.K."

That rather upset me. If you are a creative person, I do not see the point in asking somebody if you can be creative. If I get the right flowers and use them, I just bring them in; it is something that happens spontaneously and creatively. After a month, however, he said "It's O.K. You can put flowers in the novitiate. You can do it any time you want." I think he knew himself that you do not get permission to write a poem. It just comes out of you.

Brother Harold went on to talk further about Merton and the sense of beauty that Merton found not only in the artistic but the spiritual:

I remember one time when I was serving Mass, he came in from the hermitage. We took turns as priest and server in giving the responses at Mass, and that particular day everything clicked. Everything was in Latin and everything was so beautiful. It was just downright mystical. I can not put it any other way. I think that something that was present in Merton's beautiful presentations was his Christ-centeredness. That was essential. I think that answers a lot of questions. Everything focused on that for him.

All the monks agreed with Brother Harold that Merton's central love upon which "everything was focused" was his love for God. For example, in discussing Merton's relationship with Dom James, with whom Merton had both a difficult and good relationship, Father Matthew said, "They admired each other and they heard each other's confessions. Merton himself told me that he needed him and Dom James said he had no more obedient monk than Merton." Then he went on to explain what he meant by this steadfast devotion:

> I suppose the key lies in commitment, I mean the deeper commitment. He committed himself to a way of life, to a submission to a pattern of rules under the direction of an Abbot, for Christ's sake. And in a showdown, he would make it work because he saw it in terms of faith. That is the spiritual journey with Christ, and it is the game he played and he played it very seriously and the game is real. The stakes are for life.

II.

In this exploratory study based on interviews with Merton's students, four characteristics about Merton as teacher have been suggested. He was: (1) clear about his conference goals; (2) organized and articulate in lecture; (3) effective in informal discussion; (4) enthusiastic about his subject matter. Yet, Merton was thought of as more than just a good teacher; he was remembered as a teacher *extraordinaire*. As Father Timothy concluded, "Merton was just in a different league."

It can be argued that what made Merton such a powerful teacher was the beautiful unity and simplicity in the way he wove these characteristics together. One flowed into and strengthened, completed, complemented the others. In a word, the whole of his integrated and focused style was greater than the sum of the good parts. Merton's work with students issued from his true self. He taught what mattered most to him not only with clarity and structure but with passion and joy, honestly and courageously revealing himself in all his vulnerability and imperfection.

Merton's *persona* was the integrating and electrifying force. Admittedly, the Merton revealed in his conferences was complex. He was not only brilliant, playful, well meaning, but also abrupt, private, even mysterious. "Deep" is the adjective Father Matthew used to describe Merton. Complicated he was, but clear and integrated in purpose and direction he was also. Merton can be described as a centered teacher who reverently explored interrelated spiritual and aesthetic subject matter, inviting his students to join him in humility and trust in a contemplative study which all knew would lead them into eternity.

As we ended our interview, Father Matthew spoke of Merton and his search with his students. He mentioned that in preparation for our conference he had reread Merton's well-known prayer that speaks of this unending contemplative journey into the unknown. The prayer begins: "My Lord God, I have no idea where I'm going. I do not see the road ahead of me. I cannot know for certain where it will end. . . ." Father Matthew said that the prayer is perfect Merton—the man, the teacher. It expresses his spirituality perfectly, "that sense of childlikeness, of not being exactly sure of where he was at, where he was coming from, where he was going to, and yet having a pure trust in a good God who would watch over him. . . . Yeah, he was very childlike, very compassionate . . . very fragile and very clear-minded."

Bibliography

Burns, Flavian. "Merton's Contributions as Teacher, Writer, and Community Member: An Interview." Interviewer, Victor A. Kramer; Ed. Dewey Weiss Kramer. *The Merton Annual*, vol. 3. eds. Robert Daggy, Patrick Hart, Dewey Weiss Kramer, and Victor A. Kramer. New York: AMS Press, 1990. 71–92.

Casagram, Michael. Personal interview. May 10, 1992.

Conner, James. Personal interview. May 9, 1992.

Del Prete, Thomas. *Thomas Merton and the Education of the Whole Person.* Birmingham: Religious Education Press, 1990.

Kelly, Timothy. Personal interview. May 9, 1992.

Kelty, Matthew. Personal interview. May 10, 1992.

_____. "Looking Back to Merton/Memories and Impressions: An Interview." Interviewer, Victor A. Kramer, Ed.; Dewey Weiss Kramer. *The Merton Annual*, vol. 1. eds. Robert Daggy, Patrick Hart, Dewey Weiss Kramer, and Victor A. Kramer. New York: AMS Press, 1988. 55–78.

Merton, Thomas. "Learning to Live," *Love and Living*, Eds., Naomi Burton Stone and Patrick Hart. New York: Bantam, 1979. 3–14.

_____. *The Seven Storey Mountain*. New York: Harcourt, Brace and Co., 1948.

Quenon, Paul. Personal interview. May 9, 1992.

Thibodeau, Harold. Personal interview. May 10, 1992.

Weber, Columban. Personal interview. May 9, 1992.

Notes on the Monks at the Abbey of Gethsemani

MICHAEL CASAGRAM, O.C.S.O., grew up in New Philadelphia, Ohio, as a Roman Catholic. In 1955 he entered a minor seminary run by the Capuchins. After graduating from St. Fidelis Seminary in 1961, he entered Holy Cross Trappist Monastery in Berryville, Virginia. In 1963 he transferred to the Abbey of Gethsemani where he attended Merton's conferences. After studying theology at San Anselmo in Rome for three years, he was ordained in 1982. At Gethsemani, he has served as printer, tailor, cook, guest master, and vocation director. He is presently living in a Cistercian monastery in Venezuela.

JAMES CONNER, O.C.S.O., entered the Abbey of Gethsemani in 1949 at age sixteen and studied with Merton between 1951 and 1955 when Merton was Master of Students. After he was ordained in 1957, he was appointed Undermaster of Novices under Merton, and worked with him in that capacity from 1958 to 1961. His articles have appeared in such scholarly journals as *The Merton Annual* and *Cistercian Studies Quarterly*. Currently, he is Abbot of Assumption Abbey in Ava, Missouri.

PATRICK HART, O.C.S.O., was born in 1925 in Green Bay, Wisconsin. He graduated from the University of Notre Dame and after a brief teaching career entered the Abbey of Gethsemani in 1951. He served as secretary to Abbot James Fox for ten years prior to his assignment to the Cistercian Generalate in Rome. After his return to Gethsemani, he became Merton's full-time secretary in 1968. He served in this capacity until the time of Merton's death. He is the editor emeritus of *Cistercian Studies Quarterly* and one of the four editors of the first five volumes of *The Merton Annual*. He is also editor of the first volume of Merton's journals, *Run to the Mountain*.

TIMOTHY KELLY, O.C.S.O., was born in Amherstburg, Ontario. He graduated from Assumption University of Windsor in 1958 and in that year entered the Abbey of Gethsemani. He was a novice under Merton from 1958 to 1960 and served as Merton's assistant between 1964 and 1965,

the last year of Merton's tenure as Novice Master. Immediately following this service, he left for Rome where he studied for three years. In
1973 he was elected Abbot of Gethsemani. He continues to serve in this
capacity.

MATTHEW KELTY, O.C.S.O., was born in South Boston, in 1915. He began
his religious life with the Society of the Divine Word in 1935 and was
ordained in 1946. He was sent to New Guinea in 1947 and returned to
the United States in 1951 to edit the Society's magazine. At age forty-
five he entered the Abbey of Gethsemani. From 1969 to 1973 he lived
in a small experimental community in Oxford, North Carolina. In 1973
he returned to New Guinea to live as a solitary. He chose to return to
Gethsemani in 1982, and has lived there ever since, serving as tailor,
Mass office secretary, and retreat house chaplain.

HAROLD THIBODEAU, O.C.S.O., was born in 1936 in Royal Oak, Michigan. He entered the Abbey of Gethsemani in 1960 and was a novice under
Merton. In 1968 he took his solemn vows. For the past thirty-three years
he has served in a number of capacities—including working in the library and in the infirmary. He is a horticulturalist and church decorator.
He has also assisted in the making of the abbey's products—fruit cake,
cheese, and fudge. Currently, he works with the staff of the *Bulletin of
Monastic Interreligious Dialogue,* assisting with subscriptions and mailing.
In 1992 he made a pilgrimage to India, the Philippines, Taiwan, Korea,
and Japan. In India, he had rare opportunities to talk with Tibetan monks.

COLUMBAN WEBER, O.C.S.O., has been a monk of the Abbey of Gethsemani
since 1964. He was a novice under Thomas Merton and has published
extensively on Merton's life and work over the past two decades. His
articles and reviews have appeared in such popular and scholarly journals as *American Ecclesiastical Review, Bardstown Standard, Catholic Weekly,
Cistercian Studies Quarterly, Cîteaux, The Merton Annual,* and *The Merton
Seasonal.* Currently he is in Rome in the Cistercian Generalate where he
does culinary and secretarial work.

Acknowledgment

The author thanks the monks interviewed at the Abbey of Gethsemani for allowing readers to come to know them and Merton better.

Culture and the Formation of Personal Identity: Dilemma and Dialectic in Thomas Merton's Teaching

Thomas Del Prete

A recent news magazine article suggested that the current intense scientific quest to understand the origin of the cosmos is matched by, and not unrelated to, a determined effort by many in our society to understand and experience the meaning of life in spiritual terms.[1] Whether as a reaction to unfulfilling materialistic values, the confrontation of the baby boom generation with its own mortality, or the result of a collective reflective pause as a new millennium approaches, the spiritual search is apparently widespread and real, and manifested in a variety of ways in both religious and nonreligious environments. Given this climate, we might well ask how such a search might be conducted in our time and culture, and to what end. Though framed in a monastic context, these questions challenged Thomas Merton as teacher; the evolution of his efforts in response to them may be instructive for us.[2]

To understand well Thomas Merton's development as a teacher, and particularly the evolution of his approach to monastic education, would require at least some correlative study of his own continuous intellectual, monastic, and spiritual formation and his teaching activity. Conceding the value of such a comprehensive approach, what might we learn from a broad overview of Merton's life as a teacher? What

1. Sharon Begley, "Science of the Sacred," *Newsweek*, vol. CXXIV, no. 22 (November 28,1994) 56, 59.
2. This paper was developed from a draft presented at a conference entitled "Thomas Merton and the Vocation of Cultural Critic" at St. John's University in New York in October 1993. I am grateful to the National Endowment for the Humanities for funding which supported some of the research for the paper.

did the acknowledged spiritual master learn about how to support the spiritual search of his monastic charges, and how, if at all, did he take into account the cultural milieu beyond the monastic enclosure in the process? Did Merton, in keeping with his own evolving effort to understand his role as a contemplative in the modern world, develop in any sense an "anthropology" or "cultural psychology" of education, a way of addressing the influence of culture in spiritual and monastic formation, and, in turn, the potential influence of spiritual insight on society and culture?

Merton's Beginnings as a Teacher: Forming and Being Formed

Thomas Merton was a teacher for more than twenty years during a roughly thirty-year span of time. With a stint tutoring Latin during the previous year as background, Merton began teaching formally in the extension program at Columbia University during the Fall semester of 1939, responsible for a course in English composition. He was then twenty-four years old and pursuing his doctorate in English literature. The following Fall, his attempt to enter the Franciscan novitiate having been rebuffed, Merton began teaching a year-long course in English literature to sophomores as an assistant professor of English at St. Bonaventure College, Olean, New York. A year later, on December 10, 1941, having handed over some of his literature notebooks to a colleague, the twenty-six-year-old Merton entered Gethsemani Abbey. Immersed in his own monastic education, he would not shoulder teaching duties again until November 16, 1949, on the eleventh anniversary of his baptism as he notes it, beginning on that day an introductory "conference" (tantamount to a class) in theology and at about the same time a series of orientation classes for novices![3]

Merton's educational responsibilities at the monastery gradually widened. Asked to become Master of Scholastics (or Master of Students) in June 1951, he assumed responsibility for teaching philosophy and theology to those monks (the "junior professed") studying for the priesthood, and provided them with spiritual direction. In 1955 he became Master of Novices, a key monastic role involving oversight of the monastic education and spiritual formation of newly entered

---

3. Thomas Merton, *The Sign of Jonas* (Garden City, N.Y.: Doubleday, 1953) 236.

monks. Although Merton relinquished this formal teaching responsibility in 1965, he continued to teach, offering weekly conferences to his fellow monks up until his fatal trip to Bangkok in 1968.

Recalling his first teaching experience in *The Seven Storey Mountain*, Merton wrote, "I liked teaching very much." The young teacher seems to have had a rather serendipitous approach to inciting thinking and learning: "I spent most of the time throwing out ideas about what might or might not be important in life and in literature, and letting them argue about it."[4] What Merton discerned and what he evidently honored in this liberal teaching process was "a definite hunger for ideas and convictions" on the part of his first students. In what would be characteristic of his teaching at St. Bonaventure College and later at Gethsemani Abbey, a reflection of the influence of teaching mentors such as Mark Van Doren, he used literature as a lens for focusing life's meaning.

While no less oriented to establishing the meaningful and true than in his pre-monastic teaching, Merton's efforts as a monastic educator had a more explicitly spiritual, Christian, and monastic focus. As the Master of Scholastics, Merton was responsible for the theological and spiritual preparation of the growing number of monks entering Gethsemani seeking ordination. Merton's position was created in fact in response to a surge in priestly vocations, which included about thirty-five of the monastic community of 250 at the time. Anticipating the role, he reflected that "The one who is going to be most fully formed by the new scholasticate is the Master of the Scholastics."[5] He humbly assesses his initial efforts in his journal:

> It is now six months since I have been Master of the Scholastics and have looked into their hearts and taken up their burdens upon me. I have not always seen clearly and I have not carried their burdens too well and I have stumbled around a lot, and on many days we have gone around in circles and fallen into ditches because the blind was leading the blind.
>
> I do not know if they have discovered anything new, or if they are able to love God more or if I have helped them in any way to find themselves, which is to say: to lose themselves.[6]

4. Thomas Merton, *The Seven Storey Mountain* (New York: Harcourt, Brace and Co., 1948) 274.

5. Merton, *The Sign of Jonas*, 319.

6. Ibid., 323.

Merton's self-evaluation reveals his chief concern as the mentor of the scholasticate: to enable the monks to love God more and, in accordance with the paradoxical biblical prescription, to find themselves by losing themselves. Indeed, if there is a leitmotif in Merton's monastic teaching, then, as in so much of his spiritual writing and self-reflection, it is the question of finding oneself, of realizing one's whole and authentic personal identity, of self-discovery "on the deepest possible level," as he put it once in a discussion of education.[7] This theme, however, becomes less and less an abstract proposition for Merton as teacher and spiritual director; it becomes an educational as well as a deeply personal and monastic question the more he confronts the challenge of guiding others in the monastic and contemplative way. Familiar to many, the educational question, or dilemma, might be framed this way: How can we help open others to the experience of their own true identity? What approach might we take? What "curriculum" would we offer? What, if anything, ought we to know about the people in our care in answering these questions? What role, if any, does culture play in the process? Merton would perhaps learn better over time not to judge his efforts as a teacher on what was after all a spiritual plane, even as he expanded his understanding of what might be educationally helpful in the process of spiritual formation, and what discovery of one's true self in Christ, in God, might mean, for himself no less than for his students.

If somewhat uncertain about how he had affected his students during the first months of the scholasticate, and humbled by the effort, Merton realized with gratitude that teaching and "the care of souls" had drawn him into the "terrible" and "beautiful" "wilderness of compassion." His premonition that he would be the one most fully formed by this work seemed to hold true. "The more I get to know my scholastics the more reverence I have for their individuality and the more I meet them in my own solitude," he wrote. But he had also begun to develop some perspective on his students' needs and on the kind of awarenesses and understandings which might ground their spiritual aspirations. He discovered

> that after all what the monks most need is not conferences on mysticism but more light about the ordinary virtues, whether they be

7. Thomas Merton, *Love and Living*, ed. Brother Patrick Hart and Naomi Burton Stone (New York: Bantam, 1980) 3.

faith or prudence, charity or temperance, hope or justice or forti-
tude. And above all what they need and what they desire is to
penetrate the Mystery of Christ and to know Him in His Gospels
and in the whole Bible.[8]

Here Merton, the relatively young educator opening up to the experience of his students out of concern for their spiritual formation, begins
to reconstruct his monastic curriculum, giving more weight to what
might be called normal preconditions for understanding and orient-
ing oneself to the Christian spiritual and contemplative life. Confirm-
ing this view, John Eudes Bamberger, a member of the scholasticate
from 1952 to 1955, observes,

> At that period . . . he focused on spirituality and the most sig-
> nificant lectures for me, perhaps, were those on St. Paul's theology.
> His focus was decidedly and explicitly spiritual, but based on exe-
> gesis and theological reasoning. . . . He saw our greatest needs
> as getting to understand the Christian mystery in a wholesome
> and integral way, free from moralism and rigidity and a too nega-
> tive approach. He also understood that we needed to get to know
> ourselves at a deeper level, get in touch with our feelings and in-
> tuition.[9]

There is no coincidence in the fact that Merton prepared *No Man
Is An Island* while serving as Master of Students, a book which he
describes as covering the ground taken for granted in his prior work,
Seeds of Contemplation, and which addresses some of the virtues and
disciplines fundamental to the spiritual life. Merton dedicated the book
to the scholastics, who he suggested might recognize some of the "notions" in it. The prologue is replete with themes which echo some of
the concerns which surfaced in the scholasticate—the importance of
finding one's own identity through one's own experience, of saving
one's life by losing it, of facing one's limitations.

Merton's work in the scholasticate also sharpened his appreciation for the psychological issues involved in the process of spiritual
formation (if indeed these were not already eminently clear from his
own experience), and particularly the kind of pressure created by inordinate expectations or hopes. He is less than enthusiastic in describ-

8. Merton, *The Sign of Jonas*, 326–327.
9. John Eudes Bamberger, O.C.S.O., to the author, January 12, 1994.

ing the scholastics' educational needs in these terms, remarking in a letter to a fellow Trappist that one of the "problems" presented by the scholastics was "nervous trouble." He observes that some monks "come in with the jitters in the first place," or with "a false notion of the monastic life . . . the idea that they have to be something exalted and brilliant." He mentions also their effort "to force their way to sanctity by sheer strain" and the "disease of perfectionism" which afflicts them all. In his bleak view, "They are obsessed with their own miserable 'perfection' and 'imperfection,'" concentrating on themselves rather than on God, and failing to understand that God loves us because we are imperfect.[10]

If Merton's portrayal of the scholastics in this instance seems to lack sympathy and compassion, it nonetheless points to his early awareness, beyond himself, of the needs and challenges faced by those embarking with high spiritual expectation on the monastic road. It helps explain further why Merton's teaching, as Bamberger's account suggests, evolved in a spiritually-oriented, holistic, and person-centered direction, one aimed at understanding "the Christian mystery in a wholesome and integral way, free from moralism and rigidity and a too negative approach," and enabling the monks to "get to know [themselves] at a deeper level, get in touch with [their] feelings and intuition." In striving to meet this aim Merton began what would become for him a fairly steady process of expanding the boundaries of the monastic curriculum. Bamberger notes, for example, that Merton gave the monks "an appreciation of art and its place in the spiritual life and of beauty."[11] He in addition introduced them to psychology, a subject which captivated Merton especially during the 1950s, and which he clearly mined to enable both him and his students to gain perspective on the psychological challenges which one might encounter on the spiritual journey.

Joining his study of psychology to his work in monastic education and spiritual formation, Merton wrote a paper in the mid-1950s entitled "The Neurotic Personality in Monastic Life" and later on produced a set of notes in collaboration with Bamberger called "The Mature Conscience," which circulated among the monks in the noviti-

10. Merton to Abbot Augustine Moore, O.C.S.O., May 10, 1953, *The School of Charity*, ed. Patrick Hart, O.C.S.O. (New York: Farrar, Straus, Giroux, 1990) 58.
11. Op. cit., Bamberger.

ate. Merton's piece on "The Neurotic Personality" is clinical in nature, an effort to delineate healthy and unhealthy psychological states in relation to ascetic religious life.[12] The notes on "The Mature Conscience" address similar themes, but consider immature emotional and psychological states in relation to the development of conscience. Perhaps in some indirect way a response to the "disease of perfectionism" Merton perceived in his early years teaching in the scholasticate, these notes conclude somewhat pastorally: ". . . the great thing is to realize that just as we are, with our deficiencies, faults, and limitations, with our anxiety itself and our sense of guilt, we have something to contribute, we can participate validly and fruitfully in the dialogue of love."[13]

Merton's Middle Years as Novice Master: Taking Culture into Account

Merton's first seven to nine years of monastic teaching might be characterized as an effort to develop a spiritually-oriented education, to represent well the biblical and spiritual foundations of the contemplative life, and to apply his growing understanding of psychology to this work and his related role as spiritual director. While this effort does not diminish over time, beginning around 1960 there are perceptible and significant changes in content, tone, and rhetoric. For example, Merton's written introduction to the monastic vows for that year (he provided the monks with voluminous sets of carefully organized notes for each of his conferences) differs markedly from its predecessors—such as his introduction to monastic spirituality in 1955—in that it includes a commentary on modern society's treatment of the person as object.

> . . . how does one judge the value of [a person]? . . . In the old fashioned standards of the nineteenth century—how much money

12. Thomas Merton, "The Neurotic Personality in the Monastic Life," *The Merton Annual: Studies in Thomas Merton, Religion, Culture, and Social Concerns*, vol. 4, eds. Robert E. Daggy, Patrick Hart, O.C.S.O., Dewey Weiss Kramer, Victor A. Kramer (New York: AMS Press, 1991).

13. John Eudes Bamberger and Thomas Merton, "The Mature Conscience," *The Collected Essays of Thomas Merton* (Thomas Merton Studies Center, Bellarmine College, Louisville).

has he been able to make? In modern standards—how necessary
is he to an organization, to a business, to society? . . . In actual
fact [persons] exist for *things.* In our society we reverence those
who seem to *do* the most and *have* the most. There is still a shadow
of reverence for personality . . . modern society encourages [us]
to dedicate [ourselves] to *tasks,* to *things,* to spend [ourselves] as
[instruments] of production. In return [we] will be surrounded by
glamour and will have the choice of the best that is produced.
. . . God, on the other hand, does not want our works [but] our
love. That is to say, [God] wants *ourselves.* [God] seeks the person
that we *are,* in order that we may share [God's] life and [God's]
freedom, and [God's] love for all eternity . . . Our job in life is
not so much to produce anything, as *to be what we are supposed to
be.* . . .[14]

Here Merton establishes the question of personal identity as a matter
of loving relationship to God, but only after he suggests, by contrast
and in a tone which shifts from disapproving to pastoral, that several
competing and culturally seductive ways are unacceptable.

Consider another statement by Merton, by way of comparison,
delivered in 1965 during a weekly conference (he had by his time turned
over his work in the novitiate) called "Freedom and Spontaneity."
There is a tone of familiarity, and a sense of conversation based on
shared experience:

There is an inordinate worry about whether you're happy or not
happy in this present day and age, and in this country, and in this
culture, because in this culture we're surrounded by happiness
images. . . . All you've gotta do is open any magazine, and you
find pictures of all these people . . . who are ecstatically happy
because they've bought something. . . . The point is underlying
this, what is the concept of man? What is the concept of happiness?

See, our idea of our self, of the kind of person we want to be, which
everybody has—we're all stuck with a pretty big project of who
we are, of who we gotta be, who we wanna be . . . must be like
flying an airplane . . . we've got this huge psychological dash-
board of all the things that we have to watch . . . so we're on our
beam and we're getting where we want to get . . . maybe the best

14. Thomas Merton, "An Introduction to the Vows," *The Collected Essays of
Thomas Merton* (Thomas Merton Studies Center, Bellarmine College, Louisville).

thing is to forget all that, maybe that's not important at all—I mean a hundred years from now where's that all gonna be? That's all gonna disappear . . . and yet here we are living our life determined by these ideas and images which surround this self which just isn't gonna be there anymore after awhile . . . so all this is an obstacle; all this stops us from being really free. . . .[15]

An interesting aspect of Merton's introduction to the monastic vows is the cultural context he provides for his spiritual discussion. In this case, Merton notes the prevailing cultural predilection for viewing human identity in terms of tasks, productivity, or organizational efficiency. Viewed in the light of Merton's own increasingly vocalized perceptions of the needs and faults of Western culture in the early sixties, this way of introducing the vows might not be surprising. Certainly it reflects the influence of his reading in contemporary social and cultural studies—for example, W. H. Whyte's *Organization Man*—that is, his own effort to understand the evolving "modern" culture and to determine his own response to it as a monk and contemplative.

Yet there is a greater significance to the fact that Merton begins a course on the traditional monastic vows with a cultural analysis than that it parallels his own widening vision of society and his own particular relation to it. Merton's approach to introducing the vows is another example of his deliberate refashioning and expansion of the monastic curriculum over time and a sign of his own evolution as a monastic educator. It reflects in particular Merton's growing sense that his students' access to spiritual questions might be broadened if they were placed in a cultural context or perspective, if their cultural experience, more broadly, their time and place in history, were somehow taken into account.

The episode from Merton's taped conference on "Freedom and Spontaneity" is similarly revealing vis-à-vis his educational concerns. It represents Merton's effort to address, in the folksy and informal way that often characterizes his conferences, the entanglement of contemporary cultural messages and psychological pressures which accompanies the search for authentic identity in God. In both examples Merton is suggesting that one helpful way to begin the process of discovering who one is may be to learn to recognize first of all those cul-

15. Thomas Merton, "Freedom and Spontaneity," Conference Tape #230B, December 19, 1965 (Thomas Merton Studies Center, Bellarmine College, Louisville).

tural definitions which one has already absorbed, and which already bear on one's sense of self. There are other, complementary ways in which Merton approaches the topic of authentic identity in his teaching, for example, in discussing the "higher self" and the "lower self" in St. Paul (1963) and through literature, the most outstanding example of which would have to be his explication of Faulkner's "The Bear" (1967). As significant as these biblical and literary approaches are, it is his developing concern for social and cultural context, and particularly for the monk's relation to society, which is perhaps most influential in shaping Merton's distinctive contribution to a monastic and contemplative education and pedagogy.

There is much to admire in Merton's ability to elevate cultural critique to an effective pedagogical strategy meant to expose cultural messages that block the road to a deep and whole sense of self. It would be wrong to conclude, however, that Merton takes the culture of his students into account *only* in order to set them over and against it. As much as it might be at a certain stage necessary in their formation as whole persons, particularly in laying the groundwork for developing a sense of freedom beyond that which is culturally ordained, to provide a critical perspective on cultural assumptions about what it means to be a person and to live, Merton's overall understanding of culture in relation to education is much broader and more nuanced.

Merton develops what might be called an educational anthropology, as well as a cultural psychology, to guide his teaching. This development corresponds to some extent to changes in Merton's own sense of relationship to the world. In very general terms, his educational vision broadens from a focus on explicating the foundational subjects in the monastic curriculum, to responding to the more complex educational dilemmas of how to take psychology and culture and the "world" into account in providing for the formation of a whole personal identity. By tracing this development through Merton's final years as a teacher, we can gain insight into his educational efforts and suggest their significance beyond the monastic setting.

Merton's Last Years as a Teacher: Liberating Self and World

Merton seems to account increasingly for the impact of cultural versions of the self (such as the modern tendency to regard persons in terms of tasks and things and organizational results) on the capacity for realizing oneself as a whole person in his teaching. This is especially evident when he broaches directly the topic of the true self and the experience of being. In a conference on St. Basil and the natural experience of God given in 1963, for instance, he points out that to attain a simple sense of one's own being, one needs the "very deep interiority which is natural to [humanity]" and which is reflected in "primitive culture." He notes, however, the "different modes we have for keeping people outside themselves all the time—the greatest problem, psychologically speaking, of our society—people are in every way prevented from getting inside, so that actually they become afraid of getting inside [which is] dangerous because you put [people] in a state of doubt regarding what is most fundamental and most necessary for [them]."[16]

Merton also confronts the false consciousness of self fostered in modern western society indirectly in the way he draws on monastic and cultural spiritual traditions in his teaching. He communicates such tradition as a matter of lived and living experience of the deepest realities of existence, as experience which can help open one to some understanding and experience of one's whole and authentic self. As he explains in introducing St. Bernard to his fellow monks, "What I can do and what I really intend to do, is not to talk about St. Bernard exclusively but to talk about *us*."[17] The idea in studying Bernard's work is to apprehend the "resonances" of experience present there, and to transpose this experience "into our time and our way of looking at things." To instead give a review of Bernard's work would be "like school." As I have suggested elsewhere, Merton seeks to go beyond knowing *about* Bernard or what he says—beyond conceptual knowledge and beyond language—to evoke something more akin to living wisdom, or a sapiential experience, literally a "taste" of some existential truth.[18] He therefore asks the monks to consider not the words themselves but their "implications" and to listen for "echoes" of real in-

16. Thomas Merton, "Natural Experience of God—St. Basil," Conference Tape #119, August 25, 1963 (Thomas Merton Studies Center, Bellarmine College, Louisville).

17. Thomas Merton, "Love Casts Out Fear," Conference Tape (Kansas City: Credence Cassettes, 1988).

18. Thomas Del Prete, "Education in Light of the Great Joy: On Advent and Thomas Merton as Teacher," *Grail: An Ecumenical Journal* 10 (December 1994).

terior experience. There is then a kind of curriculum of "experience" at work in this instance of Merton's teaching and a pedagogical effort to introduce the monks to a contemplative way of learning, one attentive and attuned to a deep existential reality; ultimately the "echoes" are intimations of the presence of God at the heart of our own being.

Teaching for Merton clearly becomes much more than an intellectual act and more than a matter of theological or conceptual discourse. Although these discursive ways of understanding might be important for him, his interest in teaching is often to foster a more intuitive way of knowing, and a way of communicating which creates an openness to deep human experience beyond what may be culturally dictated, to something more universal on an existential plane. As he wrote, a monastic education "must seek to develop the special human capacities which will enable [the monk] to experience the deepest values of the contemplative life. These values . . . imply a certain aesthetic and intuitive awareness, a 'taste' and connaturality or a capacity to savor (in an experience that cannot easily be formulated) the deepest truths of the Christian life."[19]

When Merton introduces topics such as Bantu philosophy in conferences, he is in part recognizing the limitations of our own culturally ingrained ways of knowing and thinking vis-à-vis attaining to a deep understanding of life. "I am very interested in this whole question of primitive kinds of philosophy, and primitive outlook on life and being . . . it's closer to the Bible, for example, than some of the stuff that we have with our post-Cartesian viewpoint," he explains in opening his conference on Bantu philosophy.[20] He goes on to suggest that whereas we are accustomed to standing back and analyzing, judging, and categorizing from a distance, the Bantu apprehension of reality is more direct, immediate, and concrete. According to Merton, we may have lost "this kind of direct intuition" or "intuitive knowledge," and we need it as a basis for the contemplative life because "the contemplative life is a life of intuitive contact with reality."[21] Merton thus appropriates the experience of a "primitive" non-Western culture as a way both to understand the constraints of contemporary Western

19. Thomas Merton, *Contemplation in a World of Action*, editorial note by Naomi Burton (New York: Doubleday, 1971) 201.
20. Thomas Merton, "Bantu Philosophy," Conference Tape #220, July 11, 1965 (Thomas Merton Studies Center, Bellarmine College, Louisville).
21. Ibid.

culture and to, in some sense, transcend them as part of the process of developing a more contemplative orientation to reality.

Merton draws on many other cultural sources in his effort to open the monks to new levels of cultural understanding and awareness of who we are as whole persons. He explains Greek tragedy, for example, as a "meditation on the meaning of life" and "a celebration of what they believe to be the truth about life."[22] As he discusses Sophocles' play *Antigone,* he invites the monks to "meditate on it a bit so that you see what the real meaning is that the Greeks have got out of this, to see in other words how this meditation spells out the theme that wisdom comes from something." The point in studying Greek tragedy is "the wholeness of the development of man—behind this whole idea of Greek tragedy is this idea of the wholeness of man, and what is a whole. . . ."[23] In another extraordinary conference ("It's going to be a wild conference this morning," he begins), Merton draws parallels among ancient Greek, Confucian, and Christian understandings of human wholeness, emphasizing that wholeness for a Christian is ultimately found in Christ.[24] When the Chinese scholar John Wu wrote to Merton that he was "bewitched" by his rendering of the Taoist poems of Chuang Tzu, he was acknowledging Merton's gift of being able to elicit the deepest of human experience across boundaries of time and culture. This is reflected in his teaching.

The Merton of the Cold War Letters is not readily apparent in the monastic classroom of the early 1960s, at least as judged by the topics addressed in the taped lectures. Except for a conference on "Nuclear Testing" recorded in May 1962, virtually all of the topics during this period are what we would expect—the monastic vows, the monastic fathers, Cistercian history, and so on. We might attribute this to the fact that Merton, compelled as he was to speak out for the truth, was somewhat anxious about the implications of his doing so and unprepared to embrace educationally what was so easily perceived as a kind of illicit monastic activism. Merton's growing social awareness and social voice have a significant educational counterpart only after he changes his view of the monk's relationship to the world and re-

22. Thomas Merton, "Community and Transformation," Conference Tape (Kansas City: Credence Cassettes). First recorded in the summer 1965.

23. Ibid.

24. Thomas Merton, "Chinese Thought," Conference Tape #216, June 6, 1965 (Thomas Merton Studies Center, Bellarmine College, Louisville).

casts the purpose of monastic education in a more prophetic mold. When Merton does begin to address social issues in his conferences, his purposes are not to offer a critique *per se*, but to develop awareness and clear understanding, and to provide an informed basis for an authentic human dialogue in which a monk might engage, thus an opportunity to respond to real needs in love.

In the Fall of 1964, Merton was asked to prepare notes for a meeting of abbots held at Gethsemani that might shed light on vocational issues among postulants. Though he fretted about the task, was tired out by the day-long sessions and was dubious about the results of his effort, the meeting provided the impetus for consolidating his thought on monastic education in relation to the modern world. His resulting articles, "Vocation and Modern Thought" and "The Identity Crisis," mark a significant turning point in his educational philosophy and practice. Together with his later piece, "Renewal in Monastic Education," they lay out the groundwork for an education which embraces culture and the world and which aims to build the monk's capacity for communicating and responding to the world from the perspective of contemplative wisdom.[25] These articles help bring to fruition Merton's own learning in a variety of areas and to some extent his struggle to reconcile his own cultural criticism with his contemplative awareness of deep connectedness to the world.

Beginning in 1964 the monastic curriculum in Merton's hands undergoes dramatic change. It was actually in August of that year, just prior to the abbots' meeting, that Merton, in his words, "slip[s] in" the first of several conferences on art, to be followed by a much longer series on poetry and different poets and some on fiction. Merton characteristically links discussion to the themes of being and developing ontological awareness. "The Christian life has to have beauty in it" and "beauty is being" he declares in his first session on art.[26] Understanding poetry becomes a way of understanding a particular expression of spiritual and interior experience in one instance, and, in another, a way of coming into contact with "a statement of universal truth, of universal experience . . . what people are . . . reaching for."[27] Dis-

25. These articles are all included in *Contemplation in a World of Action*.

26. Thomas Merton, "Beauty and Art," Conference Tape #175B, August 12, 1964 (Thomas Merton Studies Center, Bellarmine College, Louisville).

27. Thomas Merton, "Poetry," Conference Tape #199, January 29, 1965, and

cussing different dimensions of Edmund Waller's seventeenth-century poem, "Go, Lovely Rose," Merton moves from the rhythm, and the silences that it creates ("Good poetry is 50 percent silence"), to the poem's structure.[28] He suggests that the fourfold structure—four stanzas each "unified by the fact that he's got a verb addressed to the rose"—forms an archetypal mandala. It is in this archetypal structure that the poem "has its effect." "Although it's saying a silly, simple, conventional message . . . actually what it is doing by its structure, and by its consistency . . . [is] getting down into this basic archetypal form which is at the heart of all life and all experience . . . it opens up this kind of inner dimension." In conferences such as these, Merton, similarly, tries to create openness to a deep inner dimension of experience. In so doing, he fulfills his own prescription for a humanities education which is sapientially oriented, that is, oriented to wisdom and developing the interior capacity for wisdom.[29]

Between the Fall of 1964 and the Fall of 1968, before his departure to Asia, Merton's conference topics diversify to include not only the humanities, but modern thought (for example, Marx), Greek tragedy, and other cultural and religious traditions. In adding these topics to the monastic curriculum, Merton is trying to help the monks build a genuine knowledge of the world and of *themselves* as one prerequisite for entering fruitfully into dialogue with it and for developing a capacity for responding to it. As he suggested to the abbots in 1964, it was of crucial importance not to view modern thought as an antagonist to spiritual life but to recognize in it a source for understanding the experience, the needs, and the consciousness of those entering the monastery. It was on this basis that one could learn to communicate better, create an existentially meaningful communication, and thus respond educationally to the monk's own consciousness, to his own time. It is certainly no accident that words such as alienation, identity, and authenticity, common to different strands of modern thinking, become part of Merton's own educational lexicon. This way of accounting for

---

"T.S. Eliot," Conference Tape #210, May 6, 1965 (Thomas Merton Studies Center, Bellarmine College, Louisville).

28. Thomas Merton, "Lyric Poetry," Conference Tape (Kansas City: Credence Cassettes). First recorded on January 7, 1965.

29. Thomas Merton, "The Need for a New Education," *Contemplation in a World of Action,* editorial note by Naomi Burton (New York: Doubleday, 1971) 201-202.

culture in the formation of personal identity again suggests an anthropology or "cultural psychology" of education at work in Merton's teaching.

By 1966 Merton was circulating in the novitiate a new reading list "on the modern world" to accompany the traditional spiritual one. The list included titles such as *Organization Man*, Riesman's *Lonely Crowd*, Jacques Ellul's *The Technological Society*, and Marcel's *Man Against Mass Society*, all grouped in categories such as "Life and Problems in the World," "Civil Rights," "Communism," "Art and Literature," and "Politics." Merton notes that "These books may help some monks to evaluate the situation in the world today, and to make accurate judgements about the monk's place in the world."[30]

Summary

To summarize, Merton's response to the dilemma of how to support the formation of whole personal identity over time takes both individual psychology and the psychological impact of culture into account. His educational response to the question of whether and how to view culture in the formation of personal identity is in part to confront false cultural versions of the self, in part to embrace culture and to promote cultural awareness and understanding, and in part to open up a realm of interior experience not bounded by culture and time. This "anthropology" of education serves several educational purposes: to enable the monks to better understand themselves as part of the process of attaining to a deeper, free, and authentic self, to develop a basis for meaningful communication on matters of existential import, and, finally, to establish "a genuine knowledge of the world" so that they might respond to it prophetically and transculturally in a spirit of Christian freedom, simplicity, and love. Merton's teaching becomes as a result more diversified and multidimensional. He tries a variety of ways to foster ontological awareness. He taps the essential biblical and spiritual sources and "transposes" the experience they represent, making it a living and actualizing experience. He likewise taps the wisdom of artistic and literary work, and other religious traditions. He

30. Thomas Merton, "Readings on the Modern World," 1966, *The Collected Essays of Thomas Merton* (Thomas Merton Studies Center, Bellarmine College, Louisville).

creatively uses the past and other cultural traditions—for example, ancient Greek culture and Bantu philosophy—to build perspective on possibilities for human wholeness in the present.

In his final talk in Bangkok Merton remarked, "The monk belongs to the world, but the world belongs to him insofar as he has dedicated himself totally to liberation from it in order to liberate it."[31] The educational process in support of liberation which Merton develops might be described as a dialectic—a dialectic between deepening understanding of culture and the world, on the one hand, and deepening awareness of being, on the other—which builds towards authentic freedom in God. This freedom then becomes a gift in love to support a dialectic of liberation in the world. Merton puts it this way:

> The task of the solitary person . . . is to realize within . . ., in a very special way, a universal consciousness and to contribute this, to feed this back insofar as he can, into the communal consciousness which is necessarily more involved in localized consciousness, and in such a way that there will be a kind of dialectical development towards a more universal consciousness.[32]

Seen in light of Merton's view of education and of teaching, the first obligation of the cultural critic is not to criticize but to understand who she or he is and to understand her or his world. Having understood, the true vocation is then to respond in loving wisdom, and in responding, to participate in the creative work of transforming culture and the world which is part and parcel of the Christian *"summons to permanent newness of life"* in the Spirit.[33]

31. Thomas Merton, *The Asian Journal*, eds. Naomi Burton Stone, Br. Patrick Hart, O.C.S.O., and James Laughlin (New York: New Directions, 1973) 341.

32. Thomas Merton, *Preview of the Asian Journey*, ed. Walter Capps (New York: Crossroad, 1991) 69.

33. Thomas Merton, *Love and Living*, 126.

A Voice in the Postmodern Wilderness: Merton on Monastic Renewal

Thomas F. McKenna, C.M.

In a frequently cited scene from a Franz Kafka novel, one traveller stops another along a highway. He asks where the other is going. The second answers, "I don't know. Only away from here. Only by so doing can I reach my destination."[1]

In this short exchange, the wanderer expresses something at the heart of the cultural mood referred to as postmodernism. There is a spreading fissure, it asserts, running down the center of all that makes up the world called "modern." If we are to be whole, we must distance ourselves from many of the tenets of this Enlightenment child. Its notion of progress, its pitting of individual against collectivity, its dominative attitude toward the earth, its commodifying compulsion, its reliance on shallowly empirical modes of knowing—these and other qualities have shown their destructive undersides in increasingly frightening ways. The Enlightenment confidence is unfounded. One cannot live as if the bankruptcies, spiritual and otherwise, of the twentieth century did not exist.[2] We have to get "away from here."

The problem, of course, is where to go. In large part postmodernism is a reaction, drawing most of its bearings and energy from what it rejects. What it proposes is another matter, and in fact it is near impossible to name any one course it sets down, so disparate are the coun-

---

1. Franz Kafka, "My Destination," *Parables and Paradoxes* (Berlin: Schocken, 1975) 189. Cited in Elizabeth Johnson, "Between the Times," *Review for Religious* 53 (January 1994) 18.
2. Ibid.

sels of its adherents.[3] Postmodernism insists that the frames of reference of the modern world are skewed, poisonous, and are to be dismantled. But the frames for a renewed world?

The more hopeful adherents (constructionists) say there are world views to be constructed, but unlike previous frameworks these new ones will not have half the applicability or staying power. Such vehicles of meaning will be helpful in different places and times but will not be able to span the gap between experience and significance in any universal way nor for very long.

Less sanguine commentators (deconstructionists) contend that the day has passed of even arriving at structures which can trustworthily carry meaning. In place are a series of arbitrary prisms through which we look at reality, which themselves have been entirely molded from the self-interests of those who sit astride the social pyramid. The task is to expose and deconstruct. After that, one must be vigilant against the forces which want to slip in new worldviews which simply switch beneficiaries. In the end it is impossible to put together basic referents (e.g., self, truth as correspondence, God, etc.) which merit our trust.

Neither position offers much firm ground on which to stand. So many of the culture's taken-for-granted beliefs about what matters and what should be passed over have been exposed as empty and merely self-serving. More reliable ones either struggle in dark and untested ambiguity, or by definition cannot be born at all.

And thus the mood. Sensing things breaking apart more than coming together, feeling contingency rather than absoluteness, aware of the fragility of human existence more than its stability, focused more on the passing scene than the permanent one, the postmodern person is wary. The best he or she can hope for is some provisional expression in which meaning might find a home—for a while. Then will come the dis-ease, the need to dismantle the tent and once again to step off onto the shifting sands. A sense of impermanence, fragmentation, disruption, constant dissolution, precariousness, and unpredictability fills the air. Confidence wanes in the advent—and even the possibility—of some new order which will hold the center.

3. Steven Payne, " 'Although It Is Night': A Carmelite Perspective on Spirituality at the Juncture of Modernity and Postmodernity," *The Merton Annual* 6 (1993) 140.

There have been a number of characteristic reactions to such a world. Certain individuals would distance themselves from all the precariousness by travelling to other times. They attempt to restore one golden age or other when things supposedly were simpler and clearer. They would create some zone of meaning outside the mainstream, using the blueprint of the earlier age, and assume their new habitation to be relatively untouched, at least on the inside, by the culture around them.

Others simply deny the postmodern temperament. Some do this by out and out rejection. Others push it aside by the more subtle stratagem of glorifying modernity. The postmoderns distort the picture, they argue, by downplaying the tremendous gains in freedom, prosperity, technology and education flowing from the Enlightenment. They make too much of the problems and conveniently overlook the many self-correcting mechanisms built into the system. They are the nay-sayers, they bite too hard at the hand that is feeding them, they show a failure of nerve in the face of the risks that life throws up at everyone. Difficulties have appeared in modern times, but not in such magnitude as to call the whole into doubt. The postmodern sensibility, stressing fragility and impermanence, simply does not mirror reality.

More explicitly religious issues also bob in these currents. While some believers do not sense the postmodern temper and others feel it mixed together with both premodern and modern moods,[4] there are those who know it in their marrow. It is these individuals especially who have increasing difficulty conceiving a God who stands untouched above the sufferings of the millions on the underside of modernity. They struggle to discern God's intervening presence in a society which keeps breaking down and breaking apart. They trip over claims that there is an inexorable plan steadily unfolding itself in history and that justice and goodness are actually making inroads.

Rather than a hovering God, these pilgrims experience an absent one. The once familiar deity who reigned over the universe in power and who existed apart, unaffected by the finitude of His (sic) creatures, is hardly imaginable.[5] And as this God recedes further and further away from lived existence, an undercurrent of loss and lost-

4. Payne, 142.
5. Michael Downey, *Worship at the Margins: Spirituality and Liturgy* (Washington, D.C.: Pastoral Press, 1994) 276.

ness seeps in. Depictions such as the "eclipse of God" (Buber), "a spirituality of bleaker times" (Rahner), and "A Cry of Absence" (Marty) probe the mood, a winter of the spirit where the comforting colors of summer and even fall have faded and trail-markers are far and few between. The tendency toward denial, restoration, despair, cynicism, and other destructive coping possibilities becomes more pronounced.

Into this unsure world, we introduce Thomas Merton. While it is anachronistic to call him a full-blown postmodern, Merton did concern himself with many of these same elements in modern life. He qualifies at least, in George Kilcourse's felicitous phrase, as "a role-model for engaging spirituality in dialogue with postmodernity."[6] And at the most, his talent for finding paths through unexplored places invests him with impressive credentials for speaking a valuable word inside this ethos.

Merton is an especially astute guide for this bare time. Granting that some[7] of the more explicitly postmodern language postdates him, Merton has clear affinities to postmodern concerns. The old maps wearing thin, the urge to move beyond established meanings, the wrestling with God's absence, the temptations to settle for an illusory stability and/or to fixate on the wrong questions, the suspicion of current methods of discourse—these issues not only caught his attention but were the fields on which he worked out his deepest questions.

It is a challenge to select a heading which draws together Merton's thought in order to focus it squarely on postmodern apprehensions. His whole corpus is about living honestly and religiously in shifting times. This essay pulls on just one thread in his writings, the renewal of monastic life in his time. In the mainlines of what he proposed are found not only some of his most telling cultural analyses but also a number of wisdoms to the late twentieth-century pilgrim.

6. "Spirituality After 'A Prayer Lip Stumbles,' " *The Merton Annual* 6 (1993) 2.

7. In a lucid treatment of Merton's late-appearing "anti-poetry," George Kilcourse traces Merton's deepening conviction about the fundamental role language plays in shaping consciousness and the catastrophic distortions modernity had inserted into much of contemporary discourse. In this respect, Merton does speak in postmodern language. *Ace of Freedoms: Thomas Merton's Christ* (Notre Dame: Notre Dame Press, 1993) ch. 5.

Monastic Renewal

It is commonplace to say that Merton's appreciation of monastic life changed over the years. In earlier writings he lionizes the monastery as the hidden-away center of the world, the prime vantage point from which lasting truth can be seen. In his middle and later years, Merton is a good deal more reserved—even suspicious—in his assessment. Both his intensifying study of the movement's founders and his renewed contact with the wider society took him to another ledge from which to look back at Trappist life. That new height was the wilderness.

He experienced a growing unease with both assumptions in place at Gethsemani and more diffusely with attitudes in society at large.[8] There was something smug and image-conscious, he felt, about each which rang hollow when heard against the experiences of those wanderers in the fourth-century deserts. These had a peril in them, a precariousness and an unpredictability. They were open-ended encounters and did not claim some insider-knowledge of a hidden trail through the wilderness.

By contrast, mid-twentieth-century America's sense of itself was sure and congratulatory, and this in spite of many indications that the country was unravelling at the edges and drying out at the center. Though many alarms were ringing warnings of rocks ahead, the culture spoke in self-assured tones that it knew just where it was going. Likewise in Cistercian life, Merton detected a wrong kind of certainty. He heard guarantees being furnished about the spiritual journey, subtle claims that "The Way" could be discovered by following certain prescriptions and techniques. Almost subliminally, a message was going out that the monastery could protect the monk. It could shield him from life's ambiguities and, more alarmingly, could flood with light the shadowy recesses of encounter with God.

Less and less for him did these outlooks square with the testimonies of the early monks. For them life was a wandering in the desert. Anything but predictable, existence was in large part unknown, much more beckoning than figured out.[9] The task in faith was to grow more

---

8. "Letter to Dom Jean Leclerq, July 18, 1967," *The School of Charity: The Letters of Thomas Merton on Religious Renewal and Spiritual Direction*, ed. Patrick Hart, O.C.S.O. (New York: Farrar, Straus, Giroux, 1990) 337.

9. Thomas Merton, *The Wisdom of The Desert* (New York: New Directions, 1960) 6 [Hereafter cited as *WD*].

supple before life's promptings. These desert fathers and mothers followed their Lord through a wilderness, that is, a place that was wild. Their greatness was to have allowed themselves to be led far out beyond the conventional into a trackless land where reckoning came only from their desire for God. And their God too was wild, a deity who could not be managed or fathomed, who lived beyond the familiar, and who forever ran ahead of their abilities to comprehend.

Merton's unease was that the Orders spoke the words of solitary search but did not really go on it. They proclaimed adherence to the ultimate but in a thousand subtle ways shifted focus to the penultimate. Merton accuses the monastery of making a grand announcement that "I am going to walk to the North Pole and then proceeding to take a walk around the block."[10]

It was not simply that they had screened out the uncertainties of the founders' experiences. These communities had also insulated themselves against the ambiguity and struggle faced by contemporaries. Done supposedly to provide an uncluttered space within which the monk could pursue God, the removal had the effect of placing him inside a bubble which was simply one more layer between the monk and the wilderness his ancestors so blessedly roamed.[11] There still were wild places, and equally to the point, there still were people who travelled through them in faith and trust. To construct a barrier between the Trappist and his peers so as to wall him off from the tracklessness these outsiders faced was to deny the monk the grist for precisely the kind of experience that shaped his forbears. Domesticating, taming, controlling, over-institutionalizing—these were *the* deadening forces, thought Merton. They cut the heart out of monastic "foolishness"—the search for the Other in the other places.[12]

Merton's Renewal Formula

For Thomas Merton, the road to religious renewal stretched out clearly. The monastic orders will come alive to the extent they re-enter the mythic time and space of their beginnings. They will catch hold

10. *Contemplation in a World of Action* (New York: Image Books, 1973) 204 [Hereafter cited as *CWA*].

11. *WD* 10.

12. "Letter to Dom Andre Louf, April 26, 1965," *The School of Charity*, 277.

again if they relearn what it is to be led by the Spirit into the wilderness. For Merton, this meant a simultaneous move along two fronts.

The first was toward the past. There had to be a sympathetic entrance into the founding events of the Order. Who were Anthony, Pachomius, and Benedict and what did they teach? What social world did they inhabit? Most importantly, along what inner paths did they walk with their God? This stage of inquiry needs assistance from the historians. The mostly unspoken assumptions of the age, the political and philosophical currents of the time, the way contemporaries reacted to the original communities—all these "facts" enter into getting a proper fix on the beginnings. But of greater importance is a more elusive type of knowing, the kind that comes from shared inner experience—of the self.

At the heart of Merton's pursuit is the search for God through discovery of his authentic self. In his arresting imagery: "If we enter into ourselves, find our true self and then pass 'beyond' the inner 'I,' we sail forth into the immense darkness in which we confront the 'I AM' of the Almighty."[13] At issue here is the manner in which this highly personal quest came to confirm Merton's choice to be a monk. The further he followed it, the deeper his realization of how much his own path was cousin to the founders'. The more his own inner road opened up to him, the more he came to appreciate theirs. The more he learned about their spiritual experience, the more he could express his own. Merton's life-journey was a trip back into the sacred spaces and times of monasticism. And that meant a walk into the wilderness, a trek into the wild places where his God dwelt.[14] The early monks became his guides, not so much marking off clear highways but mentoring him about how to comport himself. Drawing close to them, he learned how to survive and prosper in the desert, how to develop an inner compass, and most of all, how to discern God's fullness in the middle of all that emptiness. With them as soul-mates, he found a type of home in a seemingly homeless place.

Merton's second movement was toward the present—and through it toward the future. He discovered that access to the privileged experiences of the founding events passed through the portals of con-

13. "The Inner Experience," cited in *Thomas Merton: Spiritual Master*, ed. Lawrence Cunningham (New York: Paulist, 1992) 302.

14. Thomas Merton, *New Seeds of Contemplation* (New York: New Directions, 1961) 241 [Hereafter cited as *NSC*].

temporary culture.[15] While the East had its place, of itself it could not lead a person into the myth time. Only when touched to the struggles for meaning of real people in the twentieth century could knowledge about the founders reveal what of grace had happened in those Egyptian wastelands. And did not this process stand to reason since those desert mothers and fathers were seized by the Spirit precisely as they wrestled through nights with the strangers of their age?

Merton's entry into the founding vision came through engagement with the faith struggles of his era. The ones thirsting for justice in a racist and militaristic society, those lining up with the poor in a materialist culture, the ones grappling with the terrible ambiguity of claims for a good and powerful God in a world so marked with evil and suffering—these were the contemporary desert-dwellers who unveiled for him the wisdom of the ancient ones. Only in sympathetic interchange with such future-oriented groups—in Merton's phrasing, the "anonymous monks in the world"[16]—could today's monk really touch into the spiritual elan of the founders.

And so his formula for refounding: Stand simultaneously in the two streams of originating event and emerging culture. It is only when the monastery is nourished by both that it can begin to feel again the promise of the desert, to view it once more as an oasis of hope and a place of encounter. The past is accessible only through the present, and yet the present loses its depth and bearings when not anchored in the primitive experience. When the one lives from the other, there is a way in the wilderness.

Short-Circuiting Renewal

While convinced of the truth of his approach, Merton was not naive about difficulties in pursuing it. He knew too well the cold anxieties that crept in when walking through uncharted territory. For one, there was loneliness. God lived here alright, but as experienced in a paradoxical feeling of absence. At times, fears haunted the traveller: he or she might just actually be alone, emptiness might well be the last word about desert life. Still further, there was confusion. Which direction to take, what course to follow? Precious little concrete guid-

15. *CWA*, 327.
16. *CWA*, 13.

ance was given in the wilderness, at least of the kind provided by tried-and-true conventional wisdoms about the next steps to take. So much of it was testing, weighing one thing against a plausible other. The temptations to step off the road were many, and they pressed hard.

One way to withdraw was to deny the emptiness. Out of fear, a person could feign certainty (even to self) and then attribute others' doubts to frail faith, morbidity, fixation on some authority issue, or whatever. Things are not half so bleak, they would counter, and it is a disservice to the rest of us to paint so stark a picture of the present mood. The assured ones assert that the bulk of practices and categories in use do bear the warmth and light of God. The proclaimers of God's absence, they continue, are simply wrongheaded and perhaps obsessed with death.[17]

Another escape route is a return to some previous world which (seemingly) embodied the divine in clear and comforting ways. If we recreate that golden time, the restorationists contend, the present loss of nerve will evaporate. Merton was quite explicit in naming the favored eras and the kind of people who proposed to lead the Trappists back there.[18] His objection was not that those former ages were shallow or that they did not contain things which could be of help now. His unease came rather from the lulling allure such a deadening promise held out. Not only was it illusory, but it gloried in the claim that it insulated the monks from the very experience which attracted the best of them in the first place.[19]

Still one more evasion, in Merton's eyes, was to screen the voices in the wider culture which genuinely probe for the transcendent. These individuals could disturb, because from their future-sensitive stance they called present social arrangements into question. For Merton, the unpropertied intellectuals—the poets and the artists for instance—were among such searchers. Beneficiaries of the culture but not totally invested in it, they noticed parts of the society that many nearer to the center preferred to overlook.[20]

But more relevant to our reflection is another group with whom Merton felt a special kinship: people who find themselves in crises of faith which have been set off by the various dysfunctions of moder-

17. *CWA,* 101–109.
18. *CWA,* 196.
19. *WD,* 10.
20. *CWA,* 235ff.

nity.[21] These are the ones who struggle with the dimming of transcendence; in other words, with the felt withdrawal of God. They walk through the empty places of the world and from those locations are able to say something of hope to more conventional types about what it is to follow a savior who beckons from the future. Often such outriders are critics of current structures of religion. But because their faith (just as was the early monks') is shaped in struggle with the culture, they are to be heeded. Strangers themselves, they know something of the approach of the God who lives out beyond the familiar.

To use another metaphor, Merton teaches that the healthier societies are the ones that do not close their gates too quickly on the barbarians. On the contrary, they entertain the outsiders because they carry precious things. This is Merton's monastic reprise of the recurring Christian wisdom that God comes in the form of the stranger. If the Orders are not to become shells of their original selves, they are going to have to pay special attention to the groups and individuals who "unofficially" search for God in solitude. For Merton these are the unnamed monks in the world. In his more vivid language: "The monastery is not a ghetto and will not profit by being kept as one."[22] "The problem today is that there are no deserts, only dude ranches."[23] The Order will stay fresh to the extent it remains sympathetic with "what and who in the world is open to change."[24]

Merton's bracing prescription for how monasticism should respond to crisis discloses a truth at the core of his overall message. Though life can seem a wandering search for God, God will find us in the wilderness if we stay honest in the search and resist the temptations to settle for less. If we surrender to the love being given us at our true center, and trust that God is leading us every step of the sometimes comforting and clear, but more often lonely and confusing, way, we will be found.[25]

What might Merton, who approaches monastic renewal from such an angle, have to say to the postmodern traveler?

21. *CWA*, 178, 201.
22. *CWA*, 218.
23. Thomas Merton, *Zen and The Birds of Appetite* (New York: New Directions, 1968) 19.
24. *CWA*, 327.
25. Cf. *New Seeds of Contemplation*, 241, 258.

Living in the Wilds with Hope

Thomas Merton would be a soul-mate to Kafka's pilgrim, save in one fundamental respect. The Trappist certainly desired to get "away from here," "here" understood as the shallowness in much in the modern ethos. He also would admit that he does not know where he is heading, "where" in the sense of an already mapped out line of march. But that there is really no place to head, and that at the deepest, most existential of levels there is no guidance being provided, Merton would not agree.[26] Though difficult, and at times terrifying, the wanderings in the wild are not pointless. They go somewhere, granting that both the somewhere and the way to it are not apparent.

The profound strangeness of the territory "away from here" is not the echo of a bottomless chaos, insists Merton, but the mark of the profound otherness of the God whose home turf the wilderness is. In other words, even though both pilgrims experience the road as precarious and frighteningly unfamiliar, the one regards it as a dead-end and the other as a beckoning path. For reasons ultimately unexplainable, yet not absurd, Merton finds meaning on the road, even though the meaning is mostly promise and is filtered through smokey glass. He travels through the wilds in hope. It is because of such trust that Merton both joins and parts company with certain postmoderns.

He is at home with a sensitivity which names and even glories in the indeterminate. He is kin to the spirit which challenges cherished views of reality because they are built on self-interest and resist whatever cannot be folded into their outlook. Merton was intensely aware of the gap between the bounded, smug wisdoms of the age and the vast horizons within which these actually exist. He bristled at the illusion that there were charts of the infinite ocean and of the snug harbors in it. Inasmuch as he took it as a project to spring some leaks in the boats of those who claimed to be so deft at sailing that they could stay dry and on course in all weather, he did deconstruct and undermine. His hope lit up the boundaries of the conventional and revealed its limits and biases.

But his hope illuminated something more. That same borderless ocean contained hints and foretastes of the ever-faithful God. That

26. Cf. Stephen Payne's (op. cit., 158) helpful discussion of parallels between John of the Cross and Merton on confidence that there is progress on the journey through the wilderness.

Merton would unmask illusions and call the present into question, yes; but only as prerequisite for approaching the ever-receding God. While his walk through the wilderness was solitary and his steps could indeed feel random, his deeper intuitions told him he was going somewhere. The pillar of cloud which led his desert ancestors, and the Spirit who drew Jesus into the wilds, expanded inside Merton too. To paraphrase his account of it, the trail through no-where was heading somewhere. In substance, Merton sympathizes with those who testify to the tracklessness of the landscape, but not with those who conclude to the aimlessness of a journey through it.

Such confidence in destination and clues toward it grounded Merton's outlook. The path of no-path is blessing, he insisted, even though its bountifulness can, at times, clothe itself in impenetrable disguise. It is grace for a number of reasons.

For one, the various false selves are scraped away along its track.[27] There is purification in a desert. The inadequacies of present self-images come to light: their limitation and their alien character, their solipsism and destructiveness, their unworthiness before the real thing.

Second, there is progress on this journey. There is headway which is not horizontal only but a stretching of capacities to discern the underlying purpose. The traveler's spirit deepens. That is, it is not as if she or he simply tries on a succession of socially constructed selves, each one as empty as the one before it. New representations go somewhere. They conform more and more to the word of the genuine self being spoken in the person's depths. But more fundamentally, the very process of shedding of old images enables the pilgrim to establish a clearer fix on that inner homing signal which draws him or her on past all images. Authentic struggling purifies the taste for the true and the good. Masks must be peeled away—deconstructed, if you will—but the act of doing so sensitizes the individual to the deeper currents of the journey and exposes false directions along the way.

The third point is a refinement of the second. The desert is blessing because it sharpens an individual's ability to hear the future. The wilderness disciplines the traveler to listen more acutely for "the more" embedded in present life. Like no other experience, it hones the individual's discrimination for which is the genuine article among the many values jostling for a place in the culture.

27. *NSC*, 258.

It is worthwhile to highlight this theme in Merton. Certain varieties of postmodernism are heavily skeptical about avowals to sense something of the world-to-come, about claims to have gained traction from some foot planted in the future. By contrast, Merton's eschatological grounding would have him look in exactly that direction. For him, desert emptiness is the very condition for heightening sensitivity to the special grain of this horizon. It is just this receptiveness to the still-to-come which is the basis for judging the worth of any current construction of reality.

The desert is grace because in it, one meets God. Crossing into it with trepidation, Merton also senses its great prospects, the cool of eternal springs lying just beneath its forbidding surface. In the "other" place (the trackless land of his own freedom), Merton encounters "the Other."

A wilderness guide not only points forward but warns about which paths to avoid. As we have seen, Merton identifies a number of trails which, though enticing, end in box canyons.

The first is denial that one is even *in* the wilderness. The traveller insists that he or she is marching through known territory and that assertions to the contrary are alarmist. Merton acknowledges the comfort such a stance brings, but he goes on to describe the subtle way it seals off travellers from their deepest bearings.

This particular caution speaks to those who not only deny postmodernism's warnings, but regard them simply as the excuses of the unsuccessful. Modernity's difficulties, they say, are the kind of irritating shortcomings that crop up in any great civilization. And in this present one, most all problems can be weeded out by greater efficiency. Merton contends that such breakdowns are more than passing glitches. They are fruits of poisonous roots which are planted in the heart of the age and are killing off the rest of the garden.

Merton shines an especially bright light on the epistemology such a denying spirit prefers; i.e., technique and managerial rationality. He returns again and again to the deceptive circularity of the approach. Within the scope of our focus, he refers to the monastery's confidence that the recruit cannot stray if he but follow this routine or that formula. But in other places, Merton makes the larger criticism. The left-brain stance offers what it proports to be a complete, self-grounding explanation of the world. Its unquestioned success as world-view since the seventeenth century is perhaps the most powerful contributor to its own blindness. The refined analytic tools, the tendency to equate reality with its discoverable structures, the achievement itself of breaking the bonds of premodern thinking—all conspire to exalt technique and instrumentality at the expense of more holistic wisdoms. As Merton draws attention to the fathomless stretches of territory which bound this efficiency principle, he pinpoints the hubris of this managerial approach.

An especially beguiling form of denial is restoration. For the monks, it was the longing to reconstruct a favored age in order to experience again the vitality which that era supposedly provided. For the "modern," it is a wish to go back to early Enlightenment days when opponents were hard-pressed to contend against science's promised Third Age.

Merton was an irritant in this discussion. He did not believe there ever was such a secure time, and in fact was himself attracted to particular ages by their very precariousness. It was willingness to grapple with uncertainty at cultural stress-points which distinguished the truly great men and women. Even if a given era were more settled than the present one, the heroic individuals in it were those who felt the press of the unfamiliar up against the known and sought meaning at just that juncture. Excessive clarity and unassailable surety stifled Mystery. New life, thought Merton, rises from the primal waters—the chaotic primal waters. In shock from "too much future," many in the present call for return to some simpler, more purposeful age. Merton's counsel is to recognize such advice as short-sighted hunger for the safe place which, in the longer view, only builds a dangerous one.

Merton's skill for crossing the wilderness is risky art rather than sure method. Relying on intuition that is at once gift and hard-won achievement, and on candor about all he does not know, he is an exposed pilgrim in need of much sustenance. To be nourished, Merton listens inside himself for the increasingly audible voice of the Spirit working through his freedom. But the monk is also attentive to the outside.

He would capitalize on the savvy of other journeyers who have learned to walk in hope. The unpropertied intellectuals, the artists, the ones who struggle with God's absence, those thirsting for justice, his "anonymous monks"—they all know something crucial. They give powerful witness to the virtue of authentic and trusting perseverance.

Merton would alert the postmodern traveller to this mostly low-profile resource. Not everyone is without direction. For some on this road, the absence of God has not translated into the lack of experience of God. Paradoxically, God's distance from the conventional channels carries God's presence. Like everyone else they proceed in darkness, but, in some flickering sense, have begun to see light within it. Merton encourages active solidarity with these comrades-in-hope. It behooves the rest of us, he advises, to watch for compatriots who have come upon something very practical—even though expressed in different ways—about divining water in the desert. They have fought off cynicism in just that place. In the face of contingency and frightening interruption, they have been able to keep their bearings there. In a time of heightened uncertainty, alliances with such "anonymous monks" are not luxury, says Merton, but essential travelling gear.

Mutatis mutandis, could we not say that Thomas Merton himself is among the most steadfast of postmodern wanderers? Feeling the insolvency of much in modernity, he did not withdraw from it nor cease probing for a way through its brambles. He embraced the central postmodern intuitions while refusing the ministrations of would-be consolers who sought to paper over modernity's problems. Certainly in action but most helpfully in word, he makes the case that wilderness travelling can be done—because it has been done. Merton's is a path in the dark along the way of honesty, attunement and trust. He is a sympathetic and useful ally to those who are convinced of postmodernism's criticisms but not of its nihilistic conclusions.

Merton's Legacy: Perspective

Though the worlds of the 1960s and the 1990s are disparate, they do connect in at least one important respect. The hollowing-out of cherished cultural symbols which registered in those earlier years has reached middle age in the more pervasive temperament of postmodernism. From his vanguard post, Merton not only felt its chill in his bones but thought hard about how to incorporate the mood into his own spiritual life. What he offered was perspective. Individually and corporately, one can walk purposefully through the wilderness. If the group names things as they most deeply are, if it does not succumb to the allures of escapism, if (most importantly) it allows itself time and space to experience the darkness as God's own light, that community can travel confidently through the trackless places. With this acute ear, Merton heard the opening chords of postmodernism, and from his own time he continues to guide. He is not the expert whose self-assurance comes from having been there and back. He is rather the fellow-traveller who also tried to wrestle with the angel in the night and has left us a most encouraging account of how it is that the struggle is actually grace in our time. Merton moves away from "here," but helps us to believe in the reality of God's "there."

Revisiting *Zen and the Birds of Appetite* after Twenty-five Years[1]

Matthias Neuman, O.S.B.

The decree of the Second Vatican Council on Non-Christian Religions is often hailed as an entirely new beginning in the relations between the Catholic Church and other world religions. But the majority of conciliar achievements, such as liturgical renewal, a new vision of the Church and the affirmation of religious freedom, were prepared for by prophetic forerunners: the liturgical movement of the late nineteenth century, the Nouvelle Theologie of the 1920s, and writers like John Courtney Murray on church-state relations.

The area of interfaith dialogue also witnessed such pioneers. The 1950 National Conference of Indian Bishops took initial and hesitating steps away from the unilateral condemnation of other religions, which had been a hallmark of much pre-Vatican II Catholicism. Visionary individuals like Dom Bede Griffiths, Father Henri Le Saux, and Dom Aelred Graham saw prophetically that the Catholic Church needed to engage in mutual and respectful interactions with the great faith traditions of the world. They believed that religious pluralism and intercooperation would become the norm of an emerging global community.

Thomas Merton could be included among this group of interfaith pioneers. His writings on the significance of interfaith awareness impacted greatly upon the popular mentality of American Catholics. In so many areas Merton became a measuring stick of spiritual attitudes among educated Catholics. A recent article charting the shifts

1. This is an expanded version of a paper delivered at the March 17–19, 1994 Merton Conference at Bellarmine College, Louisville.

in spirituality preferences over the last quarter century calls Merton perhaps the most influential of all spiritual authors in that period.[2]

There is, therefore, a value twenty-five years after his death in reviewing his seminal insights in interfaith dialogue, surveying his hopes for Zen and Christianity, and reappropriating his suggestions which may have been overlooked. This paper undertakes three tasks: first, to review the main themes in what is perhaps Merton's most deliberate effort to address directly the possibility of interfaith dialogue, *Zen and the Birds of Appetite;*[3] second, to compare Merton's views and hopes with the actual historical and ecclesiastical developments of the past quarter century; and third, to suggest ways in which Merton's ideas still possess value as guides into interfaith understanding and practice.

Main Themes in *Zen and the Birds of Appetite*

Zen and the Birds of Appetite consists primarily of essays previously published between 1964–1967.[4] However, the second part of the book, "Dialogue on Wisdom in Emptiness," co-written with D. T. Suzuki (1961), predates the Second Vatican Council. During his collegiate days at Columbia, Merton initiated many contacts with non-Christian religious traditions, but Zen developed a growing appeal for him during the 1960s.[5] Merton was not a systematic theologian, but dealt with material in the literary style of an essayist. He did not like hard and fast definitions and thought a variety of descriptions better conveyed both the substance and feel of a subject. This makes it some-

2. Robert Hamma, "The Changing Style of Spirituality: 1968–1993," *America* 169 (November 27, 1993) 10.

3. I will not go into the genesis and evolution of Merton's interests in the East and Eastern religions. That task has been well done by others. See Bonnie Thurston, "Why Merton Looked East!" *Living Prayer* 21 (November–December 1988) 43–49; Chalmers MacCormick, "The Zen Catholicism of Thomas Merton," *Journal of Ecumenical Studies* 9 (Fall 1972) 802–818.

4. *Zen and the Birds of Appetite* (New York: New Direction Books, 1968). Henceforth referred to in the text as *ZBA*; numbers in parentheses are page references in *ZBA*.

5. Of all the Eastern religions Merton seemed most comfortable and knowledgeable with Zen, and Daisetz Suzuki seems to have been the major influence; see MacCormick, 804–805.

what difficult to select key topics, but the following issues seem to stand out.

1. In the enthusiasm surrounding the closing years of the Vatican Council, Merton was greatly concerned about the tenor of liberal Catholic attitudes toward Eastern religions. He felt that large numbers of American Catholics mistrusted Asian religions and their practices (16). The post-Vatican II Catholic was not drawn to contemplation (20), and actually disdained things metaphysical, Greek or mystical (28). Post-conciliar Catholics longed for activism, history, event, movement and progress (28–29). Perhaps such is the reason why Merton gave surprisingly little attention to the council or its decrees in *Zen and the Birds of Appetite*. He mentions the council in several brief passages, but does not quote it at length or develop its basic points (15, 40). Perhaps the documents were still too fresh for him to recognize their potential impact. Or, maybe Merton believed that real dialogue proceeds through the leadership of committed individuals.

After twenty-five years this concern about American activism and the Catholic mind might seem "unfounded," considering the many advances in dialogue, increased contacts between Buddhism and Christianity and especially in light of a Vatican letter warning against too much assimilation.[6] Others, however, could argue that the general academic religious community and the large populace of American Catholics remain woefully ignorant of Eastern religions and the significance of interfaith dialogue.

2. The main thrust of Merton's essays in *Zen and the Birds of Appetite* seeks to convey a correct understanding and appreciation of Zen to Western Christian minds. Westerners find Zen puzzling in reference to their traditional ways of thinking. Merton stresses that there are two senses of Zen which must be kept separate, yet related: Zen as a religion of belief, piety and ritual, as traditionally understood, and Zen as a transconscious "consciousness" (3–4), a pure consciousness gained by pushing beyond the formal structures of religion. Merton believes that the great world religions, Islam, Christianity, or Buddhism, inevitably push beyond the formal structures of faith to a deeper level of awareness and experience (5).

This latter perspective of Zen attracts Merton profoundly, and he labors in most of the essays to articulate it through a variety of ap-

6. "Letter to the Bishops of the Catholic Church on Some Aspects of Christian Meditation," *Buddhist-Christian Studies* 11 (1991) 123–138.

proaches. Zen in this transconscious perspective describes a striving which explodes beyond the historical and cultural bounds of Buddhism. This Zen is not kerygma or revelation, but an experience of pure awareness (47). It seeks to attain an unarticulated and unexplained ground of direct experience, to grasp reality *without* logical verbalizing (36). In this "pure consciousness of Being" the perceiving subject as subject eventually disappears (23–24). The true purpose of Zen is "awakening a deep ontological awareness, a wisdom-intuition (Prajna) in the ground of being of the one awakened" (48). In his short essay on Kitaro Nishida, Merton approves the Japanese philosopher's concern with "the primary structure of consciousness," "a pure experience of undifferentiated unity," and "the intuition of the basic unity of subject and object in being" "prior to all differentiations" (67–68).

Reaching this level of Zen consciousness smashes the mental and cultural preconceptions which so easily confine and distort our inherited or learned ways of perception and evaluation. The Zen attainment wants to just see, to wake up, to become aware . . . in the simplest and purest way possible (43). The Zen mind wants to look without any fetters; simply seeing becomes "the basic and fundamental exercise of Buddhist meditation" (53). Thus so many of the traditional Zen techniques (stories and koans) seek to explode accepted principles. Like the sudden ringing of an alarm clock, Zen tries to deliberately wake up the mind that thinks in ego-centered practicality and manipulation in order to lead that mind toward pure freedom and openness (50). This Zen escapes beyond its cultural religious boundaries and becomes a self-emptying experience found in all the great mystical traditions of the world.

3. Merton believes that this type of Zen consciousness bears a similarity to forms of Christian mysticism and has much to teach Christianity. While he does not hold all mysticisms to be identical, certain analogies and correspondences appear in widely diverse religious traditions (43). He finds one Christian analogy in the thought of Meister Eckhart and his theme of "going beyond God" (9–12).[7] In still another passage he alludes to a Christian mysticism which apprehends God neither "as Immanent or as Transcendent but as grace and presence . . . as Freedom and Love" (25). In the essay attempting to describe the meaning of "Transcendent Experience," Merton finds a basic

7. Merton's appreciation of Eckhart grew substantially through the years: MacCormick, 815.

similarity between Sufism, Christianity, and Zen. Their mysticisms all pursue a radical and unconditional questioning of the human ego. Through this questioning the individual self-consciousness must disappear before (or perhaps into) the transcendent which confronts it. In Christian terms this is like that special awareness of Christ or the Spirit within the self, which in turn absorbs the self: "I live now not I but Christ lives in me" (Gal 2:20). Or again, quoting Eckhart: "We love God with His own love; awareness of it deifies us (75)."[8] Merton maintains that in all higher religious traditions this path to transcendent realization follows the tasks of self-emptying, of negating the ego (76).

This ancient, yet modern perspective of Zen can be brought to enrich contemporary Christianity. Its nondoctrinal, concrete, direct and existential method reminds Christians of the crucial importance of regaining an immediate perception of spiritual things. Such an intuitive presence so easily gets covered over by anxieties and concern for doctrines, morality, and rituals. Zen challenges Christians to learn to pay attention, to develop a kind of consciousness that sees without preconceptions.[9] One is tempted to say that Merton's natural bent of irreverence particularly appreciated Zen's cryptic, disconcerting, and irreligious character (34). As Zen jolted traditional Buddhist minds, so also might Christians benefit spiritually from a touch of reverent iconoclasm.

Even though Zen has no direct concern with a personal God or a transcendent revelation, it does seek a purification and expansion of the mind in which subject and object ultimately become One. In this way Buddhism definitely counts as a religious philosophy (79). Merton warns Westerners not to judge Buddhism as fundamentally negative or world-denying; it has produced too much vitality, joy, literature, and art in a wide range of human civilizations (80). There is a genuine sense in which Nirvana counts much more as pure presence than absence or negation (80).

4. Merton felt that a major mistake of Christians was to begin a dialogue with Buddhism on a doctrinal rather than an experiential

8. Merton notes that Dr. Suzuki approves of Eckhart's statement: *ZBA*, 75–76.

9. Perhaps Merton was thinking of the famous beginning of the Rule of St. Benedict, "Ausculta" (Listen). *RB 1980: The Rule of St. Benedict*, ed. Timothy Fry (Collegeville: The Liturgical Press, 1981) 156–157.

basis. Catholics will find this hard to accept because doctrine has occupied such a large place in Catholic religiosity. Traditional Catholicism emphasized doctrine as the *fact* of revelation accepted in faith.
In a similar vein, historical Catholicism revered the exact transmission
and understanding of doctrine (39). These fundamental aspects of their
religious mentality mean that Western Christians give primacy of place
to "religious explanation" and concrete historical forms of religion (e.g.,
doctrine, moral laws, rituals) as the necessary foundations of faith. They
want to begin religious dialogue right there. Zen, however, resists
being easily communicable and prefers experience over explanation,
which always remains secondary (46).

In Merton's view all great religions (in their inner reality) aspire
to a direct confrontation with Absolute Being . . . Absolute Love . . .
Absolute Mercy or Absolute Void (61). In Buddhism the highest level
is reached when the individual is completely emptied of selfness and
becomes "enlightened." Christians would do better to begin dialogue
by discussing the nature of enlightenment and searching for analogies in Christian life.

5. The previous point leads to another of Merton's major ideas:
to dialogue genuinely with Buddhism, the faith of Catholicism must
be recaptured as a living experience. Too often Catholicism exalts historical doctrine over present practice. But what is desperately needed is
a practical experience of faith, different from doctrine, morality and
worship; the heart of the Catholic faith must be grasped as a living
experience of unity in Christ, a taste of eternal life (39). The spiritual
practice that Merton describes is not like following the instruction of
a blueprint. He intends spiritual practice to mean the way an artist
delves into the material of the craft—creatively, lovingly and with an
openness of purpose. The latter practice possesses a personal im-
mediacy which the former does not have.

Merton elaborates this notion of a living spiritual experience
through several dynamic images. He notes that the Bible often emphasizes themes of direct experience, such as the Old Testament notion of "knowing" and the New Testament emphasis on "Life in the
Spirit" (52). He points to Paul's two kinds of wisdom: (1) rational and
dialectical and (2) the spiritual wisdom of the Cross. Here the Cross
symbolizes a stark, existential experience of union with Christ in human
pain, suffering, tragedy and emptiness. Through such experiential symbols Christianity becomes more than an intellectual acceptance of a

religious message by a submissive faith; it is uniquely a deep, personal experience of inner spirit that gives strength and power in meeting the immediate challenges of human life (55).

6. A last major point suggested by Merton is a question: can a Christian practice Zen? In what was surely a shocking statement even for the immediate post-Vatican II world, Merton answers affirmatively. But he means Zen as a quest for pure and direct experience on a metaphysical level, free from verbal formula and linguistic preconceptions. This Zen can help Christians recapture their own spiritual paths. Soon after *Zen and the Birds of Appetite*, Merton expressed this thought more clearly:

> . . . I think we have now reached a stage of (long-overdue) religious maturity at which it may be possible for someone to remain perfectly faithful to a Christian and Western monastic commitment, and yet to learn in depth from, say, a Buddhist or Hindu discipline and experience. I believe that some of us need to do this in order to improve the quality of our own monastic life. . . .[10]

Merton and the Last Quarter Century

Thus, in the late 1960s Merton was writing about the need for Catholics to have an accurate understanding of Zen, the possibility of being in dialogue with and learning from Zen, and making the startling suggestion that a faithful, believing Christian might actually practice Zen for religious improvement. Few people were probably listening. In the full flush of those activist years, not many were ready to turn in an easterly direction or even to look inward and nurture contemplation.[11]

But times change and the practical encounters between Christianity and Buddhism mushroomed in the decades after Merton's death. Much was due to a great influx of Buddhists into the United States. The wars in Southeast Asia brought Vietnamese, Laotian, and Cambodian immigrants; the Japanese economic miracle significantly increased their presence in the United States, and the conquest of Tibet by China eventually brought many Tibetan Buddhist leaders to the

10. Thomas Merton, *The Asian Journal of Thomas Merton* (New York: New Directions, 1973) 313.
11. There were very few reviews of *ZBA* in the years following its publication.

Western world. They did not arrive only to be displaced immigrants; they have become a growing and influential presence, initiating university programs in Oriental and East Asian studies and establishing national centers for the study and practice of Buddhism (e.g., the Naropa Institute, Zen Mountain Monastery). They have also demonstrated a marvelous flexibility in adapting ancient religious teachings and practices to fit a modern, technological western culture.[12] They have made a significant and growing number of American converts to Buddhism.

All this has provided increased opportunity for contacts between Buddhism and Christianity. And while this intermingling is not widespread through the general American religious population, it is surely far more than people would have imagined when Merton was writing twenty-five years ago.

The professional theological encounter has taken major steps forward. One need only survey religious publishing houses to see the number of publications, both specialized and popular, which explore the relationships between Christian and Buddhist beliefs and practices.[13] Independent study groups of Buddhist and Christian scholars have been working together for years in trying to establish better mutual understandings.[14] Since 1980 there have been four International Buddhist-Christian Dialogue conferences which have drawn participants from all over the world.[15] The Society for Buddhist-Christian Studies recently became a participant in the Council of Societies for the Study of Religion, and its journal, *Buddhist-Christian Studies*, provides further evidence of ongoing research and professional standing in American academic circles.

12. A fine example of modernized Buddhism can be found in the works of Thich Nhat Hanh: *The Miracle of Mindfulness*, trans. Mobi Ho (Boston: Beacon, 1975) 1987; *Peace Is Every Step* (New York: Bantam, 1992).

13. A handy tool is: Educational Resources Committee of the Society for Buddhist-Christian Studies, *Resources for Buddhist-Christian Encounter: An Annotated Bibliography* (Wofford Heights, Calif.: Multifaith Resources, 1993).

14. The John Cobb-Masao Abe study group has circulated papers and held working sessions for almost fourteen years. As an example of their sharings, see Roger Corless and Paul Knitter, eds. *Buddist Emptiness and Christian Trinity* (Mahwah: Paulist, 1990).

15. International Conferences have been held at the University of Hawaii (1980, 1984), Berkeley, California (1987), and Boston University (1992). The Boston meeting drew over three hundred participants from seventeen countries.

However, the dialogue has by no means been an easy one, either in theory or practice. Roger Corless, in his introduction to *Buddhist Emptiness and Christian Trinity*, wrote some of the most honest words ever penned by one looking back over his own contributions to a collection:

> These essays . . . are exploratory and tentative, confusing, and even (speaking as much for myself as for my fellow contributors) confused. When I reread what I have written, I find that I am not sure that I know what I am trying to say, and as I was editing the essays of my distinguished colleagues, I sometimes wondered if they might not have similar reactions to their own work.[16]

If true for professional academics, imagine the troubles of the average lay person—for example those involved in the official dialogue initiated by the Roman Catholic Archdiocese of Los Angeles with the Buddhist Sangha Council of Southern California. Their initial report covering the first years of their joint venture describes the struggle: "First, we discovered that learning about each other's tradition was learning the vocabulary that it uses to express itself. This proved to be more difficult than we expected. . . . At times we spent an entire session on just one word or concept."[17] But the dialogue continues, as well it should.

On still another level the practice of shared meditation by Christian and Buddhist monastics, as well as visits to each other's monasteries, has become a part of the landscape of American Catholic religious life. Delegations from the United States have visited and lived in Buddhist monasteries in India, Japan, Thailand, and other Eastern countries, and in return hosted groups of visiting Buddhist monks and nuns. Monastic organizations like Monastic Interreligious Dialogue (MID) seek to further and deepen these contacts. And program offerings in many American retreat houses frequently utilize Eastern methods of spiritual meditation and practice.

Merton raised the issue of a Catholic practicing Zen. Yet did he ever imagine that a major issue in the professional dialogue twenty-five years later would be whether it is possible to be a Catholic priest and ordained Zen master at one and the same time? Yet such is one

16. Corless, *Buddhist Emptiness*, 1.
17. The Los Angeles Interreligious Group, "Buddhist-Catholic Dialogue: An Early Journey," *Origins* 20 (April 11, 1991) 715.

of the major issues that the Society for Buddhist-Christian Studies has been pursuing at recent meetings: What exactly is this "mixed religious practice?" Does it compromise the essential integrity of either Catholic Christianity or Zen Buddhism? Is it an entirely new kind of religion?[18]

Merton's Seminal Insights

Merton was writing at the very beginning of the modern dialogue between Christianity and Buddhism. Do his thoughts and suggestions in *Zen and the Birds of Appetite* still have merit in the wake of the rapid expansion of the last quarter century? I believe they do, although not always positively. I would like to indicate several issues where a cue from Merton would facilitate the ongoing dialogue.

First, Merton's stress on religious experience as the basis for any sound and fruitful dialogue needs to be given greater attention. The recognition that Zen can best be understood in its actual practice was the turning point in his own developing understanding. In the "Postface" of *Zen and the Birds of Appetite* he acknowledges that several pages of his 1961 essay "Wisdom in Emptiness" (coauthored with Daisetz Suzuki), need to be radically changed.[19] His initial approach relied too much upon theological understandings which were abstract and conceptual. Zen reveals its truth in concrete, actual experience and practice.

At this point we must deal with a serious lacuna in American Catholicism: its reluctance to articulate and communicate Catholic faith as a spiritual practice. That faith has been frequently spelled out in doctrinal, ritual, and institutional expressions, but less often as a spiritual discipline which incorporates a model and goal of human maturity on the way to its religious goals. Buddhism, on the other hand, possesses many practices of concentration, meditation, and physical posturing, and each can be explained in terms of the attitude sought by the practice, the religious conviction expressed, and the goal of human maturity sought. Catholics in general lag far behind in that kind

18. This topic was vigorously discussed at the 1992 International Buddhist-Christian Dialogue Conference and among the regular meetings of the Society for Buddhist-Christian studies. See *Newsletter of the Society for Buddhist-Christian Studies* 11 (Spring 1993) 3.
19. *ZBA*, 139.

of experiential awareness. Even monastic participators in interfaith dialogue frequently mention how their discussions with Buddhists have thrown them back on their own (often flimsy) resources in trying to find experiential explanations for traditional monastic observances. To the extent that Catholic participants in interfaith dialogue emphasize, nurture, and articulate their faith as a living spiritual practice, the better will they be able to share with Buddhist counterparts.

Second, Merton never ceases to stress that pure experience lies at the heart of Buddhist meditation and Christian mysticism. The need to recapture this difficult notion becomes ever more urgent as an "age of prejudice or cultural boundedness" seems to be descending upon the American mentality, both popular and academic. Increasingly ethnic groups, churches and special interest organizations seem to exalt their own particular biases and even make intolerance a virtue. Scholars proclaim with increasing insistence the impossibility of getting completely behind one's inherited cultural and experiential patterns; human beings are innately and irrevocably culturally determined. They may purify those thought patterns partially, but a transconscious consciousness is not even considered in much of today's scholarly discourse. To return to Merton is to revisit the possibility of exploding beyond one's inherited perspective. It would be extremely valuable for religious scholars to reexamine three kinds of experience and the interactions between them: (1) a transcendent metaphysical experience; (2) a religious mystical experience; and (3) religious experiences within culturally embedded forms.

Third, a minor point in *Zen and the Birds of Appetite*, but one which connects with issues raised by the recent Vatican letter,[20] deserves further exploration: whether a regular Christian life (that is, a life of basic doctrinal belief, ritual worship and affective prayer) is religiously *inferior* to the kind of deep interior experience stressed by Buddhists and contemplative Christians? In *Zen and the Birds of Appetite* Merton at times seems to incline in that direction. He intimates that there are different levels of religious experience or practice (72). He acknowledges a place for I-Thou religious practices (e.g., in liturgy and morals) at the beginning of one's faith, but in these ordinary religious experiences the subject remains conscious as a subject. The progressive

20. Op. cit., "Letter to the Bishops of the Catholic Church on Some Aspects of Christian Meditation."

religious practitioner, however, relaxes any grasp on a religious goal and contemplates in pure presence.

The Ratzinger letter[21] raises a genuine concern, one that has been longstanding in Christian tradition. Historically the basic religious measure of spiritual practice has been *loving service*. How does this loving service relate to deep, interior experiences of meditation and mystical presence, and vice versa? This is surely an issue to be explored in our expanding spiritual supermarket of Zen-Christian meditation retreats, centering prayer, and New Age spiritual happenings.

When *Zen and the Birds of Appetite* first appeared in the late 1960s, it was not hailed as a significant work. But the dialogue with Buddhism and other world religions had hardly begun. In the following years a tremendous explosion in interfaith relations has occurred. Nevertheless *Zen and the Birds of Appetite* twenty-five years later still possesses fresh and revealing insights.

21. Ibid.

Animated Outsiders:
Echoes of Merton in Hampl,
Norris, Dillard, and Ehrlich

Claire Badaracco

Among the characteristics of Thomas Merton's poetry that continue to engage audiences is a conversational style that pulls readers inside his most intimate dialogues with God. Merton's spiritual journals written from the Abbey of Gethsemani are also a familiar genre. The literary wilderness essay, perfected by Henry David Thoreau and Ralph Waldo Emerson, epitomized the nineteenth-century American philosophy of transcendentalism. As a philosophy, transcendentalism prized simplicity in "natural" religion and the idea of oratory and of writing as civic vocations, a suitable way to explain the idyllic thinker among the agrarian, utopian communities that flourished briefly in mid-nineteenth century New England. The word "natural" signified the spirituality of the "outsider" who left the village for a life outdoors. Detachment from the habits of village culture freed the observer to report on the illusions and reality of a seemingly eventless world and to seek community in a new way, through the patterns of the seasons and habitats of creatures. Above all, such a writer praised listening.

Thomas Merton's poetry and prose provide ample evidence of his reading the American transcendentalists and his regard for Emerson and Thoreau as writers, thinkers, and spiritual philosophers. Henry David Thoreau left Concord for Walden Pond because he "wished to live deliberately, to front only the essential facts of life," as Merton noted in *Sign of Jonas*, and to see, as a poet, if he could learn what nature "had to teach."[1] Emerson observed that most people had a very

1. Thomas Merton, *The Sign of Jonas* (New York: Harcourt, Brace and Co., 1953) 316.

superficial way of seeing themselves united with other humans and with nature as one community. He wrote that "nature never became a toy to a wise spirit." Only those whose "inward and outward" ways of seeing were "truly adjusted to each other" could understand the preaching of the stars and the powerful eloquence of the sun.[2] Emily Dickinson also sought refuge in her poetry from what Merton would call the "vain agitation of cities."[3]

Just as Merton sometimes mentioned the words of Thoreau and Emerson, a number of contemporary writers are turning to Merton's poetry and journals as "spiritual classics." Works by Patricia Hampl, Kathleen Norris, Annie Dillard, and Gretel Ehrlich provide some examples of a larger conversation going on in mass culture about popular religion, the perception of the beautiful in women, and the importance of integrating the feminine in achieving religious balance. What makes this curious and intriguing is the way in which women writers are using the themes of monastic simplicity to offer an alternative vision about religion to those traditions of orthodox, patriarchal culture. At the same time, one might conjecture from these works by women that there seems to be an insistence on reinventing women's religious culture as the literature of outsiders. Paradoxically, what once was weakness now is perceived as strength. Being on the outside of biblical culture enables women to reinterpret the language of the scribes.

Among such contemporary women writers are those working within a genre of "spiritual journalism." Produced for the mass marketplace, the genre is a type of wilderness essay that is part prayer, part diary, part poetry—a narrative of the animated soul in an eventless, natural world. These writers have chosen to live in places off the beaten path where the mass media cannot penetrate, or is irrelevant—the plains, desert, forest. The common ground for their shared religious perspectives is that of the silence made holy by the act of their recording the silence, and the world made up of small, inconsequential lives caught up in daily ritual and routine transformed suddenly into events of vast consequence because they occur in an otherwise eventless landscape.

Four writers are discussed in this essay as contemporary practitioners of "spiritual journalism"; they seek to transcend psyche, or-

2. *Norton Anthology of American Literature* (New York: Norton, 1989) I, 904.
3. Thomas Merton, *Life and Holiness* (New York: Doubleday, 1964) 14.

thodoxy, and culture in a way that Emerson, Thoreau, and Merton would have found congenial. In their search for a feminine spirit, for a "natural religion," these writers seek to discover and to describe for others what it means to be human. They write about natural religion—balanced, authentic, healthy, as well as ordinary and conversational—not as a matter for the intellect or even so much of the heart, but as matter for the artist's source of vision. With detachment from official religion, they bear witness to a natural order unrecognized by the secular world. The poetic dimension of "natural" religion (the "language of the spheres") provides the authentic way into the feminine soul and out of the dilemma of patriarchal culture. The purpose of prayer, for these women artists, is to listen and to observe what God is saying and doing in the world. The writers' vocation is to tell readers what they hear and see.

Among the contemporary writers working in the genre of spiritual journalism, several have created works about the geography of the soul. Each unravels the contradictions of her search for natural religion to help define what "feminine spirit" means. When Merton wrote that the "difference between the moral life and the mystical life is discovered in the presence of contradiction," he also observed that the role of discovery in the contemplative life is a process of "finding the Holy Spirit in new and unexpected places."[4] He kidded his long-faced readers that one of those surprising places "might be in moral theology." "I thought," Merton wrote, "moral theology was just a set of rules by which one learned to keep imperfect Christians and sinners from getting mad at the Church and walking out altogether."[5] For contemporary writers seeking a place in patriarchal religious culture for the feminine spirit, one of those surprises is not in moral theology but in their cultural memories of Catholicism. However, contemporary women are not revisiting Mary McCarthy's *Memories of a Catholic Girlhood*.[6] Instead, they create a bemused literary distance from the artifacts of their fathers' faith that is less nostalgic than comic. The press for relevance to the immediate moment overcomes the poignance of the past: for there is no question that the present moment is the one that counts, defines the importance of seeing things as the are,

4. Merton, *Jonas*, 188.
5. Ibid., 280–282.
6. Mary McCarthy, *Memories of a Catholic Girlhood* (New York: Harcourt, Brace, 1957).

not as they are remembered. Ironic and comedic modes sustain the contemporary narrative and encourage a dubious reader to enter the world of orthodoxy without timidity.

Drawn to the aesthetic center of the Catholic religion, several of these writers have left the attic of their girlhood to enter a dialogue with feminism itself as a belief system, with those who regard feminism in a quasi-religious light, and with those who regard the feminine spirit as a threat to official religion. They do not retreat from the religious and moral dilemma posed by patriarchal culture and orthodox faith which relegates women to the periphery. Merton acknowledged that the "artificial" system of religious hierarchies which cast women as outsiders "needs to be changed," and that change in "the whole idea of priesthood" cannot come about by women "getting all fixed up in a chasuble and biretta," but by developing "a whole new style of worship in which there is no need for one hierarchical person to have a big central place," but a form of worship in which "everyone is involved."[7]

The four writers discussed here provide narrative evidence of their search to resolve an authentic religious dilemma. Merton wrote that the essence of the mystical prayer life was the way to resolve human dilemmas "in ease and mystery," choosing at the same time "both horns of the dilemma and no horn at all and always being perfectly right." In mystical activity, he concluded, "the dilemma suddenly ceases to matter."[8] Evidence from the genre of spiritual journalism demonstrates how writers are spiritually freed by their lives as outsiders from both secular and official religious culture. Their search to understand what it means to be human in relation to an Other, not in relation to the self, is in that dimension of non-being weighted in eventlessness. It is this quality which separates these writers from the literature by eco-feminist women that is caught in its own resistance against inherited forms, its refusal to integrate spirit and culture, its "obstinancy" to borrow Martín-Barbero's phrase.[9] The writers I recommend here as being congenial with the contemplative dimension are

7. Jane Marie Richardson, ed., Thomas Merton, *The Springs of Contemplation: A Retreat at the Abbey of Gethsemani* (New York: Farrar, Straus, Giroux, 1992) 175–176.

8. Merton, *Jonas*, 280.

9. Jesús Martín-Barbero, *Communication, Culture and Hegemony: From the Media to Mediations* (London: Sage, 1993) i–iii.

engaged in a search for the transcendent, but they are not separatists. On the contrary, they use Merton, and especially his use of transcendentalism, in translating their search for a mass marketplace audience.

Eco-feminists construct political philosophy, building a goddess-system to compete with patriarchy, and treat Nature [capitalization mine] as part of a hierarchy of being. The spiritual journalists see nature as a source for instruction and conversation for humans about becoming. Further, eco-feminism is a distinct strain in American literary history, an outgrowth of the "confessional school of poetry" of the 1970s that included writers like Sylvia Plath and Anne Sexton, many of whom ended their own lives after a great deal of torment and despair. Merton argued that the resolution to any interior problem as a psychological fact lay not in the resolution of selfhood or psychology, in "what I am or what I am not," but in the "mode in which I am tending to become what I really will be."[10] In the opinion of the spiritual poet and literary critic Denise Levertov, who knew Thomas Merton and admired his writing, the confessional school produced "womb poetry," a literature of self-gestation from which emerged not a new self, but a more functional one.[11] Through contemplation, Merton might have argued, gender ceases to matter: prayer is both a "way out" of the gender-difference argument and a "way in" to unity with all people.

Patricia Hampl

Patricia Hampl is a professor of English literature at the University of Minnesota. She calls herself laughingly a "convent school ingenue who refused to convert to the secular faith of the real world." She points out in *Virgin Time* that her girlish Catholicism was an instinct about two things—the right to exercise the imagination and the need to travel. A child's interpretation of life as journey is about the freedom to move, to be "on the trail," she recalls, "I didn't know how to think about the past without going somewhere."[12] Her book is about

10. Merton, *Jonas*, 188.
11. Personal conversation with Denise Levertov at University of California at Berkeley, 1968. See also Carol P. Christ, *Diving Deep and Surfacing: Women Writers on Spiritual Quest* (Boston: Beacon, 1980).
12. Patricia Hampl, *Virgin Time* (New York: Ballantine, 1992) 206. See also, Christina Buchmann and Celina Spiegel, eds., *Out of the Garden: Women Writers on the Bible* (New York: Fawcett, 1994).

her journey toward becoming a writer of some spiritual depth and comic vision.

The journey she relates is a pilgrimage from Assisi, to Lourdes, and eventually to northern California, where she seeks definitions of mystery and connections with the human through a search for community in contemplative prayer. Along the way, her tale is imbued with an awareness of religious anachronism embodied by the human comedy. Though Hampl begins the book with the rather severe concept of journey, she discovers, having met a cast of characters in Chaucerian fashion along the route, the more complex dimensions of Merton's contemplative model as central to a reality that will take her beyond history and politics. Through the process of travelling she establishes an occasion for her spiritual conversations with the reader.

Hampl and her fellow travellers find Merton's definition of the contemplative life as "one's own time. But not dominated by one's own ego and its demands. Hence open to others—compassionate time, rooted in the sense of common illusion and in criticism of it."[13] She calls this the "timeless time, the receptive temporal pivot when being hangs suspended, unadorned by will or intention," citing Merton as her source. He had written, she notes, "For the birds, there is not a time . . . but the virgin point between darkness and light, between nonbeing and being . . . when creation in its innocence asks permission to be once again, as it did on the first morning that ever was." Hampl interprets Merton's signature moment as the difference between daybreak and dawn, a paradigm of perpetual uncovering of a darkness that does not cease.[14] The contemplative point of view, she notes, is a way of thinking about religion where "the day is a verse and the season is a stanza."[15] Nature sets the rhythms for prayer in the writer's life.

According to Hampl, the contemplative life is not a way of limiting what can be seen; it is "a habit of attention brought to bear on all that is." The contemplative dimension provides the controlling metaphor for a life of observation. The nuns who taught in her Kennedy-era convent school asked, "Who sees the parade better?"— "the baton twirler strutting along the middle of the street? Or the person with a balcony view, looking down on it all?" The person in the

13. Hampl, *Virgin Time*, 224–225.
14. Ibid., 206.
15. Ibid., 220.

balcony, Sister argued, "unobserved and hidden," "possessed the entire event" not unlike the writer, while the twirler, Sister pointed out, was a "borderline ninny," despite the "kick" of being the center of attention. The elevated status of the observer shapes Hampl's narration as well as her concept of her vocation as a writer. Because of her Catholic training, Hampl says, "self-expression became my true faith." Her education gave her the freedom to stare out the window at nothing—which was excellent training for the imagination, she observes. Of the convent school, she recalls that "the whole place was an injunction to metaphor, to the endless noticing of detail that is rendered into transformation."[16]

Hampl discovers the model of Mary as an outsider who was really on the inside, at ease with her freedom to stand aside and "ponder" the mysteries of life. Pondering assumed a high place in her girlhood religious outlook on life. The "other, richer passion, rooted early," Hampl writes, "was for the mystery of a dedicated life."[17] The very concept of vocation, a somewhat foreign notion in a consumer culture, forms her habit as a writer.

The Church offered a mature Hampl an opportunity for intimacy not afforded by the real culture and something different than the intimacy of her marriage. Beneath its theology, patriarchy, or history, Catholicism in its first state "was sheer poetry." The cultural memories Hampl transmits with *Virgin Time* are the right to observe, record, stare out the window at nothing, and the freedom to imagine the self, or to converse with God, to ponder as His mother had done the meaning of being human. "Somewhere along the years," Hampl writes, "religion passed beyond the allure of the consecration to the mystery of living itself. That mystery, elusive even in its presence in every breath we take, was represented to me as the life of contemplation. The monastery was a hive, the laboratory of life's mystery."[18]

Kathleen Norris

Kathleen Norris, a resident of a small town in South Dakota, is a poet, wife, Protestant, lay minister, and an oblate in a Benedictine

16. Ibid., 224.
17. Ibid., 14.
18. Ibid.

community of sixty-five monks in North Dakota. Norris's *Dakota: A Spiritual Geography* is best considered in the light of the literary tradition of Emily Dickinson or Flannery O'Connor—it is about making room for the spirit despite the restrictions or confinements of a place. Preferring "music and story over systematic theology," Norris describes an inner landscape as being shaped by the natural conditions of the place she and her husband prefer to their earlier life in Manhattan. "The city no longer appeals to me for the cultural experiences and possessions I might acquire there," she writes, "holiness is to be found in being open to humanity in all its diversity. And the western plains now seem bountiful in their emptiness, offering solitude and room to grow." Norris's formation responds to the ancient order, the Desert Fathers' spirituality, "not taught but caught; it was a whole way of life."

The American way of life accepts consumption of material goods as a serious matter, while talk of time and God make her peers uncomfortable. For Norris, the idea of "God's ever present hospitality in both nature and other people" is an "invitation," and in deciding to live in a place "where nothing happens," the author discovers that she "can change." In a landscape where there are few people and long winters, Norris had to give up attachment to ideas of dominance or control. Rather, she had to wait. The place would "mold" her. Norris concludes that religion is to "be participated in and not consumed— one reason why Americans are as a culture in a deep conflict about the role religion ought to play in democratic life." The silence of the plains resembles the silence of the monastery. Norris writes, "All of this reflects a truth Thomas Merton once related about his life as a Trappist monk: 'It is in deep solitude and silence that I find the gentleness with which I can truly love my brother and sister.'"

What makes monastic life interesting to her are the monks' extraordinary ideas about reality and their "relaxed attitude about the holy that can alarm the more rigidly pious." Like the monks, the small midwestern plains town is disappearing, but their responses to impending obsolescence differ. The townspeople see only that they are failing as a community, while the monks continue to care for one another and for strangers such as the author and those she brings with her to the monastery, as though time itself were irrelevant or simply part of the larger order of things, like the seasons.

The monks teach the author a lesson about natural balance in moderation. She cites the fourth-century desert nun Amma Syncletia, who wrote that "lack of proportion always corrupts," and that the center of the ascetic way required balance among food, work, prayer, rest and play." The point of religion, Norris writes, is "not what one gets out of it, but the worship of God; the service takes place both because of and despite the needs, strengths, and frailties of the people present."

So that the penultimate balance for which nature serves as a metaphor is between life and death, one season and another, night and day, spirit and matter, reality and dream, being and non-being. What sets the monks apart, Norris concludes, is their "contemplative sense of fun." For as the Trappist Matthew Kelty writes, according to Norris, "You do not have to be holy to love God. You have only to be human. Nor do you have to be holy to see God in all things. You have only to play as a child with an unselfish heart."[19]

Gretel Ehrlich and Annie Dillard

Ehrlich's *Solace of Open Spaces,* published in 1985, is patterned on Dillard's prize-winning *Pilgrim at Tinker Creek,* published in 1974. Though her voice is more mature than Dillard, Ehrlich is less defensive about her retreat from city life. In their early work, neither sees the organized Church to offer solace in religion that is comparable to that of the natural world, which offers both truth and comfort.

Ehrlich retreats to a sheep ranch in Colorado, where she recounts her life with the cowboys, hermits, and townspeople. Little happens but the revelations of nature. Like Dillard, she is more comfortable with natural science than with faith. For both women, contemplative realities in the Desert Fathers' tradition provide the counterpoint, the backdrop for what is available rather than sought. Ehrlich finds "exquisite paradox" in autumn's "double voice," the one that says everything is ripe, the other that everything is dying. Knowledge of the paradox is the center of what the Japanese monks call "awareness," according to Erhlich, "an almost untranslatable word that means beauty tinged with sadness." Indeed, nothing seems to separate these two writers from religious maturity or transformation except time: neither historical nor political events offer interference. The focus on the present

19. All references to Kathleen Norris are from her *Dakota: A Spiritual Geography* (Boston: Ticknor & Fields, 1992).

elevates the absence of events, so that it, too, plays a role in the narrative about being.

Dillard is more pragmatic than not; she admits "I see what I expect." She cites Thoreau's return to nature as a way to escape mystery. Dillard describes herself as a writer who is like the man watching a baseball game in silence in an empty stadium, cheering over and over when the imaginary players lope off the field into the dugout. "But," Dillard protests, she will "fail" or "go mad" if she tries to comprehend mystery solely through the imagination. "The secret of seeing," Dillard writes "is the pearl of great price."[20]

Dillard concludes that this secret cannot be sought. Rather, she reluctantly concludes, understanding mystery is a gift: "All I can do," she writes, "is to gag the commentator," or disbeliever, "to hush the noise of useless interior babble that keeps me from seeing just as surely as a newspaper dangled before my eyes. The effort is really a discipline requiring a lifetime of dedicated struggle; it marks the literature of saints and monks of every Order East and West, under every rule and no rule, discalced and shod." Dillard's narration is built through a meditative process that moves her beyond the "mind's muddy river." Though she is a meticulous observer of nature, she never enters the "deep light" but hovers on the perimeter, telling the reader about its value.[21] Dillard ends her narrative "dancing to the twin silver trumpets of praise," her "left foot says 'Glory' and her right foot says 'Amen.' "[22]

To have chosen a life of solitude, Ehrlich writes, is seen by the world as a sign of failure.[23] One of Ehrlich's neighbors is the granddaughter of Ralph Waldo Emerson: she ranches alone, admits that the life is hard, but achieves balance and perspective by focussing on all things rather than one. She acknowledges that "everything" is beautiful.[24] In this landscape, Ehrlich finds sacramental meaning, a text from which she can derive instruction.[25] Like Merton, Ehrlich "loves winter when the plant says nothing."[26] In the absence of anything but

20. Annie Dillard, *Pilgrim at Tinker Creek* (New York: Harper & Row, 1974) 15.
21. Ibid., 32.
22. Ibid., 271.
23. Gretel Ehrlich, *The Solace of Open Spaces* (New York: Viking, 1985) 21.
24. Ibid., 43.
25. Ibid., 71.
26. Thomas Merton, "Love Winter When the Plant Says Nothing," *Selected Poems* (New York: New Directions, 1967) 112.

whiteness, she gleans peripheral vision that leads her to the greater knowledge that "it is in the volume of life we learn life is good." Ehrlich finds the same invitation to be human in solitude that Thoreau found. He wrote that to be human is to be like the river, always in the same channel but a new water every instant.[27] In solitude Ehrlich finds the source for her renewed faith in life itself if not in any official religion. As autumn teaches her the paradox that ripeness is a form of decay and "leaves are verbs that conjugate the seasons," Erhlich concludes that the whole of nature is a metaphor for a kind of transubstantiation: "Today the sky is a wafer. Placed on my tongue, it is a wholeness that has already disintegrated; placed under the tongue, it makes my heart beat strongly enough to stretch myself over the winter brilliance to come."[28]

Conclusion

American women writers are playing an important and culturally significant role in the transmission of popular ideas about religion by producing literary works about their search for transformational community through solitude and through contemplation. As the communication scholar Jesús Martín-Barbero observed recently, he "still" needed to explain for himself the role women played in the "transmission of popular memory" and women's "obstinate rejection over centuries of the official religion and culture"[29] in Latin America. Meanwhile, North American women's resistance to "official" religion seems to have occurred primarily on an academic rather than a popular level. While there is ample evidence of examining biblical scholarship and the sociology of religion so that women are included, ideas about popular religion in America, where women are concerned, remain on the level of the enthusiastic, either eco-feminist or "new age." Writers of such recent enthusiasms intend to redistribute secular power, rather than reinterpret ancient traditions about belief. The latter, I suggest, is the work of the genre of spiritual journalists: they seek to connect with ancestral patterns of belief in order to both transcend and to reconnect their present day with the past. Perhaps women's "obstinate re-

27. Ehrlich, *Solace*, 84.
28. Ibid., 130.
29. Martín-Barbero, *Communication*, 91.

fusal" cited by Martín-Barbero in Latin America, and the resistance to official religion in North America, suggests we might consider the genre of spiritual journalism as a public explanation for what they *do* accept, and as an attempt to bridge the private world of spirit and the material culture through an aesthetic construction for the authenticity they are seeking. This is a level of reality provided neither by the secular nor the religious culture these authors have inherited.

Hampl, Norris, Dillard, and Ehrlich integrate spiritual principles drawn from the transcendentalist tradition as part of their aesthetic vision. To varying degrees, each finds congenial the virtues of simplicity, detachment, non-being, eventlessness as means to enlightenment. Monastic aestheticism has been taken up as a model for transcendence as they search for a place for the feminine spirit in orthodoxy and in mass culture. During his lifetime, Thomas Merton opened up to a wide readership his experience of religious life in the monastery by drawing readers into what had previously been quite inaccessible to most of them. As the books by these women demonstrate, it is because of Merton's efforts to make the wisdom of the monastic way available to people in all walks of life that his writing continues to shape the cultural memory of those who try to express what the Catholic tradition means in contemporary life.

Time of Transition:
A Selection of Letters from the
Earliest Correspondence of
Thomas Merton and Ernesto Cardenal

Edited by Christine M. Bochen

Translations by Roberto S. Goizueta

Introduction

The following exchange of letters represents the earliest correspondence between Thomas Merton and Ernesto Cardenal, the Nicaraguan priest, poet, and revolutionary, who was for two years a novice
of Thomas Merton's at the Abbey of Gethsemani. Written between August and December of 1959, these letters shed light on what was for
both a time of transition. Having discovered that he was not suited
for the rigors of Trappist life, Cardenal had left Gethsemani and
returned to Latin America, settling for a time in Mexico where he studied for the priesthood. At the same time increasingly frustrated with
the constraints of Gethsemani, Merton had renewed his search for a
place where he might live his monastic vocation more fully and faithfully. These letters offer an intimate record of a trying time for Cardenal
and Merton as each struggled to discern what God was calling him
to be and to do. When Merton wrote to Cardenal that "the important
thing is that you have clearly a vocation to a contemplative life . . .
the only thing that needs to be found out is exactly how and where,"
Merton could well have been speaking to himself for he was voicing
a conviction and posing questions that were very much his own.[1]

1. See letter of November 18, 1959, pp. 194–197 of this text.

Reading Merton's letters to Ernesto Cardenal, first published in *The Courage for Truth*,[2] we glimpse many facets of Thomas Merton. We meet the monk, novice master, priest, poet, and social critic as well as the friend who regarded his relationship with Cardenal among his most treasured friendships. The opportunity to read both sides of the correspondence[3] further enriches our understanding of Merton, particularly as it enables us to appreciate the significant role that Ernesto Cardenal played in Merton's life both while he was at Gethsemani and after he returned to Latin America.

For Ernesto Cardenal, to become a novice of Merton was quite unexpected:

> I learned of Merton for the first time when he began to be known in the United States, when I was 23 years old and was studying at Columbia University in New York, where he also had studied. I read his first books when they appeared and translated his poems which were published in Mexico. I always continued being a reader of his, being interested in him as much for the literary aspect as for the religious. At age 31 I had a radical conversion to God and I decided to search for the place where I could be more removed from the world and nearer to God and then I felt that my vocation was to be a Trappist.
>
> The only Trappist monastery that I knew about was the one of Gethsemani for it was the one in the books of Merton. I assumed that Merton no longer would be there because in one of his last books he had said that possibly they would send him to another foundation. It was a very great and pleasant surprise when I found

2. Thomas Merton, *The Courage for Truth*, edited by Christine M. Bochen (New York: Farrar, Straus, Giroux, 1993) 110–163. See also Thomas Merton, *Witness to Freedom*, edited by William H. Shannon (New York: Farrar, Straus, Giroux, 1994) for the full text of Merton's letter of October 8, 1959, unavailable when *The Courage for Truth* was published, and Merton's letter of October 22, 1965, which was also unavailable earlier. See 207–209 and 227–228 of *Witness to Freedom*.

Merton's letters to Ernesto Cardenal are reprinted with the permission of Farrar, Straus, Giroux.

3. The letters of Ernesto Cardenal, published here for the first time, were translated by Roberto S. Goizueta. I am grateful to Ernesto Cardenal for his enthusiastic support of the publication of these letters and for his willingness to share his reflections on his relationship to Thomas Merton, to Roberto Goizueta for translating Cardenal's letters, and to Mary Lee Bishop, S.S.J., and Dr. Edward Malinak for their assistance.

out that he was not only there but that he was the Master of Novices and the one who would be entrusted with my religious formation.[4]

Equally surprising to Cardenal was the direction his conversations with Merton took.

> The first conversation that we had he informed me that the Abbot wanted to make a Trappist foundation in Latin America. It would be with Merton, who had thought first about the Virgin Islands, then Columbia, or Ecuador, in a place in the Andes, with the indigenous people. I talked to him about Nicaragua and Nicaragua began to be another alternative, in addition to Mexico. Later he changed his mind: it wasn't practical to establish a Trappist foundation there, but rather a contemplative life more free and more simple without the rigid anachronism of the old orders, without habit, rules, bureacratic structures, a group small and poor. . . .[5]

When he met with Merton "for spiritual guidance," Merton "would ask about Nicaragua, Somoza, the poets of Nicaragua, the Nicaraguan countryside, poets from other parts of Latin America, other dictators. . . ." Though Cardenal had thought that entering the Trappist Order meant that he would "have to renounce everything . . . —my books, my interest in my country, in politics and the dictatorships of Latin America, in Nicaraguan politics, in Samoza, in everything," Merton helped him realize he would not have "to renounce anything."[6]

Though Merton's fascination with Latin America did not begin with Cardenal's arrival at Gethsemani (before entering the monastery, Merton had visited Cuba and became enthralled with the land and its people), conversations with Cardenal roused his passion for Latin American literature and culture. He read voraciously and peppered Cardenal with questions. He began to feel a deep affinity for the people of Latin America and to experience a sense of solidarity with them in their struggle for freedom. Merton began corresponding with friends of Cardenal's in Nicaragua, and before too long he was in contact with writers throughout Central and South America.[7] Just as surely as the

4. Ernesto Cardenal, unpublished comments (July 2, 1995).

5. Ibid.

6. Ernesto Cardenal in *Merton by Those Who Knew Him Best*, edited by Paul Wilkes (San Francisco: Harper 1984) 36.

7. See *The Courage for Truth*, 164–243, for Merton's letters to Latin American writers.

novice master initiated the novice into the mysterious world of the monastery, the novice drew the master into a world which both novice and master thought they had left behind when they came to Gethsemani. Merton was very much at home in that world and he felt a deep kinship with its people, particularly its writers, and in 1959 he made plans to move to Mexico, after that to Nicaragua.

Latin America appealed to more than the poet in Merton. As he and Cardenal talked, they began to envision monastic life as it might be lived in Latin America—simply and poorly—in true solitude, untethered by the restrictions of monastic life he experienced at Gethsemani. Merton's deep attraction to Latin America, his growing unrest at Gethsemani and his persistent longing for deeper solitude combined to make him very receptive to Dom Gregorio Lemercier's invitation to come live as a hermit near Cuernavaca. Dom Gregorio, Prior of a small, experimental Benedictine community, visited Merton several times during the summer of 1959. Earlier that summer, Merton had sent letters of inquiry to bishops at Bluefields, Nicaragua; Reno, Nevada; and San Juan, Puerto Rico, inquiring about the possibility of living in their dioceses. These letters and others, published in *Witness to Freedom*, chronicle Merton's "vocation crisis of 1959-1960."[8] In September, he wrote to Archbishop Larraona who headed the Sacred Congregation for Religious in Rome, to request an indult that would allow him to leave Gethsemani and live elsewhere as a monk.[9]

Throughout his monastic life, Merton's desire for the hermit life was deep and intense. That he should be a monk was never the issue, but periodically he grappled with the question of how, and where, he could best live the monastic life. The crisis of 1959-1960 needs to be read in the context of Merton's ongoing struggle with stability and his deep desire for solitude. In the early fifties he had considered joining the Carthusians or the Camoldolese, attracted by the solitude he might experience there. In 1965, when his longing for solitude was fulfilled, at least in part, by his move to a hermitage on the grounds of the monastery, Merton still did not entirely close the door on Cardenal's suggestion that he might join him at his newly founded community at Solentiname. And by 1968, Merton realized that his hermitage was far too accessible to ensure the solitude he desired, and throughout

8. See *Witness to Freedom*, 200–226.
9. Ibid., 205–207.

his travels, during the last year of his life—to New Mexico, California, Alaska, and finally the Orient, he kept his eyes open for a new site for his hermitage.

Given all that they shared—both were converts, writers, contemplatives—it is understandable that Merton and Ernesto Cardenal became close friends. "From the beginning," Cardenal writes, "there was a great affinity and friendship between us, especially because we were the only poets in the entire monastery, and also because we both had studied at Columbia."[10] But Merton was also a solicitous novice master—his deep concern and care are evident in his first letters to Cardenal; he was full of encouragement, tempering words of hope with honest realism. Cardenal's deep respect for Merton is also evident: the young poet valued Merton's advice and turned to him as he mourned what he had left behind and discovered what he would do next. Merton was doing much the same: anticipating the difficulties he would experience when he actually left Gethsemani and imagining what lay before him as a monk living in Latin America.

But as Cardenal recalls, Merton "did not want to leave in disobedience,"[11] and the indult Merton sought was not granted. Informing Cardenal of that fact in his letter of December 17, 1959, Merton appears surprisingly resigned to the decision. That letter, which Merton managed to get out in the Abbot's absence, was the last he would write to Cardenal for more than a year. Unconvinced by Merton's insistence that he was offering needed spiritual advice, Dom James Fox prohibited Merton from corresponding with Cardenal. Merton obeyed. And though he characterized himself as at peace with the decision, less than a year later, in August 1960, he wrote to Archbishop Paul Philippe, secretary of the Vatican's Congregation for Religious, once again raising the possibility of leaving Gethsemani to live as a solitary in a place like Cuernavaca.[12] Merton did not leave Gethsemani then, nor in 1965, when Cardenal invited Merton to join him at Solentiname.

In the intervening years, Merton's life changed in two important ways. In the early sixties he became an articulate and insistent witness for peace, writing against war and the proliferation of nuclear weapons and calling attention to the injustice of racism and the misuses of technology. This return to the world was followed by a retreat

10. Cardenal, unpublished comments.
11. Ibid.
12. *Witness to Freedom,* 221–223.

to the hermitage. In 1965 Merton finally received permission to live in a hermitage on the grounds of the monastery. For a time, leaving Gethsemani to live elsewhere as a monk lost its appeal for Merton. Yet thoughts of going to Latin America were not entirely behind him. Before embarking on his journey to the East, Merton shared with Cardenal "the news that he would travel to Asia and that on returning he would visit a Trappist foundation in Chile and then would go to Nicaragua to be some three months in Solentiname." Continuing his reminiscence, Cardenal wrote: "We were constructing for him a small hut with a palm roof and we were expecting him at any moment when I received the cable from Gethsemani with the news of his death in Bangkok."[13] Though Thomas Merton never visited the community at Solentiname, his influence was certainly felt there, as it was in Nicaragua where he had developed a circle of friends, and as it is throughout Latin America where Merton is known by many writers and read by countless people. Ernesto Cardenal had drawn Merton into his world—the world of Latin America, and Merton had found his place there.

Correspondence: August 9, 1959 to December 17, 1959

Ernesto Cardenal to Thomas Merton

Universidad Iberoamericana
August 9, 1959

Rev. F. M. Louis, O.C.S.O.
Gethsemani.

Dear Father Louis:

I have just arrived in Mexico because my trip took one week. There were some errors in the itinerary they gave me and it turned out to be two days later than what they had told me. Also, I arrived in New Orleans on Friday evening and had to wait there until Monday because the Nicaraguan Consulate, where I had to renew my passport, was not open on Saturday. But I did not have any other trouble, except a boring wait in New Orleans, without finding anything to do there.

13. Cardenal, unpublished comments.

The day after arriving in Mexico (the day before yesterday) I went to visit the monastery. There I told the Father Prior everything I had to say and he understood everything clearly. We agreed that I would arrive in two weeks, and that I would stay there as a guest or postulant for some months, until I could clearly see what God wants from me.

The monastery is in a very beautiful place, fairly removed from Cuernavaca (about half an hour on foot) and in an isolated place, surrounded by tropical vegetation, and with woods in front, somewhat similar to those in front of the novitiate in Gethsemani. The monastery is on a kind of hill, from where one sees a stupendous panorama of the whole valley of Cuernavaca, with the city below, and in the background great mountains and volcanoes. They are building a very revolutionary church, in accord with the most modern Mexican architecture, directed by a young monk who is an architect. Nevertheless, something strange happened to me upon my arrival: and it was that, in spite of all this which I describe to you, and which I saw that I liked, I felt sad and depressed, with a strange melancholy that I never felt in Gethsemani (where, from the moment I entered, I felt overcome by a great joy which I never lost during all the time I was there). I spoke with this young architect, who is very charming, and I found him radiant with joy, as I had always been in Gethsemani, and that made me see the difference with my current mood. I do not know if this is a passing, psychological reaction, because I do not see there any objective reason to be depressed. In any case I have resolved to enter there, whether sad or not, and to stay there as much time as is necessary until God reveals to me what I ought to do—unless my health does not allow me to do so. This does not worry me because I am completely in God's hands, and I feel that He is with me and that He directs my steps and brought me here. At the same time, I have no desire to return to the world, nor would I consider for a moment the possibility of staying in Mexico, despite the fact that here I could give classes at the National University or the Jesuit university, because there is a great scarcity of professors with university degrees and I could get them immediately if I wanted. But I cannot live in the world, because I do not belong to it. Therefore, I am sure that I have not lost my vocation, that I belong to God alone and that He will take me to where He wants me to be, and I am at peace.

My stomach is more or less the same as in Gethsemani. Sometimes I am bad and others well. During the trip I was worse, probably because I was nervous and because of the delays and the disagreeable wait in New Orleans. Upon entering the world I discovered, from my arrival in Louisville, that the world is a truly unlivable and horrible place. Especially life in the cities of the United States, because life in Mexico—even in Mexico City—is more human. In New Orleans, other than the library and the Tulane museum (which were closed almost the whole time I was there) and the churches (which are always closed or empty), I had no place to go. I spent most of the time in my hotel cell. On the streets, there are only shops and restaurants and movie theaters. Wherever one looks, there is nothing but advertisements about sex or food. There is nothing more boring than walking on these streets when one no longer has any interest in these things. In Gethsemani, I often thought that our life was monotonous. But there is no comparison between that exterior monotony accompanied by a very intense interior life and the dreadful monotony of modern city streets, all frightfully alike, and where one finds absolutely nothing interesting to do. What gave me greater sorrow was thinking about the great number of novices of Gethsemani who have left to live in these cities. And it does not surprise me that many want to return having just left, for I am sure that if I had left of my own accord to live in the world I would have immediately asked to be readmitted to Gethsemani. I tell you this because perhaps, in your lectures, you may want to give this message to your novices in Gethsemani, whom I am always remembering and for whom I always pray. I wish you would tell them that my experience of the world is that it is unlivable and if they leave because they think the world is more interesting they will be sorry as soon as they leave. Upon arriving in Louisville I went to a restaurant to eat some sandwiches because it was already noon, and upon opening the door I became horrified and retreated immediately, because inside there was noisy music coming from a juke box, so horrible and loud that I thought I would rather starve to death than eat with that music. From outside, through the glass walls, the restaurant appeared to be in profound silence, and inside it was a hell. I entered another after having determined that there was no music. But no sooner had I ordered my food than the juke box started and I had to resign myself. I have seen in this an image of what the world is: from the tranquility of the monastery it can appear calm and serene, but when one enters, it is a hell.

I received the telegram with the address of Mejía Sánchez. I am staying at the Jesuit university, because it is more monastic here and with more facilities for Mass, etc., and I am with Father [Angel] Martínez and with another Nicaraguan Jesuit who is a good friend of mine. The rector of the university is another Nicaraguan Jesuit who is also a good friend.

The translations of your poems are ready to be published and we await only [Armando] Morales' illustrations (before coming, I wrote asking him for them). The boys, friends of mine, who are in charge of the university press are very happy with the poems, which they have liked a lot, and they are very eager to publish the book. Under separate cover I am sending you a journal with [Boris] Pasternak's letter and also the last issue of the *Journal of Literature* with some poems of mine from among those of the *Hora O*. They will also publish this collection in a small book. They have also told me that they are about to publish my *Epigrams*. Mejía Sánchez has read my anti-Somoza poems in lectures and I am told that they have been very well received. They have also been published in some revolutionary journals, and in a Chilean communist one directed by [Pablo] Neruda. [Robert] Lax's translation will appear in the journal of the university.

Father Martínez received your letter and will be writing you soon. He tells me that your letter has made a great impression on him and has made him think a lot. He sees that my situation is the same as his, and he tells me that his situation is that of [Gerard Manley] Hopkins. He has suffered much like Hopkins, and still suffers, but he tells me that Hopkins resolved his problem the wrong way. I do not know if he will be able to resolve his.

The disturbances continue in Nicaragua. The day I arrived the Mexican papers carried news of a new attempted invasion on both fronts, but we do not know if it is true. There are two movements that are preparing invasions: one infiltrated by communists and the other a democratic one. But those that are infiltrated have not been able to organize themselves and the democratic ones have a greater probability of success. There have been protest demonstrations in León and Managua, and the students have been machine gunned and they have killed a number and wounded many persons. This has incited new demonstrations and protests. The clergy have acted courageously and the priests have denounced the government even from the pulpits. The invaders were accompanied by a priest chaplain, who was imprisoned. This makes more incredible the pro-government declarations which the Archbishop has made, and which I am enclosing with this letter. My cousin who had been lost in the jungle appeared after fifteen days; he was recognized by the police and is in prison. It seems to be true that, miraculously, this time they have not tortured the prisoners. I will write you again when I have more things to tell you. Do not feel obliged to respond if you do not have time. But I count on your prayers, just as you are always present in my poor prayers. As are also all the novices. In Christ.

Ernesto Cardenal

[P.S.]
I am not too sure of the price of the train ticket. On the ticket it says $50.84 but it seems odd to me that it would be so inexpensive because I thought that it cost more. Since they have sent me a $50.00 check from home I am sending it to Gethsemani, in case that is the price of the ticket. If it is not, please let me know so that I may send the remainder. Farewell.

Thomas Merton to Ernest Cardenal

August 17, 1959[14]

Dear Ernesto:

Thank you for your letter. I was relieved to hear you had finally arrived, because I thought interiorly that the plan would very probably not be quite as simple as it looked on paper. Certainly when it was expected that you would reach Mexico City from San Antonio in eight hours, I knew it was impossible. And so you had two days in New Orleans: they must indeed have been miserable. I think the weariness of the journey and the other effects of your leaving here, with the inevitable let-down, must have been chiefly responsible for your sadness. I know of course how you would feel, and it was to be expected.

14. Unless otherwise noted, Merton's letters were written at the Abbey of Gethsemani, on monastery letterhead, bearing the inscription: Our Lady of Gethsemani, Trappist, Kentucky. It was generally Merton's practice to observe the monastic habit of inscribing each letter with the letters ''jhs.''

You came here under ideal conditions, and everything was of a nature to make you happy and give you peace. You had given yourself completely to God without afterthought and without return, and He on His part had brought you to a place where the life was unexpectedly easy and pleasant and where everything went along quite smoothly for you. Hence in reality the first real Cross you met with, in your response to God's call, was the necessity to *leave* this monastery, under obedience, after having been told that it was not God's will for you to stay here.

You must not regard this as the end of your vocation, or as a break in the progress of your soul towards God. On the contrary, it is an entirely necessary step and part of the vital evolution of your vocation. It is a step in your spiritual maturity, and that is why it is difficult for you. Certainly it would have been pleasant to remain in the state of almost passive irresponsibility here—that is one of the qualities and one of the vices of this monastery: everything is geared to keep one passive and, in a certain sense, infantile. This is from a certain point of view excellent, and it can quickly bring many souls into a state of detachment and peace which favors a certain interior life. But unfortunately also the peculiar circumstances of this monastery prevent real spiritual growth. Underneath the superficial and somewhat false good humor, with its facade of juvenile insouciance, lies the deep fear and anxiety that comes from a lack of real interior life. We have the words, the slogans, the notions. We cultivate the pageantry of the monastic life. We go in for singing, ritual, and all the externals. And ceremonies are very useful in dazzling the newcomer, and keeping him happy for a while. But there seems to be a growing realization that for a great many in the community this is all a surface of piety which overlies a fake mysticism and a complete vacuity of soul. Hence the growing restlessness, the rebellions, the strange departures of priests, the hopelessness which only the very stubborn can resist, with the aid of their self-fabricated methods of reassurance.

Your own interior life was perfectly genuine. God gave you many graces and brought you close to Himself, and perhaps you would never have come so close to Him anywhere else. For these last two years, Gethsemani was ideal for you, and you must regard it as a great grace that God brought you here. It is something that has changed the whole direction of your life. But at the same time if you had remained here, the general spirit of unrest in the community and the growing fear of falsity which has disturbed so many of our best vocations and made them leave, would have reached you too. And by that time you would have been professed, and in a very difficult position.

The fact that you were in danger of developing a stomach ulcer was a warning sign of the very painful and harmful experiences that would have awaited you if you had stayed here, and I assure you that the happiness you had known in the novitiate would not have lasted long.

What next? You must wait patiently, prayerfully, and in peace. No one can say yet whether you should enter another monastery. I do not know if you will be happy in the choir anywhere, since you do not sing. I advise you not to think too much about whether or not you are happy. You will never again reduplicate the feeling of happiness which you had here, because it is not normal to do so. You would not have known such happiness even if you had remained. Your life now will be serious and even sad. This is as it should be. We have no right to escape into happiness that most of the world cannot share. This is a very grim and terrible century, and in it we must suffer sorrow and responsibility with the rest of the world. But do not think that God is less close to you now. I am sure you are closer to Him, and are on the path to a new and strange reality. Let Him lead you.

J. Laughlin tells me that he is publishing my translation of your Drake poem ["Drake in the Southern Sea"] in the New Directions annual. Along with some poems of Pablo [Antonio Cuadra]. Lax will be glad to hear that the Circus [*The Circus of the Sun*] is being printed in Mexico. Have you contacted Mira?

I have little time now, so I will finish and write you again later. Keep me posted, and let me know when you enter at Cuernavaca [Benedictine Monastery of the Resurrection in Mexico]. I told the novices your message, that the world was unlivable, and they received it with awe. I am sure they do not doubt it. If one wants a pleasant and harmless existence, certainly Gethsemani is the place for it. And I don't think the average novice who enters here will ever be deeply effected by the sense of nullity and falsity that underlies the facade. Yet it is strange how some of them remark on the tension. A more mature postulant, who stopped at a French monastery on the way here, says he felt no tension at all in the French monastery, but feels it here. It is very strange, and I think very significant.

Please give my best regards to Dom Gregorio [Lemercier, O.S.B., superior at Cuernavaca], and say I pray for him and for his monastery. Your description of it sounded very beautiful.

And now, God bless you. Best regards also to Fr. Martínez, to Mejía Sánchez, etc. And here is a letter from Morales, in Peru. Nothing from Pablo Antonio yet about the islands. With all affection, in Christ,

fm Louis

[P.S.]
The magazines just arrived—many thanks.

Ernesto Cardenal to Thomas Merton

Feast of St. Louis, King
[August 25, 1959]

Rev. Fr. Louis, O.C.S.O.
Gethsemani

Dear Father Louis:

Today, the feast of St. Louis, is my second day in Cuernavaca. The evening before coming, I received—very propitiously—your beautiful letter of the 17th, with the marvellous timeliness with which the Lord sends me everything. In it, you admirably strengthened my spirit for my entrance here. It infused me with a great peace, and I received it as coming directly from God, dictated by Him. And I remain very grateful to Him and you for this letter. It is the most important one I have received in my life. It reminds me of the first one I received from you when I was going to enter the Trappe, and which I did not dare to answer because, thinking that you did not know Spanish, I found that I could not write an adequate response in English to that letter. Now, also, I am unable to comment adequately on your letter, not even in Spanish. The following morning, I went to say good-bye to Fr. Martínez and to assist at his Mass, and, after Mass, I gave him your letter to read. Reading it with great care, he was deeply impressed, and he asked me to leave it with him so that he might read through it again and reflect on it some more, and later he came in a taxi to give me back the letter.

I'm very convinced of your advice that I should not pay too much attention to my happiness, which I enjoyed so much in the novitiate at Gethsemani, nor pretend that this can repeat itself, nor think that this is necessarily identified with union with God. Nevertheless, I am happy, not with the exalted rapture in which I entered Gethsemani, but I am truly in much peace. The oppressive experience which I had the first time I came has not repeated itself this time. But neither do I feel any attraction to becoming a Benedictine. I am with a happy peace, and with a kind of indifference, without feeling either repugnance or attraction toward them. The only thing I am sure of is that I do not want to return to the world. As he said good-bye, Fr. Martínez told me what you, too, think, and what I also think with ever greater conviction: that I should become a priest. The Jesuits recommend the seminary in El Salvador, which they administer. Because they tell me that in Nicaragua I would not be able to make progress in my studies, because there are few professors and I would have to take the courses with everyone else. In El Salvador, they would have me do my philosophy studies in one year. And, also, they would admit me for free, since the financial issue would be another problem. It will be hard for me to adapt to Jesuit formation. But every seminary will be hard, and I accept it happily if it is what God wills. The courses in El Salvador begin in February. They also recommend a seminary for delayed vocations in Salamanca, but I don't want to go to Spain.

Dom Gregorio has not even called me to speak with him and I have not even disclosed these things to him, nor have I given him your letter to read. Today he was going to Mexico City for the day.

I am in the guest house, in a marvelous room, with a large window as wide as the whole room, through which one contemplates the entire valley and the city of Cuernavaca. It is a city of some 80,000 inhabitants, and to look down there at night is a beautiful spectacle—as if from heaven—the lights of the city burning bright.

I think that the first unpleasant feeling I had when coming here was due to the fact that I had in my mind a kind of fixation on the memory of the Trappe, which imposed itself on my reality. I didn't like the Office in Spanish because the cadence was different from that of Gethsemani. I have now become accustomed to it, and I enjoy the Office intensely, much more than in Gethsemani. I didn't like the habit because I found it ugly in comparison with ours, which was so beautiful aesthetically—and which I still miss at times—and, above all, because I only saw strange faces instead of a community to which I had become accustomed. There were none of my friends from the novitiate, for whom I felt and always feel a great affection: including those who had already left before me, but who remain present in my memories of the Trappe. Tell the novices that I always pray for them, just as when I was there.

I am a Proustian and I live on memories. Above all, I'm going to be very nostalgic about those days. They were days in which, more than any others in my life, I lived least in the past, and in which I most enjoyed the beauty and happiness of the present. With the passage of time, I forget the unpleasant details and remember only what is most beautiful and poetic of the Trappe. But this is not important, because I know that these days in Cuernavaca will, later, also turn into unforgettable memories.

Dom Gregorio is constructing small groups of cells in the neighborhood of the monastery, and he told me that he would transfer me to one of them when they are finished. In time, he plans to put the entire community into small groups of 5 or 6 cells, isolated—something more like Subiaco than Monte Casino—and leave the actual monastery only for guests, novices, and community events.

They are finishing the church, built by a monk, which is the most beautiful and original I have seen in my life: it's round and constructed with a wall of unequal stones, without a single window, like a well. In the center, on a circular base of black stone, is the altar, carved from a single block of white stone. Around the altar is the choir, circular, in levels, like a small stadium. The light enters directly from the sky, through a mica opening in the ceiling, which is like a circus tent. One feels as if one were in a hole inside the earth, or in the crater of a volcano, or in a pre-historic cave.

My friends from Mexico, all leftists and some even communists, have received me with great enthusiasm. My experience in the Trappe was extremely interesting to them, and they didn't tire of asking me. And I didn't tire of telling them about it. They all want to come visit me in Cuernavaca, and I've told them all to come. The most interesting case is that of León Felipe, one of the best Spanish poets in exile. He was always very religious, but heretical and even blasphemous, and above all resentful toward the Church because of the Franco question. He is now more religious than ever, after the death of his wife, and through the friendship of Fr. Angel he is today practically converted. We have given him your books and he is reading them avidly, staying up at night. He will come to see me next week with Fr. Angel. I'll send you some of his poems. We also gave him your essay on Pasternak ["Boris Pasternak and the People with Watch Chains"] to read. (This essay is stupendous. Angel Martínez liked it a lot. Mejía Sánchez wants to see if it can be published in Mexico, even though it will also appear in *Sur* because he considers it very important.)

I'm sending you the letter from Morales which you sent me, so that you may read it. The book is ready, and they only await the illustrations. I've written to Pablo Antonio urging him to send them. "The Tower of Babel" will be published in a collection of drama of the University of Mexico, and we've given "Prometheus" and the "Signed Confession" to the Journal of the University. Lax will appear in the next issue of the *Mexican Journal of Literature*. Mejía Sánchez has been very active in arranging all of this. I'm thrilled with the publication of "Drake" in New Directions.

Fr. Martínez was going to write to you this week when he has some free time. They overwhelm him so much with work that he doesn't even have time for his Act of Thanksgiving. And he often has to stay in bed with his ulcer pains. I think he suffers tremendously.

Pardon the abuse of so long a letter. I am praying a lot for you, especially today, and every day. And also for all the novices. Give them my best.

With an embrace, in Christ,
Ernesto Cardenal

Ernesto Cardenal to Thomas Merton

September 5, 1959

Dear Fr. Louis:

I enclose some poems from Gethsemani, copied in all haste. I had them there in rough draft, and here I've given them more-or-less definitive form. I'm not too sure of them. They seem to me somewhat mediocre. I think the ones I had written before entering the Trappe are better. They're valuable for me because they're a chronicle of those days. I'm making some more, which I'll send you in the future. If I publish them, I plan to given them the title: GETHSEMANI, KY. What do you think? I've just read your article on Mt. Athos ["Mount Athos"] in JUBILEE, which the monks have lent me, and it's very interesting. Above all the end. My stomach is very well. I'm better every day. So I think I'm recovering. My spiritual life is the same: very passive and very simple, so simple that I'm almost unaware of it. I'm only aware that God resides within me because I feel a detachment from all other things and, when I'm alone and in silence, I am happy. While in Mexico, I felt strangely immunized to all city life, and I was also happy. During those days I was almost unable to pray, except for a tacit prayer, because as soon as I tried to do so more formally, I felt discomfort in my stomach. This doesn't happen any more. And I also attend all the Hours of the Office without feeling any discomfort.

I think that smoking is good for me, and I've been smoking since I left, but I do it only a little, as you told me: some 7 cigarettes a day.

Morales has given an exposition in Lima with tremendous success. Artists, critics and all the persons who attended said that it was the finest painting they've seen in a long time, and he's sold his paintings in such a way that he's broken all records.

Fr. Jacinto Herrero has written me that his directors have advised him to carry out his ministry in Avila for some two years, and that he then decide as to his contemplative vocation. He says that thus it will be, and he asks me to give you his best.

Today I read by chance a newspaper from Mexico and, in it, I found out that a friend of mine was rebelling in Argentina against the Argentine president. He is Gen. Carlos Toranzo, who was ambassador to Nicaragua. He lived across from my house and we were good friends. He was one of the principal leaders of the revolution against Perón. Now the new president has removed him and the army is in rebellion because he is very popular among them, and they don't want to honor the president's order. I don't know what's going to happen. He is very Catholic, and very democratic, and a great person. In Nicaragua they continue to prepare a larger invasion than the first. The disaster of that one was in part because Nicaraguan communists prevented Fidel Castro from sending assistance which he had offered to my first cousin Pedro Joaquín, with whom he greatly sympathized, since they told him that he was a reactionary and very pro-American, and then Fidel didn't help. Nevertheless, there are two groups fighting in the mountains. One of them seems to have assistance from Castro, because it is a Nicaraguan [group] that fought with Castro and gave him a great deal of money for his revolution. But I don't know what its leanings are. My brother Gonzalo [Cardenal] is currently head of the underground movement in Nicaragua, undertaking very dangerous activities, such as the introduction of weapons, communication with the revolutionaries outside the country, and the production of dynamite bombs which they place in buildings belonging to the Samozas or *Somocistas.* I've found this out just now, when my brother-in-law passed through Mexico and came to visit me in Cuernavaca, because earlier they couldn't inform me by letter. There is great need for our prayers.

You are always my first intention in the Mass and in many of the Hours of the Office. I also pray a lot for the novices.

Did the pieces of ceramic I sent to the oven of St. Meinrad arrive there?

In Christ,
Ernesto Cardenal

Thomas Merton to Ernesto Cardenal

September 12, 1959

Dear Ernesto:

Not only have I received two good letters from you but a charming one also from your dear Grandmother thanking me for helping you, etc. I can see indirectly from her letter and from what she says people say of you that your stay at Gethsemani made a very great difference in your life and that you have changed and developed remarkably. It is my own experience that God did much work in your soul when you were here and I believe He will continue to carry on this good work, all the more so when you are passive and quiet and content to let Him work without desiring to see anything that He is doing.

I am very pleased to hear that your stomach is better. That is a good sign also, but you must expect that in times of stress you will have the same trouble. It may happen that trouble in the stomach may come when you are evolving toward a change or a new step—when a new phase of your life is beginning to come into being. When the step is made, the stomach will be quiet.

Both Dom Gregorio and I agree that it is utterly providential that the Jesuit Fathers have offered you hospitality in their seminary and will educate you for the priesthood without charge. This is another evident sign of God's love for you, and with all peace and joy you should accept it, with no anxiety and care about where or how you will exercise this priesthood when the time comes. Simply receive the necessary education and seminary training, with great humility and love, and do not fear the effects of a different kind of formation. If for some reason it is insisted upon that you behave officially as a Jesuit-formed spirit, let your conformity with the party line make contact with only such men as Caussade, Grou, Lallemente, etc. who are all strong on peace, passivity, abandonment, and not aggressive or systematic at all. But I am sure any director will recognize in you the value of your tendency to silence, childlikeness and peace.

The pieces of ceramic work returned from St. Meinrad and the larger crucifix is definitely one of your very best works. It came out a deep brick red, and has a very heavenly and spiritual joy about it which I like greatly. I am having Fr. Gerard put it on a walnut Cross and it will hang here in our room. I will have a picture taken of it if I can. The other smaller pieces are all good. Should I try to send you any of them?

Dom G. showed me pictures of the church of the monastery at Cuernavaca and it is certainly very interesting and effective. I should imagine that saying Mass there with the roof open to heaven must be a wonderful experience. His visit here was a great success and we had some good talks. It is good to find someone who agrees so completely with one's views on the monastic life. I am sure your stay there will be very profitable and that it will carry you forward, far beyond what you reached when you were here. Gethsemani is a very limited place, in its way. The Holy Spirit is certainly working here, but there comes a point where further development is frustrated or impossible and where truth becomes seriously falsified. Of course I suppose that is true wherever human institutions are found.

Your poems about Gethsemani *[Gethsemani, Ky.]* are very effective and have a special meaning for anyone who knows the scene and the incidents. The simplest ones are the best—for instance the little song "Hay un rumor de tractores . . ." and the other one about the smell of the earth in the spring in Nicaragua, and the ones that bring to mind contrasts and comparisons with Nicaragua. The one about the snow is very effective: perhaps it is the best. Though once the statement is made here, it loses force when repeated, more diffusely, in the other poem where the pigs and the motor horn come in. The paradox there is good, but less successful.

I think you are right in saying that these are less good than the ones you wrote before coming here. Certainly they have less power. But they should be what they are, simple and quiet and direct. And with that charming Chinese brevity. On the other hand your poems in the *Revista de la Literatura* are splendid. They constitute some of the few really good political poems I have read—they have the quality, and even more, that the left-wing poets had in the thirties. They are powerful and arresting and I am very happy with them. I wish I knew more about the background and the story. I think they are clearly your best poems.

I have been reading some more of Carrera Andrade and think I will have to translate some of them. He is very good.

Stephen Spender's wife came through here and we had a very fine conversation together. She is a splendid person, very interested in religion, liturgy, St. John of the Cross, Yoga, etc., etc. I told her about Corn Island [an island off the coast of Nicaragua where Cardenal and Merton thought about locating a contemplative foundation] and she was enthusiastic. I have had no information about it though, and do not know whether the Bishop will stop by to talk about it.

Morales' letter was deeply moving and I can see part of the reason why his exhibit was a great success. The news fills me with joy and I hope to hear more about it, see some reproductions of the pictures. I hope the book of poems is coming along, with the illustrations. I am returning his letter, I pray for him as well as for you and Pablo Antonio every day at Mass, not forgetting Mejía Sánchez and P. Martínez.

Fr. Paul of the Cross left, but I am forwarding your letter to him.

I shall keep Gonzalo in my prayers and Masses. It is dangerous work but I hope it will be fruitful. I think you must all go a little slow, and don't depend too much on Castro. I think he is a little out of his depth and there is danger that he may make decisions and gestures that have no basis in reality, in order to salvage something of his own position which will be more and more menaced. Take it easy. There is great danger that the revolution in Nicaragua may serve as nothing but a cat's paw for the communists. Let *them* get burnt. However, I cannot claim to know the political situation.

I value and appreciate your prayers. Keep them up. I am sure God will hear them. I have great confidence in the future, though I do not know exactly what will come out. I think there is considerable hope of a really constructive answer and solution to everything. More later.

God bless you, and please mention to your Grandmother that I was very happy about her letter which I will try to answer when I get time.

With all affection, in Christ,
fm Louis

Thomas Merton to Ernesto Cardenal

October 8, 1959

Dear Ernesto:

I have received very good news from Dom Gregorio in Rome. He has seen Fr. Larraona and it seems that the dispensation will be granted, but still the Superiors of the Order must be consulted and this may be quite an obstacle. But it seems as if in the long run the move will be completely successful. This is very fine and encouraging news, and is certainly the result of much prayer, including your own prayers, for which I thank you. Keep them up, they are more necessary than ever.

I have written Dom Gregorio a letter which was mailed in the usual way, open, and so I was not able to speak very freely. Father Abbot [James Fox] does not know all the details as yet, as far as I can tell, though I have told him in a general way that since I cannot obtain a leave of absence from him I am appealing to Rome. I do not know whether or not Rome has as yet contacted Father Abbot. At the moment he has been in the Bardstown hospital with a hernia operation.

Since I can more easily write you a conscience matter letter, I think I will take this opportunity to send you some important remarks which you can convey to Dom Gregorio at the proper time.

First of all, about entering Mexico. I think it would be safer if I got a passport and a regular visa to enter as a permanent resident. This will take time. If there is some special difficulty I will simply enter, as you did, on a tourist card. I imagine that to obtain a visa I would have to have some kind of document or affidavit from Dom Gregorio. I hope he will know what to do, and will take steps to produce the necessary evidence that I will have a home and support in Mexico. This could be sent when it is definite that I am to come.

The plan I thought would be most convenient would be, when I get the indult, to leave here and go to Albuquerque, New Mexico, and take up the question of the visa with the Mexican consul there. While I am waiting for things to materialize I could then take a look at some of the Indian pueblos in that region, which would be very interesting. I could even perhaps spend a few days on one of the missions and make a kind of retreat in the desert.

If Dom Gregorio thinks best, I would simply come to Mexico as fast as possible on a tourist card and then get the visa later, as you have done.

From time to time I will send you packages of books—they will be our books and perhaps you could keep them for me. I think there is still one book of yours here, Max Jacob. I will enclose that in one of the packages.

One small trial is my health, at the moment. There have been some complications in my usual infirmities. I hope I do not have to spend any time in the hospital. I think it is just a providential event that will help me prepare for a new step. Often sickness has the function of slowing a man down when he is about to turn a corner. Please pray that it may be no more than this and that everything will go well. This is such a wonderful opportunity to reach out for a more simple and solitary life, and to put into practice the ideas that have come to me for so many years. It would be a shame to spoil it. I am very happy that things are turning out well, and I want to correspond perfectly with the opportunity. It is so important to try to realize in actual fact the simplicity of the monastic ideal, and to get away from all the artificiality which grows up in the monastic institution. Let us pray that we may find the ideal of a simple, non-institutional, contemplative life in the mountains, in true poverty and solitude. Meanwhile I hope there will be a little house available soon.

How are you? I have not heard anything from you since Dom Gregorio brought your poems. I am wondering if a letter of yours has failed to reach me. If you answer this one, it had better be conscience matter. Let me know any other hints or suggestions you think will be useful. When travelling in Mexico perhaps I ought simply to dress as a layman. I will need prayers in the next two or three weeks as the struggle with Father Abbot may be quite difficult though there is nothing he can do now, at least as far as I am concerned. Keep well, and God bless you.

Faithfully, in Xto [Christo] Domine,
fm Louis

[Letterhead]
St. Anthony Hospital
St. Anthony Place
Louisville, KY
October 17, 1959

Dear Ernesto:

I am in the hospital for a few days, but it is only a question of a minor operation, and everything seems to be all right. I hope to be fully recovered in a day or two.

So far there is no indication that Father Abbot has heard anything from Rome. At least he has not said anything to me about it, and his attitude does not indicate that he feels upset about anything. I should be very surprised if he had heard from Rome, & at the same time I presume that nothing will be done until he is consulted. Hence I may have to wait quite a long time. But it is worth being patient about.

Before I came to the hospital I got all the Carmelite nuns at the Louisville Carmel to pray for this intention. I also had the happiness of saying their proper Mass of St. Teresa on the Feast day—which was the day of my operation. I am sure their prayers will be very powerful.

[D.T.] Suzuki is finally sending his preface to my Desert Fathers' book [Suzuki's preface was not published in *The Wisdom of the Desert*]. It has not arrived yet but it should be very interesting. I am very happy about it. Naturally I look forward very much to coming to Mexico, and continue every day to pray that this venture may be successful for the glory of God. One must expect obstacles & difficulties but there seem to be so many indications that this is God's will & I trust He will bring it to completion in His own way. I look forward to hearing news from you when Dom Gregorio returns from Rome. I am very pleased that his requests were successful and that Cuernavaca is now established as a Priory.

I remember you everyday at Mass, along with Pablo Antonio and all your intentions for Nicaragua. And I know you will not forget to pray for us. I am expecting to return to the monastery tomorrow or the day after. There is no special news at Gethsemani—everything is as usual. There are very few new postulants, but Fr. Robert made his profession on October 4th.

With all best wishes to you, and all affection in Christ our Lord, fm Louis

Ernesto Cardenal to Thomas Merton

October 17, 1959

Dear Father Louis:

I have just received your stupendous letter, which has given me much joy. I am extremely happy and am giving many thanks to God because everything is turning out so well, as we have asked. During the Mass and all the hours of the Office I have been asking most especially for this intention, and it seems that it is God within me who has been seeing to it that I have this intention permanently in the Office, and I will do so even more during these last remaining days.

I am also very grateful to you for your other letter, after mine in which I sent the poems. I had not written you again since then because I thought that Dom Gregorio would pass through Gethsemani again on his return, and I was waiting to see what new news he would bring—and in the meantime I had nothing new to tell you. Apparently Dom Gregorio was not going to pass through Gethsemani again on his return since you have sent me this letter for him. We expect him this week and I will give him the letter as soon as he arrives.

Pablo Antonio has just sent me Morales' illustrations. They seem marvelous to me, as they do to him. I sent them to Mejía Sánchez so that he would take them to the university. They would proceed immediately to publish the book since they were eager to begin, and I told them that while they prepared to publish the text they could send you the illustrations so that you could see and approve them (which approval I was sure you would give). If they no longer had time because they were going to publish the illustrations immediately, that they would at least send you the page proofs. I do not know if they will do one or the other. But perhaps neither the one nor the other is now necessary since you are coming soon and can see them here yourself.

A guest who came to the monastery told me that some friends of his have made some translations of your poems and were expecting to publish them around December. He told me that they would bring them first to me so that I could review your translations.

I suppose that you will want to stay a few days in Mexico City before coming to Cuernavaca to see some important things (Our Lady of Guadalupe, murals, bookstores, the pyramids of Teotihuacán, some persons, etc.). In that case I would want to go spend those days in Mexico to be your guide in the city. You would have to notify me of your exact date of arrival so that I may go to meet you.

I suppose it will be best for you to come in completely secular clothes. Some priests use the Roman Collar, but it is not necessary, nor is it common.

I will keep here those books of yours which you send me. Please send the copy of the poems of Gethsemani which I sent you with Dom Gregorio, if you still have them, since I have lost one of them. You do not need to send me any of the ceramic figures which I made there, since I have the molds and can make them over again. But I would like—if you can—a photo of the crucifix in the novices' chapel.

I am sending you a letter which Pablo Antonio wrote me. Everything he says about Ometepe [another possible location for a contemplative foundation] seems very good to me. But it also seems to me that Corn Island is a marvellous place. The ideal would be to live for some time in both places. I wrote to the Bishop of Bluefields [Carthusian Bishop Matthew A. Niedhammer] when I left Gethsemani, as you had told me. I do not know if he got to talk with you. He did not respond to me, but he had no reason to do so.

I hope your illness will be nothing serious, and I will also be praying a lot for your health during these days. I have again begun to feel bad as before; at times I am better and at times worse. When Dom Gregorio comes I will ask him if I can see a doctor, since he offered me medical treatment should I need it. I do not know if this will be an obstacle to entering the seminary in February as I had planned. I will see what the doctor says, and also what you advise me. Whatever happens does not worry me because, since it is something outside my control, it will be God's will and, that being so, it will also be what is best for me. I will write Father [John] Eudes [Bamberger], because he told me to let him know how I was doing once I had been here a while, and because if I still did not feel well he could advise me what to do.

I have no apparent reason for not being well, because in every other way I live a life of total peace and much happiness, of perfect solitude and silence. I spend time on the Office, lectio divina, Latin, some literature, prayer, scripture, and a new translation of the psalms into Spanish which we are doing in the monastery and I think it is turning out to be stupendous. I do not have problems or anything that worries me. I do not think of the future, I am one with the will of God, and I live completely in the present.

I am reading *The Sign of Jonas* for the third time. I read it the first time when it was published, with a purely literary interest. I read it again, with a different interest, when I was about to enter Gethsemani. Now it has a new interest for me after having lived, more or less, the whole book. I was planning to read only certain passages because I had already read it twice, but I found that all of it interested me and I could not skip even one line.

Mira is here in the guest house waiting for Father Prior in order to enter the novitiate. He is very happy to have come here and not to Gethsemani. Also in the community is Franco, the one from Oaxaca, who applied for admission to Gethsemani and you advised him to reenter this monastery. He is very happy to have done so. He says he is very happy and is very grateful to you for your advice, and he has asked me to give you his best. I hope that God will continue to hear our prayers. In Christ.

Ernesto Cardenal

Thomas Merton to Ernesto Cardenal

October 24, 1959

Dear Ernesto:

I got your letter of the 17th safely yesterday when I returned from the hospital, so everything is ok. Father Abbot left this morning for California and will return before November 1st. Things are evidently going to move quite slowly, but I have every hope of success, but I have not the slightest idea what is taking place. But that is very well. The thing is in the hands of God and we must let Him work it out as He pleases. Certainly our prayers are being answered, in due season. The only thing that surprises me is that so far nothing difficult or unpleasant has occurred, and somewhere along the line there is going to be a hard and nerve racking obstacle to negotiate, in the very difficult rupture that will have to be made with Gethsemani and with its Father Abbot. That is what I most dread and feel will be most difficult, because of all the personal ties and even obligations that exist. This is what . . . will now require the most prayers and the greatest help of the Holy Spirit. A work of God can often and usually does demand a complete uprooting that is extremely painful and disconcerting, and which requires great fidelity in the one called to do the work. The difficulty comes in the darkness and possibility of doubt, in the mystical risk involved. I am very glad that the danger and the risk appear very clearly to me, and I am resolved to be faithful in this risk and not cling to the security of the established position I have here. But I dread going off with imprecations hurled after me, and being treated as a traitor, etc. This must not be allowed to affect things so much that I become influenced by it. Yesterday I had a very fine long conversation with the Prioress of the Louisville Carmel [Mother Angela Collins] who is a fine person and who has her nuns praying for our project. But we will all have to be very determined and struggle without discouragement, trusting in God and accepting difficulty and delay.

That brings me to the question of your own health. I certainly do not think that the stomach trouble you had here will necessarily be an obstacle to your entering the seminary, and I would not let it become an obstacle by worrying about it. The reason for your leaving here was that this life puts an exceptional pressure on one who tends to have ulcers: but seminary life is closer to normal and it would hardly burden you more than an ordinary life would. You will doubtless always be molested with stomach trouble in one form or other so I would just make the best of it, do not let it deter you from undertaking the things that are for God's glory; accept the handicap He has willed for you and take the normal care of your health that will enable you to support the work you have to do.

Pablo Antonio's letter contains a lot of wisdom, and I agree with him that a place like Ometepe has about it all the elements that are called for in a contemplative foundation that is to play a really vital role in Latin American culture and society. It will take a little time before we might be ready for Ometepe but that is the kind of thing that really makes sense. Corn Island has natural advantages, but that is all. I feel, as does Pablo Antonio, that one must also be rooted in the Indian and Latin cultural complex in a very definite way. Besides that, the Bishop of Bluefields, when he finally got around to replying to my second letter, became very timorous and told me that he could not take me unless I were actually *sent* by my Superiors. My explanation of this is that I sent the letter to him open, with permission of Father Abbot, and Father Abbot evidently enclosed a letter of his own which put the fear of God into the good bishop and told him, in no uncertain terms, to steer clear of anyone who wanted to leave Gethsemani. The bishop really sounded frightened.

It would do no harm to send proofs of Armando Morales' pictures, as I may yet be a month here, if not more. I am glad that they are very good, and think the whole edition sounds very promising.

I will certainly let you know when I can hope to come to Mexico and it would be wonderful to look at the city and its environs together. I shall want to see all the best things and meet your friends. It will be necessary for me to really soak in the atmosphere of Mexico and get thoroughly acclimatized, though naturally I am not looking for a lot of hectic social life. But it is certainly a duty to become quietly and gradually really a part of the nation and of its life and not simply be a gringo tourist. I just want to look and learn and be quietly receptive for a very long time, and become integrated in the whole cultural atmosphere of the city and the nation. Above all I hope no one will expect me to come as a kind of celebrity with something to say and a part to play, because that would be very harmful to the whole project. Everything should be done quietly and discretely, for very many reasons—first of all for my own personal and spiritual good, and secondly for the success and right working of the plan. Because it is very important that no publicity be given to the fact that I have left Gethsemani and the Order, but that even those who know about it should understand it simply as a normal leave of absence. Later when the new venture begins, it will make itself understood on its own terms. Above all nothing must be said about new or special projects, and the worst thing that could happen would be for me to be surrounded by eager inquirers and prospective postulants ready to join a "new Order." That would be fatal.

I am glad to hear of Mira and Franco being there, and the fact thay they are happy about it sounds very good and augurs well for the future. Give them my best wishes and my blessing, and I will keep praying for them.

I shall take your advice about wearing plain secular clothes. I don't even want to wear black. If I don't look like a priest, at least I don't want to look like a Jehovah's witness. But of course it all depends what I can get. The suitcase they gave me, to take to the hospital, fell open in the middle of a street in Louisville and I was scrambling around to put books, shirts, etc., back in. It was raining, too. I haven't sent the books yet but I am getting together a package today.

My regards to Dom Gregorio—he will have received the letter from you and one I wrote the last day at the hospital. I still am not sure whether the indult is to be sent to him or to me—or both. The simplest would be, if he gets the original, to send me a photostat. But he doubtless has thought out what he intends to do, and I leave the whole thing in his hands and those of God. When I told the Carmelite Prioress how Dom G. had come here and proposed his plan, etc., all unexpectedly, her simple comment was: "He who is sent by God speaks the words of God."

So let us keep up our hope and our desire to serve Him truly and sincerely, devoting our limited and fallible wills to Him with all purity and fidelity of heart. It is not a question of building a great edifice, but of living a simple life and preserving as much as possible of the values we already have found, in experience, here and elsewhere—eliminating as far as possible the great defects and obstacles of a highly organized life. A woman wrote recently to the monks: "We would have expected the Trappists more than anyone else to put Christ back into Christmas, and instead you have put cheese into the Mass."

With all affection and blessings, and with great gratitude for your prayers. I remember you every day by name in the memento, with Pablo Antonio, Mejía Sánchez, Armando Morales, etc. God bless you all.

fm Louis

Ernesto Cardenal to Thomas Merton

October 27, 1959

Dear Father Louis:

I have just received your letter of the 24th, and I have also received the one you wrote me from the hospital. I am very happy to know that your stay there was very short because it indicates that your operation was not serious.

Dom Gregorio came two days ago. I gave him your letters and I have just spoken with him today. He told me to write you that you should come with a *tourist visa*, since the other was currently very difficult to obtain and one would have to wait an extremely long time. Being here, it would be very easy to renew this visa, or, as well, exchange it for a residency visa. He has done this with some foreigners staying here. But it would not be advantageous to give the address of this monastery to the Mexican authorities, because these procedures for exchanging visas are somewhat illegal; and it is best if they do not know the foreigner's place of residence; that way, they will be unable to carry out any vigilance or to maintain any records on him (records and vigilance that hardly exist in any case).

I can only imagine how difficult the departure from Gethsemani must be for you. I had been thinking about that for days. It is a very great test which very few religious have. It is like leaving one's home and family for a second time. But I was also thinking that perhaps God would make this departure unexpectedly easy for you. As was my departure from my home, which I had feared so much, and which nevertheless was later, by some miracle, so easy that I felt as if I had taken some sort of drug (and my departure from Gethsemani, which was already for me like a second home, was equally simple). I am fully convinced of the immense good that your coming will do for Hispanic

America. As are the three or four persons in this monastery who are aware of your visit (the superiors, since the community knows nothing), and who are waiting for you with extremely intense interest and a great deal of prayer.

It was precisely yesterday that, during the Mass, I was inspired to offer up all my stomach ailments for your plans. But don't think that these ailments are very great, because, on the contrary, they are extremely easy to tolerate. Nevertheless, they are the only ones I can offer up since I have no others, either physical or moral or of any kind; and I think that few people—religious or otherwise—suffer less than I do.

Next Sunday Mejía Sánchez will come to visit me. He will bring the illustrations and poems so that here we can make arrangements for their distribution. I understand that soon he will be able to send you copies of the illustrations, since the university told him that he should personally be in charge of making the prints and I suppose that he was going to proceed to do so immediately.

Morales has just returned to Nicaragua after his trip through South America, where he had great success. He was in the Sao Paulo Biennial Exposition and there received an award as the best Hispanic American painter, or something like that. He has participated in five international expositions and has received awards in all five.

It is possible that [José] Coronel [Urtecho] will also come to Mexico soon. Fortunately for him, he no longer has a diplomatic post in the government, and he has a son in jail as a revolutionary. He currently does not have economic opportunities in Nicaragua and it is possible that he will come to Mexico in December, where he could give classes in both universities, the national university and the Jesuit university. It would be great if his stay in Mexico coincided with yours.

I have been thinking about which place of residence would be most suitable for you during your stay in Mexico City. Perhaps in a small hotel, discreet and quiet? Or perhaps also in the Jesuits' Universidad Iberoamericana, which will be quiet and empty since the students are leaving on vacation in November. There you could choose to live in two parts: in the university itself, staying in the Jesuit community, which is small since there are only five or six living there and some of them will also be on vacation; or in the student residence, where I stayed, which is directed by a Nicaraguan Jesuit who is a very good friend of ours, and which will also be empty. They could give you an apartment there by yourself; in both places you would have a chapel to celebrate Mass.

It would be much better if you came in common, everyday, colored clothing, which is how the Jesuits dress, and that way your presence will be more inconspicuous. It seems to me that we will be able to avoid all undesirable and sensationalist publicity. For that, it would perhaps be advisable that you come with your maternal last name, or simply as Father Louis. Several friends of ours work in the newspapers, and we could later make arrangements with them for a serious, official version of the news, and when it is opportune.

I want to tell you again that the good which your presence will do here is incalculable, especially among certain people—the leftists—which are the most important and most energetic groups in Mexico (the Catholic groups are mediocre and reactionary and it is necessary not to mix with them or collaborate in their publications so as not to lose one's reputation). When I have spoken with them I have been impressed with how they go about seeking God along odd paths, or how God mysteriously seeks them within themselves. All they need is the apostolate of a presence such as yours, without preaching, since it is the preaching which has alienated them.

Father Prior has told me that he will make me see Dr. Garza, a famous psychoanalyst in Cuernavaca, a friend of Suzuki, and a disciple of Dr. [Erich] Fromm (though they have told me that Dr. Fromm himself has not been able to cure his own ulcer and, not long ago, was very ill because of it). I think all I need is some orientation talks so that I can treat myself, and so my ailments will not interfere with my vocation, since I do not pretend to be without any suffering.

My cousin Luis Cardenal escaped from the prison in which they were holding him strictly incommunicado, at the foot of the Presidential Mansion, leaving at night in military dress. Pedro Joaquín Chamorro and one hundred others are being tried in a War Council which has already become long and tedious.

This morning the monastery is marvelous because the whole community went to some priestly ordination in Cuernavaca and the only ones left in the house are a postulant and myself. I end this letter in order to pray a while for the things which I write you about here, in this empty monastery. I embrace you, in Christ.

Ernesto Cardenal

P.S.

Dom G. asks me to tell you that the normal procedure for the indult is that they send it to you. In case it comes to him, he will send it to you immediately. And that in case there is some delay, he will get in touch with their Procurator in Rome in order to accelerate the process.

Also that I tell you that he spoke with Father [Jean] Danielou in France and that he is in complete agreement with all the steps you have taken and approves it all.

Also that you should look at number 50 of the *Supplement de La Vie Spirituelle*, where there appears an article on the statutes for hermits, and in which it is stated that the only solution to this problem is exclaustration.

I have received a very charming and friendly letter from Laughlin asking me about you and your plans. I have just answered him bringing him up to date on how things are going.

Odilie Pallais, in Nicaragua, who is interested in this, is offering many prayers for the success of your plans (from her sick bed). And surely also offering up much suffering, because her best prayer is her illness.

Affectionately in Christ,
Ernesto Cardenal

Thomas Merton to Ernesto Cardenal

November 18, 1959

Dear Ernesto:

When your letter arrived three, or maybe two weeks ago, Father Abbot made a lot of difficulty about giving it to me, but he eventually did so. There was not much else he could do, since it was a conscience matter letter. I was glad to get it. And I made known to him that I thought such correspondence should not be interfered with. At the same time I told him that I would assure you that he was unfavorable to it. In a word, there is considerable opposition to the correspondence. But still the rights of conscience remain, and if there is something important then I think he is bound to allow a conscience matter letter to pass. He probably will not pass any other kind of letter, that is from you at Cuernavaca.

The other day Rev. Father left quite suddenly for Rome. I have no doubt his journey was intimately connected with the matter which interests me closely. At first I thought he had left of his own volition. Later I realized that he had been summoned to Rome, in actual fact, by the Abbot General. No one knows exactly what is the purpose of this journey, but if he was summoned to Rome against his own will, that puts a different complexion on the matter. However, prayers are certainly needed at the moment. I just learned today that Fr. Larraona, the head of the Congregation of the Religious, has been made a Cardinal. That seems to be very good news, as far as I am concerned. I am sure Dom Gregorio will be equally pleased by it.

I was very interested to hear of the progress on the book of poems. New Directions is bringing out a paperback of my *Selected Poems*, almost the same selection but not quite. Mark Van Doren has written a very fine preface. I wonder if you heard about the trouble his son Charles got into. That TV program, on which he won so much money last year, was "rigged" and unfortunately Charles was an accomplice to the whole thing, which was very unfortunate. I don't think he clearly realized where it would lead, and he was not the most guilty one. Still, there has been a big fuss about it, with a lot of self-righteous speeches by senators on the shame of lying! As if senators were notable for telling the truth.

I am very happy to hear of the wonderful success of Armando Morales and I hope he will keep it up, though success is not the important thing, but the spiritual work of the artist. And I look forward to receiving copies of his illustrations from Mejía Sánchez—they have not yet arrived but I will inquire about them. It is a pleasure to know that [José] Coronel [Urtecho] may be in Mexico soon. Incidentally, Laughlin will probably be stopping here in December. I will be glad to see him.

About your own difficulties: I hope and pray that your conversations with Dr. Garza will be helpful. Of course, you understand that you will never be completely without difficulties and I would not be discouraged at all from continuing either in the seminary or at the monastery, whichever you prefer. You certainly have a vocation, but not necessarily a conventional type of vocation. Whether you are actually called to the priesthood cannot be decided without further trial, but the important thing is that you have clearly a vocation to a contemplative life, in a general way, and the only thing that needs to be found out is exactly how or where. And that is not too important because wherever you are you will be tending to the same end. The only problem about the priesthood is whether you can be a priest without getting too involved in an exhausting and time-consuming ministry. That is the question. But for the rest you need have no doubts and no fears. God is with you. Incidentally I am touched by the simplicity and kindness with which you offer your troubles for me. With so many friends praying for me I am sure everything must inevitably go very well with me, and no matter how dark and obstructed things may sometimes appear, I have great confidence that everything will eventually work out well. But there is need for patience. I am glad too that Odilie is praying for me. I greatly value her prayers.

Prayers are the most important thing at the moment. And deep faith. The inertia of conventional religious life is like a deep sleep from which one only awakens from time to time, to realize how deeply he has been sleeping. Then he falls back into it. It is true that God works here also, but there are so many influences to deaden and falsify the interior life. A kind of perpetual danger of sclerosis. The psalms become more and more of a comfort, more and more full of meaning when one realizes that they do *not* apply to the conventional situation, but to another kind of situation altogether. The psalms are for poor men, or solitary men, or men who suffer: not for liturgical enthusiasts in a comfortable, well-heated choir. I am sure you have greatly enjoyed the work of translating them.

In a couple of days they will dedicate at Washington the immense new shrine of the Blessed Virgin which looks like a big substantial bank. Strictly official architecture, and the thing that strikes me most forcibly is its evident Soviet quality. There is a kind of ironical levelling process that makes Soviet and capitalist materialism more and more alike as time goes on. Who is more bourgeois than Krushchev? And he made a very "good" impression in the USA, except on the fanatics who refused to see him as one of their own. A successful gangster, who is now affable and a good family man in his declining years.

I will not continue this letter, as there is not much more news. We wait in silence and in peace for the coming of the Savior—in an advent atmosphere. I pray constantly to Our Lady of Guadalupe. Thank you again for all your prayers and your faith. I agree with everything you said in your letter, everything hopeful and all the positive outlook you express for the future. I think the University would be the best place for the stay you plan in the city.

Trusting that nothing will happen to prevent this letter reaching you, and with all blessings and regards to you—kind memories to Dom Gregorio. I wrote him the other day, and wonder if he received the letter.

With all affection, in Christ,
fm Louis

Thomas Merton to Ernesto Cardenal

The Brown Hotel,
Louisville
November 24 [1959]

Dear Ernesto:

I told Fr. Abbot I would write you a conscience matter letter and did so at Gethsemani but I don't know if it was sent. Do not be misled by the stationery. I have *not* started on the trip. The indult has not yet arrived & I have no news of it. But Father Abbot has *gone to Rome* & is evidently opposing everything with his power. But I also think he has been called to Rome to answer some questions. He may be back this week.

If the indult is coming, it should come about next week. If you do not hear from me soon—say by December 8th—then perhaps there is something wrong. J. Laughlin is coming here in the middle of December & if you write to him he might get it in time to relay information to me. Father Abbot is very difficult about conscience matter letters now but I still think he will *have to* let one through. Put not only "conscience matter" on the inner envelope but also "sub gravi."

If all goes well I hope to be there before Christmas. I will come by plane, I hope, & will arrive in the evening about 6:30 or 7 & we can go to the University. If you are not at the airport I will go to the University by taxi & ask for Fr. Martínez.

Gethsemani is *terrible*. Tremendous commerce—everybody is going mad with the cheese business. I want to leave very badly.

Today I said Mass for the F[east] of St. John of the Cross at
Carmel. The nuns are praying very hard.

My mind is completely made up to totally cut off all ties that attach me here. It is *essential* not just for my own peace but for the glory
of God. I must advance in the way He has chosen for me & I am sure
He will make everything easy.

My best regards to Dom Gregorio—it is impossible to say all the
things I want to say to you & to him. Pray that we may meet soon.
I pray to Our Lady of Guadalupe.

I'll send a telegram to Cuernavaca as soon as I am ready to leave
& have freedom to do so.

If things get very difficult, I can be reached via Fr. Danielou who
can always get a conscience matter letter to me but I think yours will
still get through—but there may be difficulties.

God bless you all—pray for me. Thanks for offering your
suffering.

If things get *very bad*—I will be in Louisville in January for one
day & can be reached through the Prioress of the Louisville Carmel,
1746 Newburg Road, Louisville.

With affection, in Christ,
fm Louis

*The letter from Rome for which Merton was waiting was sent on December
7 and arrived on December 17. The indult Merton had sought was not granted.*

Thomas Merton to Ernesto Cardenal

December 17, 1959

My dear Ernesto:

Fr. Prior has given me permission to write Dom Gregorio in the
absence of Rev. Father and this is my last chance to get a note to you
also. As Dom G. will tell you, a letter from Rome has given absolutely
final negative decision of my case. Or at least, a decision so final that
I am not at liberty to take any further steps on my own behalf, but

can only accept and obey. I must stay here until the Church herself places me somewhere else. I still believe that the mercy of God can and perhaps will accomplish this, but I can only wait in darkness and in faith, without making any move. I have hopes that Dom Gregorio will still be able to do something for me. But what?

I think the reason the Congregation swung in favor of Dom James is that he told them a lot of irresponsible remarks about me by Gregory Zilboorg, a famous Freudian psychiatrist who is respected in Rome and has died recently. Zilboorg said of my desire of solitude that I just wanted to get out from under obedience and that if I were allowed a little liberty I would probably run away with a woman. I don't pretend to be an angel, but these remarks of Gregory Zilboorg were passing remarks made without any deep knowledge of me—he had seen me around for a week at a conference at St. John's [University, Collegeville, Minnesota]. We had not had much to do with each other, he never analyzed me, and Fr. Eudes said that Z. frequently made rash statements on the spur of the moment, which he later changed. Well, anyway, I think that is why Rome rejected my case, for certainly Dom James will have made everything possible out of these statements of Zilboorg. He has probably made enough out of them to queer my reputation in Rome forever. I remember now that you may have seen Zilboorg when he came here—or was that before your time?

I have seen the illustrations of Morales and they are fabulous—I wrote Mejía Sánchez about them. I think Mejía Sánchez will be able to reach me still with correspondence about the poems. I would like half a dozen copies of the book at least, and be sure to send me yours when they appear. Could I have a subscription to the *Revista Mexicana de Literatura* and to the *Revista de la Universidad*? I think they will still get through. Of course there is always Laughlin, if there is something important. He will be down in January. However, as I say, for my own part I can only obey the Congregation and remain passive and I have no hope of making any move to leave this Order. I have in fact promised not to leave, but will only await the action of the Church to move me elsewhere if she sees fit.

So many people have prayed hard for me: their prayers will not be lost. I received the decision of Rome without emotion and without the slightest anger. I accept it completely in faith, and feel a great interior liberty and emptiness in doing so. This acceptance has completely liberated me from Gethsemani, which is to me no longer an obstacle or a prison, and to which I am indifferent, though I will do all in my power to love and help those whom God entrusts to me here. I know we will always be united in prayer, and I assure you of all my affection and of the joy I have had in our association. Do continue to write poetry, or above all continue with your art. Everyone thinks highly of your poetry. Laughlin will probably come and see you some day. I must now get this letter out before Rev. Father returns. I close with all love to all of you. I suppose Pablo Antonio will still be able to write. God bless all of you—all my affection in Christ Crucified and Risen. *Christus Vincit, alleluia.*

fm Louis

Merton's exchange of letters with Cardenal was interrupted when Dom James Fox prohibited him from corresponding with Cardenal. Merton resumed writing to Cardenal in March 1961.

Daughter of Carmel; Son of Cîteaux:
A Friendship Endures
An Interview about Thomas Merton
with Angela Collins, O.C.D.

Conducted by Michael Downey
Edited by R. Andrew Hartmans

Sister Angela of the Eucharist (née Collins), O.C.D., was born in 1917 in Irvington, New Jersey, and entered the Carmelite Monastery in Louisville, Kentucky, in 1937. In 1957 she was elected Prioress of the Louisville Carmel and served in this capacity for three years after which she became Mistress of Novices. It was while serving as Novice Mistress in 1965 that Mother Angela went to the Carmel in Savannah, Georgia, to serve as Prioress. She has served the Savannah Carmel as its Prioress for the majority of years since her arrival there.

It was while Prioress at the Louisville Carmel that Mother Angela first came in contact with Thomas Merton. Some of his letters to her are published in *The School of Charity*, the third volume of Merton's letters, edited by Patrick Hart, O.C.S.O. She is currently Prioress of the Carmelite Monastery in Savannah. This interview was conducted there in January 1995.   M.D.

Downey: How did you come to know Thomas Merton?

Sister Angela: Before I became Prioress, Thomas Merton used to come into Louisville for medical treatment. He went to the hospital and he would also see his doctor at the same time. But because his visits to the hospital did not consume that much time, and because he was brought into Louisville by lay brothers as they distributed bread, fruitcake, and cheese to stores in the Louisville area, he asked if he could come and spend that interim time at the Carmelite Monastery chapel in prayer.

Sometimes the brothers would take longer than anticipated and he would ask if he could speak to the Prioress who was Mother Seraphim. She used to speak with him in our "speak room" in the old house on Park Avenue. The speak room had grates that crisscrossed, plus spikes that pointed outward and a heavy black curtain inside. She never opened the curtain. She just talked with him through it.

Now as far as myself, at this early period I had developed a rather negative attitude toward Father Merton, because of things that I had heard about him. It wasn't scandalous. Maybe I was a perfectionist. I was deeply rooted in our tradition as Carmelites. I didn't understand his situation and I felt that he was not giving a good example of contemplative life. We had heard stories of different nurses with whom he had come into contact at the hospital. Sometimes he would be waiting for the brothers to pick him up at the hospital, and the nurses would gather around him and they would talk with him. This might have been okay, but I didn't feel that way. I felt that he should not have involved himself in that kind of petty conversation while he was out of enclosure for the specific reason of taking care of his health.

Downey: Are you saying that within the setting of the Carmelite Monastery you had the impression that Thomas Merton had been interacting with the nurses and perhaps that there may have been a little bit more of this sort of thing? And this as early as the 1950s?

Sister Angela: Yes. Shortly after I became Prioress in 1957 he came to visit our Carmel. He asked if he could speak with the Prioress. He was told that we had a new Prioress, named Mother Angela, who was just elected. The Sister added that she would have to ask me if I had time to talk to him in the speak room. She came and told me that he was there and I said to her: "I really do not want to continue this. I'm just against these elongated conferences with this Trappist monk." She thought that this was terrible, and begged saying: "Please. What would Mother Seraphim ever think?" And I replied, "Well, she's in heaven now!" She kept pleading. Finally, I gave in and told her she could go and tell him that I would have only about fifteen or twenty minutes to talk with him in the speak room. So he came back to the speak room and we talked. But the atmosphere was very frigid. I was very cold and just listened to what he said and gave brief answers.

Downey: If I understand correctly, you did more of the listening and Thomas Merton did more of the talking. It seems as though he was looking to you as a sounding board. It does not seem to have been a conversation between peers.

Sister Angela: That could be. Yes. I like the term "sounding board," because he didn't know me at all. We had our fifteen or twenty minutes. I told him that I would be praying for him, and the other nuns would too, because we knew he was having health problems, although we didn't know what they were.

About a month later he came back to Louisville to see the doctor, and he came to the monastery again. He asked if he could speak with me. The Sister said, "Father, I'm very sorry, but we're in retreat now, and the Prioress doesn't usually have visitors during this period." And Father Merton said, "Oh, I understand. I didn't realize that you were in retreat. Maybe the next time I come I will be able to talk with her." Sister made no promises and said that she would give me the message. But while he was there, he wrote a note to me. It was just scribbled on yellow paper. It said, "I'm so sorry that I missed you because you were in retreat. Possibly the next time I come I can talk with you." I thought to myself, "Well, we will see." I didn't really want to start something that would become a regular thing.

After that note, he came to the monastery a month or so later. He asked if he could speak with me again. This time I was a little warmer. I was still very opposed to the idea that this would become a regular program, and that I would have to talk to him all the time. However, he kept coming to visit and asking for me, so I began to talk more kindly to him. All I can say is that our relationship grew from there as time moved on. I came to know him very intimately from the things he would share with me. He would tell me about various problems that he was having at the monastery, at Gethsemani, and, particularly, the problems with Dom James Fox. He would be all over the place. He would talk about Vietnam and the monastery and the problems with the Abbot. All different topics, including the scruples he suffered from continuing to be a writer, even in the monastery. He was involved in many things. I didn't know much about Vietnam or any of the political situations.

Downey: That being the case, what do you think he was looking for from you?

Sister Angela: I never felt that he was looking for something from me. He just instinctively felt that I was someone he could trust. He felt that right away. He felt that it was very freeing for him to talk to me about the problems he was having at the monastery and many deep issues as well. I think he felt a sense of trust. He told others, "I have always had a deep affection for Mother Angela." And I, myself, didn't know that affection was involved. But it was a very good kind of affection.

Downey: Did he write to you while you were Prioress in Louisville?

Sister Angela: Yes. Many of the letters and notes that I would receive from him were given to me during my term as Prioress in Louisville. And they were in the packet that I burned before I came to Savannah.

Downey: But you kept the ones that you received while you were in Savannah?

Sister Angela: Pretty much. Except for these top three. [Sister Angela had a stack of letters at hand during the interview, M.D.] These three I received in Louisville. The rest of the letters that I received while in Louisville, I burned. Some of the information that I now have came through John Howard Griffin. It was through him, after Father Louis' [Merton's] death, that I learned some things about Merton, in connection with me, that I did not know at the time. They were excerpts from Merton's diary and not intended for publication.

Downey: Would you care to say something about your reasons for letting the letters go? Why did you burn them?

Sister Angela: One of the reasons was detachment; probably not the right kind of detachment. I recalled that the Carmelites, St. John of the Cross and St. Teresa of Avila did the same thing. They burned each other's letters during the Inquisition for reasons of safety. Once I knew that I was going to Savannah to another Carmel, and that it was open-ended—for three years and possibly more—I thought about what I would do with the letters. I didn't want to bring them with me and I didn't want to just leave them there in my old cell. They probably wouldn't have been destroyed, but I just didn't want someone else to read them. Others wouldn't understand to begin with. So I decided that the best thing to do was to burn them. Part of the reason for burning them was detachment and part of the reason was for privacy. I also burned a number of letters from Abbot Fox. You see, both Thomas Merton and Dom James had been writing to me; each on a very personal level. In addition, each one had been *speaking* with me at various times about very *confidential* matters.

Downey: So you knew Dom James Fox as well?

Sister Angela: Yes. Abbot Fox used to come in to Louisville occasionally on business or for other reasons. He sometimes stopped at our monastery and would speak with the Prioress.

Downey: Recognizing and respecting the confidential nature of your conversations with these two men, is there anything you might say that would throw light on the nature of their relationship?

Sister Angela: There is not much I would add to what is now generally known through various publications. It is fairly well known that their relationship was strained. I might add this, however. It seemed to me that there was a certain element of jealousy on the part of Abbot Fox in respect to my relationship with Father Louis. Abbot Fox did some mean things to Father Louis, and Merton would talk to me at times about these things. He was deeply hurt and angry—justifiably so. My heart went out to him fully. I felt the depth of his suffering and shared it with him.

Downey: You were in an intriguing position in that you did not initiate the conversations with Merton. Rather, he initiated conversations with you. It is striking to me that Merton is a kind of a spiritual guide for so many people. Many would think that he was coming into Louisville to listen to Mother Angela, when in fact it was the other way around. The priest or the monk is usually thought to be the confessor to the nun. And so this is a new twist on what many think about Merton. It was not that you were going to him. He sought counsel from you.

Sister Angela: Well, not counsel, but sharing. He was suffering so much; from Dom James particularly. He had an immediate sense of trust in me. There were times in our conversations when he would upbraid the Abbot and get really worked up. His voice was shaking. Later I learned of many more or less trivial things that Dom James was responsible for. Some of these were very funny to me. One time he said that Dom James tweaked his hair as he walked by him. Father Louis, it seems, was typing and Abbot James came into the room and, as he went by, he tweaked Father Louis' hair. Merton said that he just wanted to swear, but instead he kept silent. In relating this he said to me, "Aren't you proud of me?" This was a real conflict for him. I came to feel that Abbot James was, perhaps, somewhat jealous of the relationship that he sensed existed between Thomas Merton and myself.

Downey: Was that because of the trust that Merton placed in you? Perhaps Dom James thought that such trust should have been in the context of the relationship between Abbot and monk. Would that be fair to say?

Sister Angela: It would be reasonably fair. There were times when Thomas Merton was very upset about various other matters that would strike me as funny. One time he was close to tears and I burst out laughing. He questioned why I was laughing and I said, "Well, Father, it's so funny what you're saying." He replied, "It is funny, but he's driving me nuts." Another time the brothers came into Louisville, and John of the Cross [one of the monks of Gethsemani at the time] brought me a letter from Father Louis saying that he wanted to apologize for upbraiding the Abbot. Merton explained in the letter that he was sorry for losing his cool and that the Abbot must have had his good reasons. Father Louis was truly very humble. There were many experiences where I was witness to his humility. Many people don't connect humility with him, but he *was* very humble.

Downey: You talk about his humility as being, in some ways, exemplary. What did you gain from the interchange that you had with him? Obviously, he was not the spiritual guide for you that he has become to so many others. But in the course of your interaction did you learn something about the Christian life or the spiritual life?

Sister Angela: That is very hard for me to evaluate. I know that at one point I wrote to him with the feeling that much of what we were sharing was of deep spiritual value to me, and I asked him if he would ever become my spiritual director. He wrote back and said that I could try but if he knew anything about Dom James, Dom James would never let something like that go through.

Downey: Do you think that was because of the jealousy you speak of?

Sister Angela: I don't think so. I think at that point Thomas Merton was getting more and more known. And it's not their [the Cistercians'] tradition to have their priests giving spiritual direction outside their own community. Thomas Merton was growing so fast. He couldn't help it. Because of the books he was writing, hundreds of people were writing to him and all wanted special relationships and favors. I thought that was so comical.

Downey: So did he become your spiritual director? Or your confessor?

Sister Angela: Well it would have been more in the area of spiritual direction for me. Questions like: Where was I at in this stage of my life? What was I experiencing in prayer? Was it "for the birds" or was it a development in growing closer to a union with Christ? That's where our conversation was. I did seek his guidance and gifted knowledge in spiritual matters. He would know instantly if someone was genuine or phony!

Downey: Even though you considered him something of a spiritual director, it never came to pass that he served in this capacity in any formal way, let's say with the approval of his Abbot. Is that correct?

Sister Angela: Yes! We had been sharing anyway, but it wasn't a spiritual director relationship. And anything he would say to me that wasn't in specific connection with my own spiritual development was in our own mutual sharing with one another. There was a sharing on both sides. He would tell me things such as that he felt like he was so engulfted in God's presence that he just wanted to dance. They weren't things that he would just tell anybody, I don't think. It was more in connection with his own prayer development and union with God. Sometimes he would express these things in amusing ways, but I always knew what he was saying. For instance, one time he spoke of spiritual delights in this way: "All day I was experiencing soft punches in my heart."

Downey: What other kinds of things did you share with him?

Sister Angela: After I was no longer Prioress, I didn't have the freedom to visit with him. So most of my communication with him was by letter.

Downey: So most of your conversations with him were exclusively when you were serving as Prioress.

Sister Angela: Yes. And then whatever letters I wrote when I was still in Louisville and not Prioress. These were not simply on a spiritual level, but also concerned with problems that I saw in the community. I asked him how to deal with them.

Downey: Did he give you some tips on dealing with problems?

Sister Angela: He really did. Some of that is in this letter. [Sister Angela held up one of three of Merton's letters written to her while she was still in Louisville, and which she had saved. M.D.]

Downey: Did you find him insightful?

Sister Angela: Oh yes. Very much. Father Louis and I were talking about education for the nuns. He said perhaps there would be a way for some of the nuns to attend a conference or symposium outside the community. However he said that we would have to be careful. That's what I liked about him. Some people felt that he was *avant garde* about things and that nothing mattered. But it did matter to him that we wouldn't go out on any and every occasion in order to get educated. He told me that we would have to be very discreet about letting people go out of the monastery. To a question about whether one of our nuns should be permitted to go to a music festival in Miami, he responded that it was one thing to go out for education, but it was quite another thing to go out for a musical event. He said, "I don't go for that. And besides," he said, "I've been in Miami and it's a dump."

He didn't just go along with everything I said. Sometimes he said, "I think that's a mistake." Thomas Merton was very practical and that's why I could always trust him.

Downey: You and Merton were both trying to live deeply contemplative lives. Did he help you to understand the contemplative life better?

Sister Angela: I don't think he really did. He was immersed in a spirituality that was wholly Cistercian and I was very immersed in mine [Carmelite]. We were each deeply rooted in our own tradition. There are some differences, but not a great deal, between the two. They are both traditions of silence, solitude and prayer. We [Carmelites] had built-in recreation times following in the Teresian charism. I don't know if they [Cistercians] did. The one thing that Father Louis and I focused on the most, what we found the most resonance on, was the hermit life within Carmel. I felt that there could be some addition to our Constitutions that would allow some of the nuns to spend some time in complete solitude. They [Cistercians] did eventually let Thomas Merton become a hermit, so I congratulated him. He was concerned about other areas like education, as well. The monks there at that time were—I can't find the word he used—totally uneducated.

Downey: Do you mean illiterate? Or, perhaps, uneducated in theology and spirituality?

Sister Angela: Something like that. It seemed from what he said that many remained at an immature stage and they never grew beyond it. But as far as Merton himself influencing me to live a deeper prayer life, we just never really discussed that. Our traditions were basically the same. They were calls to contemplative living.

Downey: The call that you both felt—one Cistercian and one Carmelite—you both saw as the same type of call?

Sister Angela: Yes. The minor difference: Saint Teresa was a very practical woman and she thought that women needed to have a period of recreation. She felt that the Sisters needed to break that total solitude. The Trappist monks didn't. They might now. I don't know. What I feel is that basically Father Louis and I felt that this was God's call to us and we responded to it where it was. The Cistercian for him and the Carmelite for me. But we both felt that there should be a provision for a hermit-type life within these traditions.

Downey: You suggest that you were each called to a different place. It seems to me that you are happy as a result of your response to that call. In your judgment, was he happy in his walk of life?

Sister Angela: I really think he was.

Downey: Even with all the conflicts that he experienced?

Sister Angela: Yes. I believe he was. It was only after he died, and through John Howard Griffin's book *Follow the Ecstasy* that I found out more. There Griffin talks about how Merton would have picnics out in the woods with different people. The names are people that I knew about in Louisville. I didn't have direct contact with them, but they were familiar names. One of them was a psychiatric doctor who would even invite his wife and other friends to the picnic. They would have these picnics out in the woods. I would just cringe inside when I was reading that. A lot of that was going on while we were still in touch in Louisville. And then that whole affair with Margie came out. That I learned about later through my reading. Now *that* truly devastated me.

Downey: Could you say a little about that?

Sister Angela: Yes. When I first read it, I was in a state of shock. It was like someone you thought highly of had betrayed you. How could he ever, ever have followed along with that?

Downey: Are you saying that he followed along with that and at the same time had such a trusting communication with you and did not give any indication about what was going on?

Sister Angela: Yes. He never spoke of this. I felt such a sense of betrayal, although he didn't owe anything to *me*. He mentions in one of his letters that he was very fond of Mother Angela and he said, "I have shared with her the very deepest aspirations of my soul and she has with me."

How could he say that and then do what he was doing? And some of that was in 1966, shortly after I left Louisville to come to Savannah Carmel. It really devastated me. I earnestly prayed to God. For a month I was like a zombie. I couldn't lift the tragedy off of me. I kept praying to God to help me understand it. And of course Merton was dead when I found out the story about him and Margie.

Then the thought came to me that this was perhaps sinful on his part. But only God is the judge. I also thought of other great sinners. I thought of St. Augustine, for instance. He was in sin, but he became a great saint. And I thought of the Old Testament, of Abraham. God tested him. God told him to kill his son. He went up the mountain to obey. And when he was about to slay the child, God stopped his hand. Abraham's faith proved him worthy of God. At that time it came to me that possibly it could be a test that God sent to Thomas Merton to test *his* fidelity. And he came through it. It was a terrible struggle, but he did come through it. So then I felt a peace about it. Nobody knows the judgments of God. Here on earth we look at the externals. And we can be very rigid in our expectations of how people are living out their commitments. I felt that I, myself, could not judge it. I was sorry that it happened. I only knew that in some way he proved his fidelity to God through that, because he certainly loved the woman tremendously.

The other thing that connects with that is a strange thing. There are pictures of us [nuns from different contemplative religious orders] all around a table when we attended a series of Merton's lectures at a retreat at Gethsemani.

Downey: What was the purpose of that conference?

Sister Angela: It was to try to bring out our common spiritual and contemplative ground. It was to show that various contemplative Orders still had a common ground.

Downey: What did Merton understand that to be? Did he listen to the Sisters, or did he do more of the talking?

Sister Angela: He talked. But he also wanted feed-back. The nuns would say what they thought. They had questions about his lectures and he would explain what he meant. One thing that struck me much later was that, in the course of one of those talks, he began to talk about passion. He said that passion was one of the most devastating things that a person would ever have to grapple with. He went into such description about the pain and the struggle of passion. I felt uncomfortable almost.

Years later, I was talking to Carmelite nuns who had also attended that retreat at Gethsemani. In the meantime we had heard about the affair with Margie. They said to me: "Sister Angela, Do you remember a lecture that Thomas Merton gave that was kind of surprising?" I said, "Do you mean the reference to passion?" They said, "Yes!" We all had funny vibrations about that, but nobody surfaced it. He put so much stress on the struggle of passion. Now we know why.

I thought about this and the great sinners who had been converted. Some said that he should have known better, but we don't know what he knew. He was just enthralled with that woman. It came about from a simple association in a hospital. She was his nurse. She spoke more intelligently than the other nurses taking care of him. It was just one of those freak meetings where two people click. They weren't meant to click in the sense that he would leave and get married to her. But he had to go through that and he proved himself. Thomas Merton must have written it all down. In John Howard Griffin's book Merton is quoted as to what he was thinking at the time. That helped me a great deal to realize what a struggle he was going through. Now I am peaceful on that. I think that it is in God's hands and it was a test and Merton made it.

Downey: I am interested in going back to that conference of contemplative superiors. You said that he tried to get people to talk about a common ground. Do you remember what he focused on?

Sister Angela: What he focused on most was that we were basically too isolated and needed some form of communication among us all. We needed some form of association or some approved body that we could all meet in. For example, the Carmels were all autonomous houses or monasteries. We communicated with other Carmels to a small extent, but this was on a social basis. There was no official bond or meeting place so to speak. He felt that the isolation was unhealthy. We were stagnant in mind to some extent. We weren't being stimulated at all.

Downey: It seems to me that, in his mind, this conference would have been a kind of springboard for "ongoing formation" in the contemplative life. On one hand he was deeply rooted in the tradition, and on the other hand he was encouraging creativity.

Sister Angela: Yes, but with great discretion! The big fruit of that meeting is that we realized that we were so bound by our rules that we could not even grapple with the subject of change in order to get it started. We thought someone should write a letter to the Holy See. A Sister suggested that he write the letter. Later he said that he would write something down as a rough copy for the next conference [which never happened, M.D.]. He did send a petition to the Holy See requesting some minor changes and diversity in living out our charisms.

Downey: This was at least one small effort at renewal. In many ways he was at the forefront of renewal. What did he mean by the renewal of religious life?

Sister Angela: He meant that we should come to terms with the age in which we were living. He felt that since much of the legislation was written four or five hundred years ago, it could not be applied literally in our day and age. Some of the things were archaic. That was the word he used: "archaic." He felt that the legislation needed to be translated into current spirituality and that it needed to be in touch with the times in which we live. He also felt that we were not provided with enough education.

Downey: Could you say a little more about that?

Sister Angela: At that time most of us had no kind of formal education within the monastery, except for retreats with priests and periodic conferences. There were great advancements that had been made in theology, philosophy, and psychology. He hoped that somehow we could tie into those gifts to bring a greater fullness to our own life within the monastery.

Downey: While he didn't necessarily support sending people away for studies, he was firm in his conviction that contemplative superiors did need to provide for some educational formation.

Sister Angela: Right. Either in the monastery itself or, on occasion, somewhere else.

Downey: You mentioned theology, philosophy and psychology. Did he see anything helpful in the "new" theology?

Sister Angela: Very much so. He felt you couldn't send everyone in the monastery away for their education, but he said occasionally it would be helpful to send one individual. He also encouraged us to bring in speakers who were very good and well known for their knowledge and their expertise and their ability to give lectures on various subjects. It was then that we began to have someone come to the monastery at least once a year here in our community.

Downey: You spoke of Merton gathering contemplatives together at Gethsemani. How did he understand the contemplative life?

Sister Angela: Well I think that he would have understood it as we all do; that is, the *ideal* of contemplative life. The giving of yourself totally to God without too much external association with people— which in his own particular life was not possible. This withdrawal is not in a selfish way, but in a way that you feel drawn to give yourself totally to God in prayer and to a life distanced from the world, but still very much in the world.

Downey: Some people say that toward the end of his life Merton had a wide understanding of contemplation. Some would say that one of his great contributions to the history of Western Christian spirituality is that he introduced the notion of contemplation to people living "in the world." Some interpreters say that he believed that one could live a contemplative life in the world and that there is a contemplative aspect of everyday living. Would that ring true to the Merton you knew?

Sister Angela: Yes it would. It really would. Even in a contemplative community in which you have every opportunity to give yourself totally to God, many times people who are living in the contemplative life are not growing spiritually.

Downey: He was aware of that, was he?

Sister Angela: Yes he was. There were those who would just go through the motions. He told me about Sundays at Gethsemani when they would have certain hours that were free. He always wanted to go to the chapel [church] to pray. It struck him how few of the other monks ever came to the chapel. He said he wasn't saying that they weren't praying. Maybe they were somewhere else. But he mentioned that it was something that he found painful. They all had an opportunity to have more quiet prayer and there were so few who seemed to want that. He would also speak of their strict silence and their sign language. He said that a lot of people using sign language made more distraction than if they just said a word. They would go through all these complicated signs when all they wanted to do was simply say, "Pass the bread!" It was very distracting. He said that it became a fetish—if that's the right word—of following these things externally, but they weren't lived internally.

Downey: Increasing numbers of people see in Merton someone who invited them to believe that there is a contemplative dimension to every walk of life beneath the external differences. Would you agree?

Sister Angela: I would agree with that definitely.

Downey: Let me ask a related question. It seems that in every life there is a central image that expresses a particular spirituality. Is there any image that, in your view, is the central feature of Merton's spirituality?

Sister Angela: It seemed to me that he was very focused on Christ. He had also become very attracted to Eastern spirituality, and there was a lot about it which he found wonderful. He just loved it. He had many friends like the Dalai Lama and other people. I remember one time—in a book or in one of his letters—he said something along the lines that the Eastern methods of meditation and discipline impressed him deeply. The methods by which they strip themselves and give themselves totally to God. But for Merton I come back to the inexplicable, unbelievable, wonderful figure of Christ. Nothing comes close to that. To me, Merton really had a very deep focus on the figure of Christ. He believed that total redemption came to us through Christ.

Downey: Was there a particular dimension of Christ's life or the Christian mystery through which Merton would have sought meaning?

Sister Angela: I think that would probably be the Cross. I think that the Cross revealed to him the meaning of suffering. In it we identify with Christ in our own suffering. Other people might think differently, but this is the Merton I knew.

Our relationship was very special. It was very simple. It probably seems trite, but I can compare it to young innocent children running through fields of daisies with great joy. There was always a carefree joy in our being together. It was so innocent and so pure. I didn't think of it that way at the time; it just was. We spoke of love, but there was no aspect of love like in a sexual or physical way. Not at all. It was a really spiritual love.

Downey: But in the beginning you found him to be something of a nuisance!

Sister Angela: I did! I did! In the very beginning. At first I got involved out of a sense of duty as Prioress. But in speaking with him I really began to see the type of man that he was. He was humble, simple, honest, direct and he was willing to expose his own weaknesses and limitations. He wouldn't even mind saying that he had had a terrible day. He would say that he was hateful with some of the monks. He would say that it wasn't their fault. It was because he was in a bad mood. I would try to be supportive and say that we all have bad days.

Downey: What was most memorable about him? Some people say that he had wonderful crystal blue eyes. Others say that he had a great big laugh.

Sister Angela: You know, I am at a disadvantage for that because I always spoke to him through the grate and curtain. I had no direct face to face contact with him. The only time I really saw him personally was when he had the meeting of contemplative superiors at Gethsemani not long before he died so unexpectedly.

Downey: What do you remember most about him? What were his strengths and weaknesses?

Sister Angela: What I remember most of all was his total love of God. That came through most strongly for me; especially in the person of Christ. His weakness was his love of people. It was a clash; more so when he was in Gethsemani. A close friend of Merton was very against his affair with Margie. He told him that it was really wrong to hide this from the Abbot. It was a struggle for Merton, because he loved people so much. And he enjoyed people. But he also liked simple people—I, myself, am a very simple person. Whatever it was that attracted him—ours developed into a very intimate friendship. I feel that his love for God and love for people were both his greatest strength and his greatest weakness. There was always something of a clash between his love for people and his commitments to the monastery. I perceived this conflict within him, but I never made any comments about it. There was always a great pull between his genuine love for God and his love for people.

Downey: What leads you to say that his love of God was so full?

Sister Angela: From my experience with him I think he was a friend of God. For example, he talked about his own prayer. Its hard to remember thirty years ago, but I always remember that he had a forceful drive to give himself to God in deep unity. I can't say whether this was a mystical state or what. I remember one time that someone asked me if Thomas Merton was a saint. I am not in any place to judge. I think that he was a very holy person, but he had many complications within his being. Sometimes he would just go out into the woods and dance. He was so filled with the love of God. Maybe it was just an emotional surge. Maybe he just felt happy that day. Other days he was plunged into doubt about himself. No one can judge. He really did love God, yet he was pulled in many other directions that weren't part of his life. But I thought he needed to find this out for himself. He had a natural gift to love people. His love for God and people was in conflict to some extent.

Downey: Would you see his insatiable desire to write as compatible or conflicting with his contemplative life?

Sister Angela: I don't know. He wrote so many books. He gave me some of his poetry once. I suppose there are many people who love his poems, but many of them just didn't make sense to me. Only one poem appealed to me and that was "The Quickening of John the Baptist." I did read several of his books, but far from all of them! He, himself, sent me some—others came from Abbot Fox.

Downey: Let me ask you more about the renewal of religious life. You said that his vision of renewal went beyond the external. Has the renewal of contemplative life following the Second Vatican Council been in step with what he envisioned?

Sister Angela: I can't say what he would have said about renewal. But in my own experience of renewal I think that we have lost a lot. In other ways we have come full circle. We tried many things, but we realized that this was not it. The big thing at that time was to be outgoing. We would welcome anyone as visitors to the Carmel. We did not want people to think that we were more special to God than they were. This was Thomas Merton's feeling too. You don't have to be in a monastery to be a contemplative. But we learned from our mistakes. This was not the way to get that message across to people. Renewal now has gone beyond even what Father Merton sought.

Downey: What do you think he would have thought renewal should entail?

Sister Angela: I think that it was much more of an interior thing with him. I feel that he was strong on going back to the sources. I don't think that he implied that we should go back to the customs of four hundred years ago with St. Teresa. The essence of the renewal is not in externals. It is internal!

Downey: What do you think was Merton's greatest gift to the contemplative life?

Sister Angela: I don't know. I have so many mixed feelings about him. Much of what he worked for has come to pass. But I don't think that I can credit him as being the source of *all* that, although I love him deeply as a friend. I could identify with him, support him, and understand him. I love truth, so that even if Thomas Merton would say something that didn't ring true to me, I would tell him.

Downey: What would you say was Merton's greatest gift to you?

Sister Angela: I guess that it was affirmation. I could talk to him about the hermit life. In these pursuits and others he did really affirm me very much. Most of them have come to pass. When I went to Gethsemani, it was the first time that I had laid eyes on him personally. I went up to him and introduced myself and we almost hugged each other, but we were restrained. I think his greatest gift to me though, was affirmation.

Downey: You were a good friend of Merton's, but are you a great fan of his writings?

Sister Angela: No. I'm really not. I find a great deal of it to be beyond me. However, I don't mean to imply that I didn't read his books. But perhaps I could say, for me, that they were somewhat sophisticated. One of the ones he wrote, *The Sign of Jonas*, was most like the person I knew him to be.

Downey: It's very intriguing that Merton's writings don't have great appeal to you, because many people who read him find that no matter what their walk of life, he really speaks to them.

Sister Angela: His words and his presence spoke to me. And part of that was our common love for the hermit life. We wanted to bring that into our traditions. He was allowed to do this. They built a hermitage for him. But I was never able to realize this desire in my own life. One time I gave a five-minute talk on the life of solitude within the Carmelites at a national meeting, but it wasn't well received. It wasn't accepted. But almost everything that I said then is now in practice thirty years later.

Downey: Did he ever talk to you about St. John of the Cross?

Sister Angela: He spoke to me about St. John of the Cross a lot. I'm not sure what it was that he felt about him. He spoke of him often.

I can't remember. Maybe it was in one of Merton's books. He loved St. John of the Cross' writings. He was astonished by all that he had to suffer and was amazed that a great deal of his suffering was inflicted by his own Order—the Carmelites themselves!

Downey: Do you think that Merton identified with St. John of the Cross because of his own sufferings?

Sister Angela: It could well be. It didn't occur to me. It seems to me that Merton said when we were speaking that he, himself, was an upsetting figure to some of the people in Gethsemani. Maybe it was the things he said or did or wrote. Or maybe it was because he wanted to be a hermit. He often spoke of the criticism, but he didn't say exactly what it was about. I did pick up that there were a few who thought that he was given too much leniency to do things and go places that monks should not do or go to.

Downey: He must have been a very strong person to endure this.

Sister Angela: I can't really say. But he loved St. John of the Cross and he loved Teresa, too. She was a strong woman and determined. He admired this greatly. I was very surprised one time when John Howard Griffin wrote to me that Father Louis had written in his diary that I was a woman of great femininity and a woman of great courage. I think he also liked St. Teresa for her determination. And he liked Joan Baez. I don't know her, but he thought very highly of her. He also seemed to respect Mother Luke Tobin highly, but I don't know what he felt for her.

Downey: In general, then, he liked strong women?

Sister Angela: He liked women who had accomplished things in their lives. I have this letter here from John Howard Griffin. Would you like to read it?

Downey: Would you mind reading it to me?

Sister Angela: No, I don't mind. This is what Thomas Merton wrote in his diary on July 2, 1965; that was the year I came here to Savannah. He says [according to Griffin's transcription],

> This morning I had a long morning up in the hermitage. The main event of the morning: Mother Angela my friend in the Louisville Carmel, who I have not seen much of since she was Prioress, wrote

the other day that she was going south to Savannah to be Prioress at the Carmel there. I was expecting her plane, for the south-bound planes out of Louisville—at least the ones to Atlanta and Florida—go right over here fairly low. The ones from Chicago are very high.

Sister Angela: He had all these things figured out!

I walked on to the pines and soon the plane appeared on time and went over very fast. It was a beautiful big new jet with wings almost as far back as the tail. It was really a beautiful sight. And as I had told her to look out for us, I suppose she saw the monastery and perhaps even picked out the hermitage as I told her where to look.

Sister Angela: He told me all that, but I never could see it!

I was happy for her up there in the sky and was even very moved. I was always quite fond of her. She was one of the few people I could talk to absolutely freely about my ideas and hopes for the solitary life, which, to a great extent, she shared and which she completely understands. She was very frank about some things I needed to know about Dom James and very much of a support. I felt that she was very much of a sister to me and I am grateful for her. I will miss her and I hope she will write.

Thousands of Words:
A Bibliographical Review

**Some of Merton's "Difficulties"; His Continual Writing Process;
and Some Implications for Readers "Caught in Civilization"**

Victor A. Kramer

"Most sorry. If you knew. I get buried under manuscripts everyday of my life, they are lying all over the place, they are blocking
the view, they are falling in my food" (Letter, 9-13-65).

I.

Merton's thousands of letters will NOT be assimilated quickly.
Similarly, this is the case for the entire body of his writing about which
he himself admits he had a hard time keeping track. He spent his
mature life learning how to work *and* pray, and he wrote hundreds
of persons for thousands of reasons. It is therefore (especially at this
early stage of knowledge about the complexity of the correspondence
and its relationship to his other projects—poetry, journal, essays, etc.)
presumptuous to think an individual or group of scholars can now assimilate such remnants and reflections of Merton's energetic diversity
and awe of God. Yet because he wrote so much we enter into dialogue.
Clearly for this monk/artist—pen, pencil, or typewriter close at hand—
the process of building language systems to ponder mysteries became
basic. Paradoxically, this meant he could never fully think things
through as he dealt with the continuing crises of his life because ultimately he was able to sense that for many things no definitive answer
exists. However, he spent his monastic vocation writing and clarify-
ing intuitions about his understanding of humankind's relationship
to God and the intricate web of culture.

We also remember that Merton came to the realization that over-used words can sometimes be hindrance as well as help, and thus readers have to bear a similar lesson in mind: sometimes it is best not to pursue "understanding." Yet all those words are there, and we keep returning to them, as best we can. Merton was, no doubt, a compulsive notetaker, writing first to himself and for himself, but always also for others. He was ceaselessly writing poems, essays, journal entries, letters and in the process outlining correspondences between insights and situations within and beyond himself, and thereby constantly asking questions and seeking to encourage others.

This review-essay builds on the idea that his many and continuing "difficulties," and questions, are a gift to an immense range of readers, but a gift exceedingly difficult to assimilate because of size and complexity. His range of interests and varieties of writing were continually expanding. To absorb the bulk of such an enormous deposit, Merton's gift of openness, is more than isolated readers can even imagine. Scholars have only begun such an endeavor. In the meantime individuals must remain content with nuggets extracted from the motherload of total accomplishment. Much can be utilized, but (and this is the paradoxical key) the ultimate assimilation cannot be done only through words. Merton teaches his readers to accept, to celebrate, but also to be quiet in addition to pouring out words in lamentation.

As the mature Merton (the final decade) became more aware of his need to reach out and make connections beyond the monastery, he also found methods to focus energy (prayer and work) and to devise ways to write about subjects of increasing importance in relation to issues beyond the cloister. This necessitated a kind of balancing between assuming too much responsibility and involvement and retreating into solitude and the pursuit of the contemplative life. Because of his enormous energy, it remains questionable that he himself felt he fully achieved a correct balance. He often expressed his realization that he wrote too much, and thus it is not accidental that (as scholars and readers) we continue to have a difficult time knowing what to focus upon. All Merton's words seem valuable, but at this point it is clearly impossible to absorb it all, or even the bulk of it. We have to learn to be content with a myriad of glittering pieces and this can be frustrating. We wonder if our difficulty is not like Merton's, finding it hard to know when to speak, and when to be quiet? We have to be satisfied with questions but few definitive answers, and we have to realize that Merton's engagement in the mystery of questioning is part of his gift.

Some 7,500 letters of Merton's are extant. There may be hundreds more because we suspect some letter holders have not surrendered them to research libraries. To read all of these letters in their proper context—which would necessitate reading both sides of the correspondence and understanding what caused Merton to generate related work—would be an immense chore. In the five volumes of selected letters now published, we have access to the bulk of approximately 2,252 of these letters. (There are omissions of passages.) This project, a labor of love by the four editors involved, is now complete and will be the subject of some limited comments at the conclusion of this review-essay. The General Editor of the correspondence, William H. Shannon, is to be commended for designing and shepherding this immense project. His fellow editors, Robert E. Daggy, Patrick Hart, and Christine Bochen have provided a valuable compilation of primary materials and related editorial information.

The final volume, *Witness to Freedom*, subtitled "Letters in Times of Crisis" (Farrar, Straus, Giroux, 1994, $25.00) is quite interesting *both* because it helps frame the continuing complex concerns of the writer and because it also clearly reflects some of the difficulties which the editor must have faced as he made selections and arranged them under the categories developed for this book. Shannon must have felt many constraints of choice and space at every step of the way as this final selection of letters was executed precisely because Merton never ceased to be engaged in overlapping issues, or crises, while he also saw involvement as necessary, yet, a trap. But what is any crisis, Ezra Pound reminds us in his *ABC of Reading*, but opportunity?

Pound also noted that the Chinese calligraphic symbols for crisis and opportunity are the same. Merton clearly sensed something like Pound, and such a realization contributed to advances both in his writing and in his spiritual life. During his final decade, as insights came flooding in, Merton found himself working and praying through a continual series of questions, opportunities, and crises. Any easy separation of living, spiritual life, and writing about life must have largely ceased to seem valid. Father Louis's need then, especially in the 1960s, and that is when the bulk of these letters were written, was to write carefully so he would not feel guilty of inaction during a time of genuine civic, political, and racial disorder, yet also to write in ways

which reflected prudence, and hopefulness, and even the need sometimes for inaction.

Continually, he found himself expressing thoughts of urgency,
as on November 30, 1962, perhaps one of the most critical moments
of his life because of questions about impending nuclear war:

> . . . Let me say . . . my own position here is one that puts me
> in difficulties. As a member of the Order I have to be careful not
> to involve the Order itself in my statements. . . . I have been asked
> to go easy in controversial statements, but I generally do not go
> easy enough (*Witness to Freedom*, 85).

Such an honest statement serves as a paradigm for much of Merton's
continuing and sometimes perplexing involvement in a myriad of interrelated issues. Sometimes he felt he had to speak, while at other
times he knew he should be silent. The question always seemed to
remain, how to produce the correct letter (or essay, or poem) at any
particular moment. Such a convergence of questions and opportunities, especially toward the end of his life, must have been exceedingly
complicated. Merton recognized the range of contemporary issues
which demanded examination while he also realized more that he was
called to center his own life. Also, his many questions were often about
interrelated issues: Solitude, Monastic Life, War, Grace, Church,
Ecumenism, Race, the question of Writing itself, etc.

It is also significant that toward the end of his life the pace of
Merton's writing activities and letter production sped up. Several
things converged. He had become more a quasi-public figure; this was
the time (after 1965) when he was freed of being Novice Master, and
at least theoretically when he had more time for reflection, while it
also was a time when many crucial issues seemed unavoidable for a
reflective person. Thus, he felt compelled to pursue a range of questions. The four preceding volumes of letters would also illustrate this
accelerated change of pace—a sense of urgency which came as his last
decade unfolded. It is as if Merton knew he might not live a long time,
and therefore had to speak, to exchange ideas, and encourage others
as they too puzzled through the entrance into the post-Christian era.
Such a pattern flashes throughout *Witness to Freedom*, but interestingly,
there is also a calmness radiated throughout the bulk of this collection
which is also worth observing in detail because it reveals the complexity

of Merton's letter-writing process. Sometimes his calmness is expressed through humor and irony.

Merton is engaged, always involved, yet he usually remains quite careful about his language (Is it in some cases that Shannon deletes a controversial item?). Generally he does an excellent job of sorting out individual pieces observed in relation to his life, the life of his community, Church, and the wider society. In fact, often his sought-for balance is achieved. But to perceive such balance—and here we return to the difficulties of reading Merton—we have to accept the separate letters as only nuggets from that bigger motherload. Scholars are now learning to do this with still other parts of the Merton canon as well.

II.

Recent books about Merton clearly reflect interpretative difficulties which radiate from the immense volume of the total body of his writing. Ultimately it becomes a matter of how to choose items and thereby to make sense of these vast literary remains, that is to choose words to make sense of living as Merton did. There are no easy answers especially when there are so many words, but opportunities are everywhere. Basic to the dilemma of sorting through the immensity of Merton's work (published, unpublished, edited, selected) is how to remain calm and focused when the possibilities for interpretation and inspiration are vast. Two 1994 books reflect the opportunities for mining Merton's gift from the myriads of possibilities of potential catalytic materials. These books reflect trends: others like them exist. (We now have, for example, a small shelf of books which provide quotations from Merton's goldmine: for meditations; for retreat; as reflections, etc. . . . Jim Forest published such a book in 1994: *Finding Your Centre, A Journey with Thomas Merton* [London, Hunt & Thorpe]. It is in that publisher's Everyday Spirituality Series.)

As already indicated, apparently it is Merton's quality of calmness, sometimes a hidden serenity in the writing, which allows admirers to choose what seems to be needed for particular interpretations. This is what the editors of the five volumes of selected letters must have learned as they carefully selected items to make the relatively compact selections for those books: social concerns; friendship; religious life; literary matters. Editors must pick, choose, and focus, yet this is both asset and liability for with any selection from Merton we always think we have answers, but, of course, what is proven is that we have only part of one.

The 1994 books by Waldron and Simsic demonstrate both the complexity and value, but the difficulty, even the allusiveness of reading Merton. Each is quite limited in approach, yet both promise to be of value for particular readers who seek models for particular ways of spiritual searching. It is not very helpful to schematize what these quite different authors offer from Merton, for one suspects that both studies were conceived with the hope that an active reader-participant would use these overviews as beginning points for what must be a journey. It occurs to me that one problem with Merton's life journey is that while he had accepted the vow of stability, in some ways he could never really feel at home. Thus his voluminous writings, and especially the letters, became his way to journey beyond the confines of his adopted home, a place about which he continued to feel ambivalent for most of his life. (That ambivalence is fundamental to the writing process itself.) A danger of Robert Waldron's book is that it appears to provide answers which are too easy, even simplistic.

Waldron has provided a Jungian reading which suggests Merton's life was a successful integration: Merton himself would not be so sure. Called *Thomas Merton in Search of His Soul, A Jungian Perspective* (Notre Dame: Ava Maria Press, 1994, 157 pp., $7.95), this quiet book (reviewed elsewhere in this volume) could serve to introduce Merton to persons with a Jungian interest, or it could demonstrate how Jung can be used to interpret Merton. (A glossary of terms is included, so this is fairly basic material.) Waldron's approach is limited in what it can do to illuminate Merton's "search." It is sometimes oversimplified, and as a perhaps strained overview of parallels between Jung's insights and Merton's spiritual journey it seldom goes beyond the predictable.

Merton in Search covers only a small amount of material and this is squeezed to fit the mold. There are useful comparisons made between Jung's perspectives about individuation and integration and Merton's spiritual journey, and no doubt Merton's spiritual movements can be profitably viewed with such a grid. (But so could all lives.) And as Walker Percy has insisted when asked about the Jungian patterns in his fiction (and life), such psychologizing cannot ever account for the mystery of how a particular individual exists in the intersection of space and time, nor account for the relationship of that person to Jesus Christ who entered history and thereby changed all history. What remains unique is the mercy of God and grace for each separate individual.

Waldron's book is a "commentary" about limited aspects of Merton's life. Valuable points are made as he illustrates Merton's movement toward "completeness" (15). In Chapter One (Death of a father and shadow); in Two (about early years and shadow projection); in Three ("Experimentation with Personae") and in succeeding chapters basic patterns are isolated and described. Chapter Four is about "False Self and True Self." Chapters Five through Eight—often through a consideration of particular passages—demonstrate how Merton clearly sensed that he should better integrate his personality. (Don't we all?) In the parts about "Anima" and "Dreams" (Chapters Six and Seven) basic patterns of synthesis are observed. The problem seems to be that Waldron squints to provide his reading of the data. He rightly points out that more evidence is probably available in unpublished materials. As an exploratory first step this commentary will be helpful to some. As an examination of Merton's psyche, this must remain a severely limited beginning.

The second book, by Wayne Simsic, by its nature, provides no easy answers because it seeks to put the reader to work. Merton becomes a companion, someone as friend who reveals himself to readers who dispose themselves to prayer. Simsic's book *Praying with Thomas Merton* (Winona, Minnesota: St. Mary's Press, 1994, 125 pp., $9.95) is altogether different from Waldron's grid. It is a guide for praying, and while its organization is clearly defined, responsibility is placed on the active reader. As a means toward contemplative prayer, Simsic uses basic patterns in Merton's writing which will serve either to introduce readers to Merton, or utilize Merton as a means for refining one's need for quiet prayer.

Simsic's procedure is to present basic Merton themes and quotations so the reader can build. Thus, general suggestions are made about how to pray (with Merton as the resource person) and how to employ these materials to one's advantage. An overview of Merton's life (15–32) sets the stage. Then fifteen "Meditations" are provided: "Turning Back to the True Self" (#1); "Prayer of the Heart" (#6); "Social Concerns" (#11); and "The Quest for Unity" (#15). In each instance a story about Merton is provided; then an appropriate selection of his words; a reflection, or some suggestions; and a closing "God's Word." Simsic stresses that the person who uses his book is under no obligation to follow all its exercises. The book is meant as stimulant and will serve well those who can enter into its suggested quietness, but then move on from Merton. The book is nicely printed, attractively designed, and will work well to draw properly disposed persons into the life of prayer.

Still another related book, while it appeared two years earlier in Germany, can be mentioned for it neither imposes a grid nor provides explicit directions about how to use Merton. Since it is an example of a book similar in intention to both the Forest and Simsic books (someone should write an extended essay and compare all such books), and also because it is an example of Merton's widening worldwide appeal and usefulness, how Merton is mined, it seems appropriate to provide limited commentary about it because it is unknown to North American readers. This recent German collection of Merton pieces done by Bernardin Schellenberger, *Zeiten der Stille* [Times of Stillness], is skillfully collected, translated and commented upon (Ausgewahlt, herausgegeben und erlautert: Freiberg: Herder, 1992 [Band 4107 in Spektrum Series]). It is evidence of Merton's widening audience and clearly designed for European readers unfamiliar with Merton. It is a success because, it seems to me, it demonstrates the open-endedness fundamental to Merton's life quest.

Schellenberger's book is arranged thematically with editorial connections dispersed throughout. With selections from *Raids on the Unspeakable*, other pieces on silence, and careful selections from *The Sign of Jonas* near the beginning, a quiet tone is set. The commentary is excellent. As the book evolves (and it is more than just selections plunked down) Schellenberger speaks less and less, and Merton is allowed to take over. Toward the end of the book poetry is included. There are sixty-two items of commentary, but these editorial comments become shorter and shorter as the book develops. The book is a success because it hints at questions Merton raised about monasticism, love, the world, etc., but it does not push any radical interpretation. This is truly a collection of texts which allows the reader to participate in interpreting Merton. Shellenberger's commentary is insightful, good enough that the German could be translated into English and Merton's words printed again to provide a valuable introduction for English speakers who need to hear about these themes of solitude and quiet.

III.

Much recent periodical scholarship about Merton also recognizes that, for the time being, we will have to remain content with looking carefully at separate reflections of his sometimes frustrated, yet ever-widening consciousness, a consciousness also of human limitations in the presence of God pondered, and only slowly articulated. I have selected four representative articles which are valuable in this connection for this essay because they represent scholarship which recognizes difficulties of analysis, but which do not force an interpretation. Each article also reveals aspects of Merton's continuing (continual) writing process.

Michael Casey's "Merton's Notes on 'Inner Experience' Twenty Years Afterwards" (originally published in *Tjurunga* (1993) is included in *The Undivided Heart: The Western Monastic Approach to Contemplation*, (St. Bede's, Petersham, Mass., 1994). While I have not examined this book, I can recommend it on the basis of this "Inner Experience" article which feeds into the book: Casey demonstrates how Merton's unfinished manuscript reveals a continuing process of pondering.

Casey's analysis of the unpublished "Inner Experience: Some Notes on Contemplation" confronts the fact of its "eclectic juxtaposition of *overlapping*, but not synonymous propositions" [my emphasis] which creates both a sense of incompleteness and a total effect "which is dynamic" (21). Thus, Merton sees that contemplatives can serve as "bridges between different traditions" (34). Casey shows how Merton drew on St. Thomas, Maritain, and the wisdom literature of the Christian tradition and he also points out that for Merton dread remains a fundamental ingredient of what any serious contemplative must face. As an overview (See especially Section 4 "Experience of Contemplation"), Casey's synthesis is incisive. The article is a good example of a scholar dealing with the complexity of Merton's never remaining satisfied with straightforward answers. It is also quite a valuable analysis of this never-to-be finished manuscript which contains many valuable insights despite the fact that all its pieces cannot fit perfectly together.

Two more articles which merit extended notice appeared recently in *Cisterican Studies Quarterly*. They also approach Merton's work in a related manner by dealing with the incomplete nature of fundamental aspects of his work:

1) William R. [should be H.] Shannon's "Reflections on Thomas Merton's Article: 'Notes for a Philosophy of Solitude' " (vol. 29, no. 1, 1994, 83–91) is a longer version of the address which Shannon gave at the Third International Thomas Merton Society Meeting at Colorado College in 1993. That "Keynote" lecture was planned so various respondents provided reactions in panels. Two of those responses, by David Belcastro and Patrick Eastman, were revised for *The Merton Annual,* vol. 7 (1994).

The beauty of Shannon's expanded article is that he provides considerable information about the textual history of Merton's "Notes" as well as information about censorship, revisions, etc. Shannon suggests the complex development of this article, and importantly, explains his own difficulty in understanding these "Notes" because he first thought the essay must contain "a full blown philosophy of solitude" (89), yet he finally states "there is no careful progression of thought . . ." (89). It is unfortunate that this longer version was not made available for the respondents at the I.T.M.S. Meeting—although it is interesting to see that both Belcastro and Eastman, in the preceding volume of this annual, do develop many of the questions which Shannon examines, especially about the dangers of solitude.

2) Richard E. Getty's "The Polychrome Face of Contradiction: Assessing Inconsistencies in Thomas Merton" (vol. 28, 3–4 [1993, published 1994], 281–296) is a thorough study of some not so surprising aspects of Merton's thought. This analysis is valuable because it both traces contradictions and inconsistencies and assures us because Merton kept growing, and therefore remained "critical of himself" (295), we must admire and learn from him. Therefore as Getty draws some implications, he stresses:

> The stark face of contradiction, as illustrated in Merton and present in ourselves, invites us to stay close to the actual terms of our personal experience. If we are honest about the presence of contradiction in ourselves, we will be led to reaffirm that we are saved *through* our humanity and not *from* it (295).

A final article to be commented upon in some detail helps explain what some observers might consider to be inconsistencies in Merton's religious preoccupations. Bonnie Thurston's "Thomas Merton's Interest in Islam: The Example of *Dhikr*" (*American Benedictine*

Review, 45, no. 2 [June 1994] 131–141) stresses that while Merton has been recognized as a figure in Buddhist-Christian dialogue, his interest in Islam remains less well-known. Thurston points out that Merton's interest in Islam goes far beyond "scattered references in talks and writings." The question addressed skillfully by her is why? Several answers are provided: first, Merton held many beliefs in common with the Muslim community including central Islamic concepts "like the unity of God *(Tawhid)* and the revelation of God *(Tanzil)* (135); second, he found the Sufi's metaphorical and "nonlogical" expression of the truths of religion "congenial" (135); and third, and most importantly, his interest in Sufism went beyond themes or style. "He deeply appreciated the Sufi analysis of the human spiritual condition" (135).

Thurston's article focuses primarily on the prayer method called *dhikr*, the final and characteristic Sufi practice, translated "recollection" and "invocation." This practice has been described by Islamic scholars as "the central means of worshiping God and invoking his presence" (138). This technical term, signifying the "glorifying of Allah" is, in fact, a means whereby God can be known experientially. This is basic to Merton's insight and it is clear that he spent considerable time in the study of *dhikr*. He was also well aware that this form of prayer was similar to that "practiced by the hesychasts in Christianity" (138). Merton had isolated an important point for dialogue between Christianity and Islam. Similarities between this practice and the invocation of the Jesus prayer are noted by Thurston, and what Merton learned, for example, from a correspondent, Abdul Aziz and other sources, suggests his profound understanding of the relationship between our being named by God and our naming of God "might never have occurred had he not studied Islam" (140). The article emphasizes that the issue of Merton's interest in Islam cannot be definitely answered, yet it is clear Merton's knowledge of *dhikr* allowed him to strengthen his Christian vocation.

The four articles singled out for commentary in the preceding section (about "inner experience," solitude, contradictions, and Islam) suggest the range of good work being done on Merton, but also suggest the difficulty of keeping materials in focus which are far ranging. In each instance, Merton's subject matter pursued might allow book length studies about these large subjects. The same is true of many of the germinal suggestions, articles and notes which appear frequently in *The Merton Seasonal*.

Most readers familiar with *The Merton Annual* will know the *Seasonal* for it serves as a kind of clearinghouse for persons with Merton interests including the members of the International Thomas Merton Society. With editor's comments, bibliographical listings, poems, sermons or homilies, articles, notes and announcements it is also a mine of information. Interestingly, its format reflects some of the problems of assimilation noted earlier. There is so much, by and about Merton, that to sift all becomes difficult. In the bibliographical listings for the four 1994 issues there are 216 items by and about Merton listed. Within the *Seasonal* during 1994, along with comments, notes, memoirs, etc., there were at least eight short articles, and two are especially significant in the light of the points I have already made in this essay: they suggest large subjects waiting for further investigation. In fact, books might develop from the methodology used in the articles by Gary Charas Behara ("Thomas Merton's *The Geography of Lograire:* A Poem of Psychotherapy" (vol. 19, no. 2, 14–17); and Patrick O'Connell, *Thirty Poems After Fifty Years* (vol. 19, no. 3, 13–17). In both these instances careful acknowledgement of preceding scholarship reveals systematic thought. Both these insightful articles suggest more book-by-book analysis of Merton's work would be rewarding. We might also note as Behara does *The Geography of Lograire* (also a draft, a beginning like all those letters) "does not end with solution . . ." (18).

IV.

Considerable recent writing about Merton, especially because the twenty-fifth anniversary of his death was commemorated in 1993, has either a celebratory or commemorative tone. This large body of material will not be commented upon here in any detail, yet it should be noted that it frequently reveals some of the difficulties of assimilation about which I have been commenting. His fellow Cistercians (in Spain, France, etc.) have provided collections of articles in quarterlies: testimonials and articles which outline his accomplishments. Many of the pieces published in the *Seasonal* work the same way. All this is too numerous to analyze here.

In the quarterly, *Collectanea Cisterciensia*, published by the French-speaking Cistercians, there are several articles which provide an overview of Merton's accomplishment. These can be found in vol. 56, no. 1 (1994); the authors are Charles Dumont, André Louf, Jacques Brière,

Bruno Ranford, and Robert Lecharlier. Similarly, an issue of the Cistercian publication of the Spanish speaking branch of the Order, *Cistercium*, 197 (1994) also recognizes Merton's accomplishment with a special section of articles. That group of pieces reprints some Merton poems, and includes articles by Robert Daggy, Fernando Beltran Salvador, and Francisco R. de Pascual.

A new publication in England, *The Merton Journal*, produced by the Merton Society of England, published two issues in 1994, and produced eight brief articles. These range from short pieces by well-known Merton commentators including Monica Furlong and Esther de Waal to reflective pieces about general topics, talks given in churches, or an examination of a well-known poem, "Grace's House." Bernard van Waes's essay on Merton and the Shakers draws some valuable parallels (vol. 1, no. 2, 44–51). An article by Thomas Del Prete on ". . . Merton's Admiration of Julian of Norwich" (vol. 1, no. 2) is almost identical to the piece which he published in *Spiritual Life* in 1993 (vol. 39, no. 4 [Winter 1993] 209–217). All this activity is clear indication of Merton's growing appeal.

Still more international activity is evident from Asia to South America. An article about some of Merton's interest in Spanish language writers was published in a Japanese publication: "Lo español en Merton" appeared in *Sapientia, The Eichi University Review* (Osaka) about Merton's Spanish language interests (no. 28, February 1994). Still other evidence of a continuing interest in Merton is reflected in a collection of his writings produced in Argentina in 1993, *Hermana American*, with a reprinted preface by Ernesto Cardenal and a new essay by the compiler Miguel Grinberg. Still other publications have recently appeared in Sweden, Germany, and England. Kurt Remele's "Prophetischer Radikalismus und seine Kritiker" (*Stimmen Der Zeit, Marz 1994, Band 212*) is an overview of the Berrigan brothers' activities with some mention of Merton's relationship to them. Catharine Stenqvist's "Thomas Merton and his view on Contemplation" (*Studies in Spirituality*, 3/1993) provides an overview of Merton's views about contemplation, most notably Zen Buddhism. Paul Pearson, from England, published an article in *Hallel*, an Irish publication, "Celtic Monasticism as a Metaphor for Thomas Merton's Journey" (vol. 19, no. 1, 1994, 50–57). Most of the international publications which I have surveyed remain fairly basic in their analysis of Merton. Pearson's competent essay (derived from an I.T.M.S. paper in 1991) is superior both as a specific analysis of parallels which Merton realized between the monastic life and *The Voyage of St. Brendan* and as a hint for Merton scholars about how they need to come to understand that Merton's journey is one that takes place on several levels—self, humanity, and God blend when one sees that reading, praying, journeying, appreciation, loving (indeed writing itself) are things done not just as an exercise for self, but as ways of being unified with others in the mystery of existence in God.

V.

In the preceding parts of this review-essay, I have suggested both assets and liabilities of Merton having written so much and the difficulties of assimilating this vast body of material. In sections II–IV I outlined recent studies about Merton and suggested that often there is more there than can be easily chewed and digested. Now I want to focus on the fifth volume of selected letters because this book, discussed earlier, *Witness to Freedom*, will be of immense value for Merton readers, just as the preceding four books of letters. But as also already suggested, as selections (often with ellipsis marks indicating an omission, and (alas) sometimes with omissions lacking any editorial signpost) these letters ultimately must be approached as reflections of Merton's immersion in the process of thinking things through. The following remarks about the complexity of Merton's letter writing would, I hope, apply to the limitations in using all the other letters collected in the preceding four selected letters volumes.

Shannon's excellent rubric of "crisis" is effective as an organizational device. Many types of crisis are readily apparent throughout these letters. Clearly one of the most important set of questions which Merton continued to face once he knew this was part of his responsibility was to face the dilemma of the Church's position concerning war. For Merton, of course, this meant that he had to work out a position for himself, and that required lots of words. Merton saw this as his opportunity to speak, but there are many difficulties too.

In the early 1960s the possibility of war was one of Merton's key concerns. And, for William Shannon who has edited still another book, *Passion for Peace*, which makes available most of Merton's writings about peace and war, this is also clearly the case. Probably this is one reason why all of the "Cold War Letters" are listed chronologically within the fifth volume, and therefore all can be easily located as they appear in the preceding four books. We hope that the new volume contains the complete "Cold War Letters" with no omissions. My cursory survey of Merton's bound mimeographed (unpublished) Cold War Letters reveals that in *Witness to Freedom* some significant omissions are made, sometimes with ellipsis and sometimes with no indications of an editorial change. (Why were not these letters included as a group in the original plans for selected letters?)

Witness to Freedom is much more than a collection of letters about peace and war, however, and just as the preceding four books of correspondence edited under the supervision of William Shannon, it covers a wide range of issues which radiate outward. This fifth book of selected letters therefore reflects Merton's ability to keep asking questions about a whole range of questions, from the nature of art to questions about vocation, about language abuse, as well as peace, etc. There are, as I said earlier, no easy answers. What is obvious is that there is much to be pursued while Merton insists there will be no quick answers. He ponders wisdom with his fellow artist Victor Hammer:

> I have not rushed to reply . . . because it is most difficult to write anything that really makes sense about *this* most mysterious reality . . . the mystery of God—Hagia Sophia [Holy Wisdom]. The first thing to be said, of course, is that Hagia Sophia is God Himself. God is not only a Father but a Mother. He is both at the same-time, and it is the "feminine aspect" or "feminine principle" in the divinity that is the Hagia Sophia. But of course as soon as you say this the whole thing becomes misleading: a division of an "abstract" divinity into two abstract principles. Nevertheless, to ignore this distinction is to lose touch with the fullness of God. This is a very ancient intuition of reality which goes back to the oldest Oriental thought (4).

Here is the record of a monk/artist who will not stop thinking about the difficulty of expressing the most fundamental ideas about the mystery of God. He must therefore be cautious. Yet almost simultaneously he can pen other letters which reflect not particulars about theory, art, and theology, but his growing conviction that modern humankind has gone radically astray. In May 1962 he writes:

> More and more I see that it is not the moral principles which are at stake, but, more radically, the whole outlook of modern man,

at least in America, and the basic assumptions which tend to guide
his thought, if it can be called thought. We are living in an absurd
dream, and a very bad one. And it is the fruit of all sorts of things
we ought not to have done. But the whole world is in turmoil,
spiritually, morally, socially. We are sitting on a thin crust above
an immense lake of molten lava that is stirring and getting ready
to erupt. Nothing will stop this eruption. But at least we can re-
frain from setting off bombs that will start it in some far worse way
than it normally would (7).

His statement reflects an extreme urgency which he often felt as he
announced the turmoil which was part of the entire culture. This is
from that group of letters he called "Cold War Letters" and which were
circulated in mimeographed form.

Shannon's inclusion of Merton's "Preface" to these letters establishes the context for what follows throughout the volume. (The
other Cold War letters, as noted, are also listed.) Merton's sense of
urgency is quite strong:

The protest in these letters is not, however, merely against the danger or the horror of war. It is not dictated by the fear that few lives
might be lost, or that property might be destroyed, or even that
millions of lives might be lost and civilization itself destroyed. The
protest is not merely against physical destruction, still less against
physical danger, but against a suicidal moral evil and a total lack
of ethics and rationality with which international policies tend to
be conducted (20–21).

We look forward to a single collection which will pull all these letters
together with *no* omissions because Merton's urgency makes this group
interesting as cultural commentary.

In Merton's view, humankind in the 1960s was standing at the
edge of an abyss: Merton's call is for repentance, yet because he is capable of saying this in so many ways his words vary immensely according to circumstance. Thus, in December 1961:

. . . repentance means something far deeper than we have sus-
pected: it can no longer be a matter of setting things right according to the norms of our own small group, the immediate society
in which we live. We have to open our hearts to a universal and
all-embracing love that knows no limits and no obstacles, a love
that is not scandalized by the sinner, a love that takes upon itself

the sins of the world. There must be total love of all, even of the most distant, even of the most hostile. Without the gift of the Holy Spirit this is mere idealism, mere dreaming (23).

But this is also quite an opportunity. Other opportunities reveal themselves throughout the collection. In January 1963, he writes about his obligation, to a fellow priest, the Jesuit, John Ford:

> . . . I am obliged, out of fidelity to Our Lord and to my priestly and religious vocation, to state very definitely some alternative to this awful passivity and lotus-eating irresponsibility which, in the end, delivers us all over bound hand and foot into the power of political forces that know nothing of God and morality, whether natural or divine. Sure, the theologians are divided, and the bishops rely on the theologians. But can't the theologians and the bishops say something? (29–30)

Which is to say, he, the monk/artist will speak. In May of the same year, with a large degree of irony, he writes to Justus George Lawler:

> I am in trouble with my own book about peace. It appears that the Higher Superiors have suddenly decided that my writing about peace "falsifies the monastic message." Can you imagine that?. . . . Let our ears not be contaminated with any news of what is happening. Let us go up in radioactive dust still blissfully imagining it is the twelfth century and that St. Bernard is roving up and down the highways and byways of old France preaching the crusade to troubadours and occasional jolly goliards, but not too jolly, it would falsify a message. Monks must preach to the birds, for the birds, and only for the birds (50–51).

He realizes his role is a limited one, but he also knows that by thinking things through, and continually writing, eventually he may be preaching for more than "the birds." Little by little the truth must be exposed.

Thus he keeps on addressing many issues. The following comment leads into an extremely perceptive comment about the feminine and false images. In June 1962 he writes to Valeria Delacorte:

> The crisis of the world is, for one thing, a crisis of falsity. The enormous lies by which we live have reached a point of such obvious contradiction with the truth that everything is contradiction and absurdity (52).

In each of the four instances quoted it is as if we have a totally different writer. Merton adapts himself and the tone of his letter to the particular recipient and the circumstances of his relationship with that person. Sometimes severe, and sometimes witty, he can play many different roles. Keeping all those roles sorted out becomes a big job for the reader.

Often Merton's Cold War documents allowed him to move beyond concerns only about the dangers of war. It is especially significant to note that his "Postscript" for these letters was written to Rachel Carson, who anticipated much of the present ecological crisis. He wrote her on January 12, 1963:

> Man's vocation was to be in this cosmic creation, so to speak, as the eye in the body. What I say now is a religious, not a scientific statement. That is to say, man is at once a part of nature and he transcends it. In maintaining this delicate balance, he must make use of nature wisely, and understand his position, ultimately relating both himself and visible nature to the invisible—in my terms, to the Creator, in any case, to the source and exemplar of all being and all life.
>
> But man has lost his "sight" and is blundering around aimlessly in the midst of the wonderful works of God (71).

It is also important to note, however, that while he was urgently writing such letters Merton remained hopeful in the midst of perceptions of a world in crisis. He frequently stresses the interconnectedness of world issues and each person's individual responsibility. This is probably the chief reason why he wrote so many letters.

One of the most significant themes throughout these letters is the need for individuals to act. The individual, he was convinced, must assume responsibility, and for him that meant he had to keep on thinking and qualifying. Merton does this in myriads of ways: On May 15, 1961, he urges: ". . . we must purify our hearts and our faith, seeking the will of God not in a negative resignation only, but with every hope that He may show us some positive way of action that can counteract the forces that are inexorably advancing against the Church" (77). On February 12, 1963, he leaps in:

> . . . you can quote me anytime as being wholeheartedly in favor of your plan, which seems to me to be a bold and original effort to meet the inhuman situation with some kind of human response:

with a gesture that focuses attention on the fact that what is at
stake is man and not just a lot of pompous abstractions (86).

Or, in an "Open Letter to the Hierarchy" (which he must have wanted
to be noticed), he writes:

> Let us return to our principle: the task of the Council is to affirm
> the Church's eschatological message of love and salvation in terms
> which are most relevant to the modern world (91).

He can also write (on January 17, 1963), "I am very interested now
in pushing forward the study of the more positive aspects of the question of peace—i.e., the theological bases of non-violence and of a social action based on redemptive love" (97).

Related to this unceasing conviction that individual responsibility
is a key are Merton's frequent reflections about still another type of
crisis—his personal reactions about his own life—which are reflected
in all kinds of ways throughout the majority of these letters. Above
all, Merton learned to face his own ambivalence, doubts, needs. There
are numerous excellent reflections of this tendency which demonstrated
his rethinking: In 1956 he can comment on the complexity of his life,
one at that time filled with disappointments, yet also later qualified
by his recognitions of his continuing need to write and qualify, to accept and celebrate. This letter is quite direct and honest:

> The bitterness in me comes from the fact that I have at last opened
> up the area in which it is impossible not to notice that in all this
> solitude business and in my other outbursts of idealism I have been
> reliving all the brat experiences of my childhood, magnified and
> adorned (131).

Earlier (1954) he could carefully qualify his 1930s remembrances of his
school recollections of Oakham. He insists the situation was much more
complex than revealed in his autobiography. He writes:

> . . . I am glad to be able to tell someone at Oakham that I really
> bear the school a deep affection, with sentiments of gratitude that
> will not die. I know that what I wrote about the school in my book
> was perhaps not flattering. But I am sure readers will have seen
> that I was not trying to describe the school objectively, but rather
> the state of my own mind there (155).

Letter by letter it becomes a matter of rethinking and qualifying and doing so to encourage others.

The monastic vocation he had settled into was worth pursuing, yet for others and for himself he had to keep asking questions. To a Carmelite nun he writes in 1952: "Do not feel that you have to wait until you find an ideal Carmel. There is nothing ideal on this earth. When I came to Gethsemani I knew it was only going to be partly what I 'wanted,' but I found God here anyway" (178). (Why isn't this letter in vol. 3?) Or he can write about his own situation in 1959, stressing that he has an obligation to his community: "Meanwhile I have modified my hopes and ideas by renouncing as impractical the thought of starting something among Indians. Whatever I do will have to have a clearly monastic stamp on it, one way or another, otherwise people just would not understand it" (205).

We learn that as early as 1947, he was writing notes and letters about the nature of contemplation: ". . . do we need a different system of contemplation (a different method of disposing ourselves for infused c[ontemplation]?" "In all the contemp. orders . . . spiritualities are all very much the same with only very minor differences. The problems are all the same: prayer based on the Presence of God, and kept as simple as possible, constant return to God's presence, . . ." (235), he asserts rather dogmatically.

However, by 1965 we have a different writer, and a far less dogmatic one, for now he knows he is not an authority:

> At the moment I am trying not to be an authority on everything, so I am becoming silent on a lot of things I spoke of before and not speaking of new ones. I am getting out of anything that savors of politics, and I don't want to start talking about marriage since in any case I am not married and what I know of sexual love goes back to a rather selfish period of my life when I was thinking of getting and not giving. I am not qualified to speak on this subject, but I recognize your rightness, especially the excellent point about the imaginary woman replacing the concrete flesh-and-blood ones. This is really the key to the whole thing (248).

Clearly *Witness to Freedom* is a gold mine. Honest questions abound. Many sides of Merton are reflected. Many crises. But not all the crises are major ones. Humor is also important. Sometimes his job is simply to entertain. As he is contemplating his Asian trip he can question (August 3, 1968) where the money is to come from for such extravagance!

> I do have one little problem: that of raising some money to pay for the extra leg of my journey. My monastic rules don't allow me much freedom in going around giving talks, especially here. Exceptions are the benevolence of a few generous souls to help out. If you have any other ideas I would be happy to hear them. I am utterly innocent in the methods of getting money from foundations. I can always borrow on a future book (257).

Such money concerns are not for selfish reasons. At this point Merton seems almost like an "operator," but he is interested in making connections, religious and ecumenical, so that he can continue to make still more connections.

Taking any of these letters out of context for a book, or (much worse) for a review-essay such as this, makes it difficult to see the whole man and the total picture. I have quoted frequently to suggest the complexity of the volume and the enormous difficulties which the editor must have experienced as he made these selections from times of crisis. Merton keeps asking and planning and pondering, and wondering, and adjusting. We come along and read a letter or so, and think that we have an answer. Only partial answers are revealed. More complexities become apparent. He will write (June 6, 1959) that

> it is true that there is a certain nobility in fighting for what we already have, because if we fail to do this we do not really have it. But it is best to remember that we already have it and that everything does not depend on the fighting. It is the great mystery of grace. Not grace in the sense of a kind of theological gasoline that you get by performing virtuous actions (that is the sin we commit!), but grace in the fact that God has given Himself completely to us already. Completely. But we have to enter into the darkness of His presence (261).

In other words, don't worry. Everything we have is already here.

A wonderful letter to Louis Massignon says this differently. It demands quotation and comment:

> Louis, one thing strikes me and moves most of all. It is the idea of the *point vierge, ou le désespoir accule le coeur de l'excommunié* ["the virginal point, the center of the soul, where despair corners the

heart of the outsider"]. What a very fine analysis, and how true. We in our turn have to reach that same *point vierge* in a kind of despair at the hypocrisy of our own world. It is dawning more and more on me that I have been caught in civilization as in a kind of spider's web, and I am beginning to say "No" louder and louder, though surrounded by the solicitude of those who ask me why I do so (278).

Here it is also a matter, perhaps, of translation: Should this word *accule* be translated differently? Is this a rather prudish rendering? Should *l'excommunié* be translated "excommunicated"? Are there other places where other languages need to be more carefully translated? Is this the case for Merton essays, poems, and books translated into other languages? The important thing is that much can be inferred from this one enthusiastic comment to Massignon. It is perhaps the genesis of the basic organization of the volume *Conjectures of a Guilty Bystander*. It is a wonderful example of Merton's continual thinking things through.

What all these letters demonstrate is a writer who can both realize the fact of continual crisis *and* continual opportunity. He realizes when we do have a responsibility to act, yet he frequently reminds readers that they are where they should be in relation to God. Yet we continue to act strangely. He keeps wondering why it should be that humankind should act so oddly:

> We are living in a condition of endemic self-contradiction and frustration which is extremely dangerous, because each new move, each new spasm that goes through the Body of the Church makes us momentarily hope and imagine that we have not stifled the Holy Spirit: but then we discover, once again, or are in danger of discovering that we really have. (His voice, after all, is not easy to silence.) Then a new and more violent spasm becomes necessary, lest we hear Him and live (291).

And if this is the case, then it seems to Merton that

> there is a most awful problem in this rootedness of the Church in permitted social structures and traditions, and the inevitability with which even in the best of moods and intentions we all fall back into a bland bourgeois stupor of self-congratulation and inertia. Even a lot of the activity has a character of inertia about it, it is so crude and so futile (308).

These 1963 and 1964 letters make it quite clear that for Merton contemporary culture is in a time of crisis and that the Church is part of the total mess. My point, and Merton's, is that it never becomes a matter of hopelessness. Thus he can say of the new *Constitution on the Church in the Modern World*, on August 30, 1966:

> The situation of man today is one of dreadful crisis. We are in full revolution, but it is not the simple, straightforward old-fashioned political revolution. It is a far-reaching, uncontrolled, and largely unconscious revolution pervading every sphere of his existence and often developing new critical tendencies before anyone realizes what is happening. Now, I think that the Constitution, though it does vaguely recognize this, does not say enough to underline the real seriousness of the situation. . . .

Yet he will immediately qualify:

> On the other hand I do not feel, as some do that the Constitution should simply have admitted frankly that the future promises little more than apocalyptic horror (316).

If we had unlimited time and space for analysis, similar patterns of crisis and hopefulness could be isolated and outlined from throughout all of the five volumes of correspondence now published.

What is needed is a way to study *all* of Merton's letters. We need to know what has been omitted; what other letters exist; the order in which all of them were composed, etc. To whom, for example, is Merton writing day-by-day and week-by-week? Such comprehensive studies might reveal paradoxically that the more he wrote—the more analytical and critical *and* hopeful he became, aware both of the complexity of a world in crisis and opportunities in that world—he also became more aware of a God whose mercy will not be easily explained.

VI.

As has been demonstrated with the preceding analysis of some 1994 publications by and about Merton, and especially in the diversity reflected in volume 5 of the selected correspondence, we keep getting glimpses of a Merton-in-process. We will need far more details for future study and better ways of putting together the pieces. There is no doubt that more and more primary material will appear. For the time being we will have to be patient.

In 1995 Orbis Books brought out a book of letters exchanged between Merton and Rosemary Ruether. Another large book of letters between Merton and his publisher, Jay Laughlin, is also scheduled to appear in the near future. Other correspondents, such as Jacques Maritain, and Jean Leclercq, are candidates for volumes of complete exchanges. The letters between Merton and Ernesto Cardenal, edited for this volume of *The Merton Annual*, also are evidence that there are many big projects waiting for other editors. Letters exchanged with various abbot generals would probably make a separate and revealing volume. All this will eventually be made available and will therefore slowly help us put some of the pieces together.

A similar kind of filling out of detail is in process with the voluminous journals. In 1995 the first of the complete journals of Thomas Merton (1939–1941) appeared under the title *Run to the Mountain*. The general editor for this journal project is Brother Patrick Hart, O.C.S.O., and with a team of five additional editors who are preparing individual volumes, the complete journals will appear during the next several years under the imprint of HarperCollins. This too is a mine of information which will eventually have to be related to what we already have.

What is ironic is the fact that Merton's life was one devoted in large part (at least his hope was this!) to moving away from words. The paradox of course is that he made such gestures continually, but he always had to do this with words. Obviously as readers we are stuck with this legacy. We learn to do the same thing which Merton learned to do over and over. The complete journals will give us one more layer of this complicated person, a Merton-in-process thinking things through, so that we might do some of the same.

Other primary documents exist which will also inevitably be made available for readers. There are scores of "Working Notebooks" which are records of Merton's voracious reading and note taking. There are also many obscure articles which have not yet been collected. There are, as has been noted, thousands more letters.

What is needed is word listings and indexes, and word studies which will help us to keep track of Merton's energy. A complete index for all five volumes of the published letters would be a help to readers. A chronological listing of when letters were composed would also help.

Where is the concordance to his poetry? Indeed to all his works? Such projects would be a good start for a group of computer scholars. But, we must remember it would only be a start and to enter fully into what Merton has accomplished we will have to enter into his world *both* of prayer *and* work. We have to see all these thousands of words and letters as but hints, invitations, suggestions, opportunities. Then we will have to be quiet.

Reviews

Thomas Merton. *Witness to Freedom: Letters in Times of Crisis.*
Selected and edited with introduction by William H. Shannon. New York: Farrar, Straus, Giroux, 1994. xii + 352 pages. $25.00.

Reviewed by Douglas Burton-Christie

In 1965 as Thomas Merton was preparing to enter his hermitage on a more permanent basis, he addressed the Gethsemani community on the theme "A Life Free From Care." He spoke of his hopes for realizing within himself a genuine "transparency"—a freedom from the constraints borne of convention and fear—through which the radiant light of Christ might shine. As this fifth and final volume of Thomas Merton's letters shows, this longing freedom was neither a casual nor occasional occupation for Merton, but a passionate, life-long pursuit.

The editor William Shannon describes three stages in Merton's developing sense of freedom, each of which finds expression in this volume. During the first half of Merton's life, it meant largely the "removal of restraints that prevented him from doing what he wanted to do." The second stage in his journey to freedom began, according to Shannon, when Merton arrived at Gethsemani in 1941. This period was characterized by the monk's *outward focus*—he looked to the monastic rule and to the decisions of his superiors as a "mediated way of exercising freedom." The third stage was marked by Merton's growing sense of freedom as an "inner reality, guided much more from within than without." Realizing this kind of freedom included both struggling to rid his life of the fictions and illusions we so often live by and uncovering his true identity. And it necessarily involved him in prophetic witness.

This growth in freedom did not come easily or without a cost. One of the unfortunate things about the way Merton's story is often told is that one is left with no real sense of *how* he managed to undergo such radical change from the earlier to the later part of his life, no sense of what he had to struggle through to reach the admirable transparency of his last years. His rough edges are softened; his neurotic and compulsive tendencies are obscured; the immense *uncertainty* that plagued him at crucial moments of his life is ignored. This is perhaps a natural tendency of the "canonization" process, official or unofficial. It is, however, unfortunate. For in the process, we lose the sense of what it involved for Merton to enter into the crucible—of his own life and the times in which he lived—and emerge on the other side, bruised, scarred but also purified, free. We should be thankful for these letters, for they reveal Merton's journey toward freedom in all its particularity and help us see how much it cost him personally to arrive at the profound integration of his later life. They also remind us how willingly he entered into the struggles of others who were striving to realize freedom in their own lives.

A brief word about the content and organization of this volume: it is organized under four major headings—Art and Freedom, War and Freedom, Merton's Life and Works, and Religious Thought and Dialogue. These are broad categories that attempt, with only partial success, to give order to the letters within. This is probably the most varied and least thematically coherent collection of letters in the series, and it is difficult to imagine how it could have been organized any differently. Still, the reader should recognize that this final volume presents particular challenges: one is compelled to travel back and forth across significant stretches of time, and read letters that are grouped in a variety of ways—by chronology, by correspondent, by theme. This volume in a sense catches up all the loose ends of Merton's correspondence.

There is something positive to be said about this profusion of letters on every conceivable topic: one sees clearly just how capacious Merton's interests were and how much effort he was willing to expend to cultivate friendships or answer simple queries concerning shared interests. There is a wonderful set of letters to Victor Hammer on art and spirituality; one senses from the tone of the letters that friendship and contact with this sensitive artist meant a great deal to Merton. There is a letter to Rachel Carson, the great environmental visionary, testifying to Merton's early grasp of the importance of this issue. There is a set of letters to Naomi Burton Stone, Merton's literary agent, that spans twenty years and that provides new insight into an important friendship and into the often tortured relationship Merton had with his writing. He addresses a moving series of letters to Evora Arca de Sardinia, whose husband was a victim of the Bay of Pigs invasion. He writes to religious men and women caught in the changes wrought by Vatican II and wondering what sense they might yet make out of religious life. He addresses the American bishops, urging them to take a strong stand on Schema XIII at the Second Vatican Council. There are letters to Louis Massignon and Herbert Mason on Islam (that complement those to Abdul Aziz and others found in *The Hidden Ground of Love*) that reveal Merton's clear intuitive grasp of the spiritual wisdom of Islam. There is a fierce, impassioned correspondence with Leslie Dewart on the Cold War in general and the Bay of Pigs in particular. He also answers queries on "the meaning of life," on his "formula for success," on "books that have influenced him," on "how a Catholic writer can have the greatest possible influence on his public."

Here is Merton in full sail, responding enthusiastically to the myriad questions of his correspondents, stretching himself to encompass their concerns. Three themes pertaining directly to freedom warrant a closer examination, and I will devote the remainder of the review to these: Merton's "vocation crisis," war and freedom, and what I refer to as the movement toward "freedom of spirit."

* * *

There is an interesting and revealing selection of letters in this volume that Shannon has placed under the heading: "Vocation Crisis: 1959-1960." These letters echo others from earlier in the 1950s (found in *The School of Charity*) and suggest a recurring theme in Merton's life: his struggle to find a way of living within the structures of cenobitic monasticism while honoring his own deep call to a more solitary life. The issue of freedom for Merton here was his desire to find a way of realizing his authentic vocation within what he increasingly came to perceive as the restrictive and artificial confines of communal monastic living. The letters reveal Merton's feelings of growing enmity toward cenobitic monasticism in general and Gethsemani in particular during the late 1950s, his capacity for stealth and political intrigue, and his seeming inability to find any reasonable balance on this question.

During the period covered in these letters, he attempts to find a place for himself in Nicaragua, the Virgin Islands, Reno, Nevada, and Cuernavaca, Mexico, among others. There can be no question that at this stage in his journey, Merton felt the solution to his particular vocational crisis was to leave Gethsemani. Freedom meant getting out. The issue was, for Merton, a matter of conscience. He writes to Archbishop Larraona, head of the Sacred Congregation for Religious at the Vatican, describing "the problem of conscience which seriously threatens my spiritual life and my psychological health." The source of this problem? What he refers to as his ongoing "participation in a monastic facade" (206). He puts the issue in even stronger terms in a letter to Father Jean Danielou: "It is a question of choice between a bourgeois, inert, decadent façade of monasticism, and a genuine living attempt to renew the inner spirit of monastic life" (211).

Merton does not succeed in convincing his superiors and eventually accepts their decision that he should remain at Gethsemani. But it is a decision only half-heartedly accepted by Merton. The process continues with endless stops and starts, during which time a great deal of ill-will builds up between Merton and his superiors. He accuses Dom James Fox of plotting against him in Rome, of keeping important mail from him, of "having an arbitrary and tyrannical spirit (216)." He describes his superiors as "having the self-righteous, deluded complacency of their class" (211). And he does this even while he is "accepting," "consenting" to the will of God expressed through his superiors, and expressing his enduring love for Gethsemani (215). But within a month, he is writing again to Cardinal Valeri to, in effect, restate his case. Within six months, he is writing to Archbishop Philippe, secretary to the Sacred Congregation for Religious, to officially reopen the case. None of these efforts bore any immediate fruit. It would be five years until Merton was allowed to become a hermit at Gethsemani. But the episode as a whole reveals with new clarity how fundamentally conflicted he was over the course his life should take, how hostile his negotiations with his superiors became, how erratic his own behavior could be, in short, how long and hard he struggled to realize a level of genuine freedom and authenticity in his monastic life.

* * *

The letters under the section "War and Freedom" contain the largest single collection of the "Cold War Letters" (smaller numbers of which have appeared in earlier volumes), a series of letters Merton wrote from October 1961 to October 1962 concerning issues of war and peace. Taken together with numerous other letters in this section on war and non-violent resistance, the "Cold War Letters" give us new insight into the evolution of Merton's thinking during one of the most creative and tension-filled periods of his life. Here he addresses the issue of fundamental human freedom under siege by the collectivist, materialist structures of power that dominate the contemporary world. The preface to the "Cold War Letters" sounds a note we will hear again and again, that the root of the Cold War mentality is a profound cultural and moral decay: "during the Cold War . . . this country has become frankly a warfare state built on affluence, a power structure in which the interests of big business, the obsessions of the military, and the phobias of political extremists both dominate and dictate our national policy" (20). He says, "we are living in a condition where we are afraid to see the total immorality and absurdity of total war" (22). In a postscript to the "Cold War Letters," written to Rachel Carson, Merton speaks of the profound cultural sickness at the heart of the ecological crisis: "I would almost dare to say that the sickness is perhaps a very real and dreadful hatred of life as such, of course subconscious, buried under our pitiful and superficial optimism about ourselves and our affluent society" (71).

He offers this diagnosis as a member of an ecclesial community, and he takes his ecclesial identity seriously. Yet, Merton expresses deep skepticism about the possibility of finding the necessary moral integrity and courage for resisting this decay within the Catholic Church. To John Ford he writes, "I am very deeply concerned with what seems to me to be the extreme reticence and hesitation on the part of Catholics who might take a position for peace . . ." (29). He writes to Gerald Landry about his feeling of helplessness: "not only helpless to understand God's designs in allowing his Church to become so completely implicated in the motives and ideals of the secular world, and its obsessions (some of which are pathological), but helpless to know what we should do about it ourselves" (44).

The struggle to speak out against what he perceived to be a great moral evil appears to have affected Merton on a deep level. Writing to Edward Deming Andrews, he speaks of "the ghastly feeling that we are all on the brink of spiritual defection and betrayal of Christ" (25). To Archbishop Thomas Robert, Merton says: "this is . . . to me a shattering and totally disconcerting question [that] . . . reaches down into the very foundations of my life" (24). Writing to Clare Booth Luce in December 1961, he speaks of the past Christmas as having been "the darkest in my life" (25). Nor is this sense of desolation merely personal. It is theological, even cosmological. Merton writes to Rabbi Steven Schwarzschild of "God's absence . . . His loneliness, His lostness among us . . . He waits among us unknown and silent, patiently, for the moment when we will finally destroy Him utterly in His image . . . And leave Him alone again in the empty cosmos" (36).

We also hear in these letters more positive, hopeful notes, attempts to respond constructively to these grave threats and give voice to the sources of hope. He writes to Stephen James, whose peace hostage program Merton supported as being "a bold and original effort to meet the inhuman situation with some kind of human response" (87). In an open letter to the Catholic bishops who were about to deliberate on Schema XIII at the Second Vatican Council, Merton urges them "to bear witness clearly and without any confusion to the Church's belief in the power of love to save and transform not only individuals but society." He asks: "Do we or do we not believe that love has this power? If we believe it, what point is there in splitting hairs about the superior morality of killing a thousand defenseless noncombatants rather than a million?" (92). And to Barbara Hubbard, he speaks of the necessity of highlighting the "religious dimension" to the current thinking about the massive death wish pervading society. The religious dimension, he says, shows itself in "radical self-criticism and openness and a profound ability to *trust* not only in our chances of a winning gamble, but in an inner dynamism of life itself, a basic creativity, a power of life to win over entropy and death" (73). This section of *Witness to Freedom* gives new depth and texture to our understanding of Merton's commitment to justice and of his acute diagnosis of the pervasive social, cultural religious malaise pervading American life in the early 1960s.

* * *

Another expression of Merton's growing sense of freedom seen in this collection of letters is the transition from an early, more structured, devotional form of piety, to a more profound, expansive, integrative, encompassing sense of the spiritual life. Freedom here is expressed through Merton's insistence on the need to throw off unnecessary structures and systems in religious life and in the Church in order to pursue God and the true self with naked honesty. Writing to Sister Anita Wasserman, a Carmelite, in 1952, one senses already Merton's intuitive vision of contemplative simplicity, a vision that would deepen in later years: "Do you really think that you will find Jesus in Carmel? Then go. What you are looking for is Jesus, and He is hidden. You are not just looking for an interesting life with him: you are looking for Him. To find Him is to be hidden even from oneself" (178). To a religious who is striving to uncover within herself and her community an authentic spirituality, in spite of the difficulties presented by formal religious life, Merton counsels simplicity. One should "teach people to seek continual, conscious awareness of God . . . continual openness to God, attentiveness, listening, disposability, etc. In terms of Zen, it is not awareness of but simple awareness" (197).

Stripping away the external, the superficial, the unnecessary—this is what Merton seeks for himself and for others. Merton concurs with Sister Maria Blanca Olim, who writes to him about her concerns about overactivity in Benedictine monasticism, that this is indeed a serious threat to the whole monastic enterprise. Monastic communities need to take care not to disregard what is after all the primary motivation (especially among the young) for those entering monastic life: "a great desire for freedom, simplicity, spontaneity, true poverty, authenticity in everything, and the total absence of formality and pretense" (198). To Fr. David Kirk, he writes of the need to focus on that which is essential in the spiritual life—life itself: "What is badly, urgently wanted is *life* and not this frozen, living death formula for 'perfection' in which all vital development is forcible crushed and negated from the very start" (307). It is consistent with Merton's lifelong attraction to the apophatic way, the way of emptiness, that he seeks the heart of life by simplifying, uncluttering. In this spirit, he counsels another religious that: "There is a certain value in just disciplining oneself to be 'empty' and to spend a certain time *doing nothing*" (199).

One sees in these letters how Merton's increasing capacity to encounter God in naked unknowing bore fruit in a spirit of genuine spontaneity and freedom. The spirituality of his later years is marked by this unerring sense of God's hidden presence in the heart of *life*. A man named John Brooks, writing a book on the habits of successful persons, asks Merton about his "formula for success." Merton senses the irony inherent in the question, but responds sincerely of his quest for truth: "My 'formula for success' actually has no bearing on success itself. My aim in life is to live as I think I was created to live: in truth, in simplicity with all my attention devoted to what is higher and greater than I: the God I serve and the world of man I believe he redeemed" (253). To Robert Menchin, who writes to him in 1966 asking for advice on making career changes, Merton offers this: "In all the changes we make in life, we should decide . . . in view of becoming *more* real, entering more authentically into direct contact with life, living more as a free and mature human person, able to give myself more to others, able to understand myself and the world better" (255).

* * *

This is the voice of a person who has himself reached a place of profound freedom, who has developed a keen sense of God's vital presence in the ordinary, and who bears witness to the enormous power of such freedom for a world snared in a web of fear and evasion. One of the most impressive things about Merton's witness to freedom is that he was able to bear witness even when he could not see clearly himself. Here we see two prominent themes in Merton's life—darkness and freedom—converge.

In a letter written to Herbert Mason in 1959, during the period when Merton was in the throes of his vocational crisis, he expresses his gratitude for the presence of grace in his life—"the fact that God has given Himself completely to us already. Completely. But we have to enter into the darkness of His presence. Not tragic darkness, just ordinariness: but above all what does not appear to be religion" (262). And a few months later: "When it is dark, it is dark and you go in the dark as if it were light. *Nox illuminatio mea*. The darkness is our light and that is all. The light remains, simply, our everyday mind, such as it is, floating on a sea of darkness which we do not have to observe. But it carries us with great power. It is the being carried that is, actually, its light. Float then. And trust the winds of God, which you do not see either, but they are cool" (263). Freedom then, is realized only in darkness, only in abandoning every support that is less than God. In that darkness one is carried, endlessly, effortlessly on the cool winds of God. This is the heart of Merton's enduring witness to freedom.

Thomas Merton and Robert Lax. *A Catch of Anti-Letters.* Foreword by Br. Patrick Hart. Kansas City: Sheed and Ward, 1994. 128 pages. $9.95.

Reviewed by Erlinda G. Paguio

In an interview Robert Lax gave to Paul Wilkes for a film on Thomas Merton, Lax remembers the certainty of his friendship with Merton from the moment they met in 1936 while working as editors of Columbia University's *Jester.*

A small collection of "A Catch of Anti-letters" first appeared in a short-lived literary journal called *Voyages.* When it was published as a book in 1978, some reviewers considered it as nothing more than just the record of two friends enjoying themselves in correspondence. Its reprinting in 1994 is a timely and welcome complement to the five-volume collection of Merton's letters published within the last ten years. This collection of correspondence between Merton and Lax differs from the others because Merton himself selected and edited them a year before his accidental death in December 1968. They are anti-letters because both friends deliberately discard all the formalities of letter writing while engaged in a lively and humorous exchange of ideas and experiences. Merton was a monk at the Abbey of Gethsemani while Lax was in self-imposed exile in Greece.

They address each other in many ways, some of which are familiar only to themselves. Merton greets Lax with "Dear Waldo," "Ho Lexos," "Cher Monty," "Dear Most," etc. Lax is equally endearing in his salutation: "Dear Captain Thurston," "Dear Arthur," "Dear Zwow," "Dear Hoopsaboy," etc. Imaginative are the ways in which they end their letters. Merton closes with: "Yrs. Demosthenes," "Yr. pal Cassidy," etc. Lax often uses "yrs, Sam," but will also sign "yrs. Lycourges," or "yrs. Tiger," etc.

Although they continuously write run-on sentences, consciously forget all the rules of grammar, punctuation, spelling and syntax, their repartee is captivating, especially when they pun. Mt. Athos becomes "Mt. Arthur." A Guggenheim fellowship is a "Guggenhappy fellowspot." Erich Fromm is "erich up" and "erich of." St. John of the Cross is "St. John of the Crux," and Albert Camus degenerates into "Albert Camels."

They appear to be joking all the time, but they are truly two wise and concerned men. Mark Van Doren, their teacher and friend, referred to Merton as his mirthful student, his merry friend, who was utterly serious and utterly free. He described Lax as one who could not state his bliss, which is his love for the world and everyone and everything in it. In one letter Lax describes for Merton the blue rooms he occupied in Kalymnos. He notes that over his bed was a box full of icons which could easily fall over him with the slightest tremor. "i am only telling you this. but i have the consolations of a solitary life. i stay in my cell and it becomes sweet" (47). Merton shares his solitary life, too: "The secret of the hermit life is that it remove the foundations and take away the building and there is no roof left and one float down the stream like a chip in the waters" (68).

His living among Greek Orthodox Christians led Lax to raise the question of who was right and who was wrong. Merton's reply was not theology, but a combination of wit, simplicity, and common sense: "Between us and them is no difference of faith, is no difference. . . . Difference between us and them is politics, chum. . . . Let the politicians figure it out. . . . It is to my mind that in the Holy Ghost and in Christ we are one and as for the visibility it is now obscure. I do not wish to explain to the guys how it is we are one because I don't know. Each one has to sit in his hutch and do his best . . ." (40–41).

Included in this book are some of their poems and Merton's calligraphies. Lax is most impressed by "Night-flowering cactus" which he considers as "some one hell of a poem." The following lines evoke the pristine character of the true self in *The Inner Experience:*

Though I show my true self in the dark and to no man
(For I appear by day as serpent)
I belong neither to night nor day (13).

The imagery of "a white cavern without explanation" recalls the mystical experience of the Bride in *The Spiritual Canticle* and *The Living Flame of Love* of St. John of the Cross.

The short poem "Seneca" which Lax appreciated immensely, portrays the Roman philosopher Seneca as the exterior self and his wife as the inner self. While he promenades within his own temple, "policing the streets of this secret Rome," his wife listens:

> While the wife
> Silent as a sea
> Policing nothing
> Waits in darkness
> For the Night Bird's
> Inscrutable cry (21).

Lax considered this a great poem because of the unity of the words and the music. He advised Merton to write more poems like it: "as reinhardt makes now all the time the same black painting, make you also all the time the same dark poem; all the time, just that one poem: here a word, there a word, maybe a little different; . . . the music always the same . . ." (24). He encouraged him to make more calligraphies because they helped the poems as much as the poems helped the calligraphies.

Merton sent Lax a copy of his message to the new Latin American poets meeting in Mexico City. Lax's reaction to it is profuse pleasure: "it is wow wow wow: just what the poets is needing; just what i felt i was coming to see in the graces of yesterday afternoon; that this is what poems is all about, this what every poet should know" (37–38). In the message Merton affirmed that for the poet "There is only life in all its unpredictability and all its freedom" (*Raids on the Unspeakable*, 159).

Merton appreciated Lax's experimental concrete poetry. "Your two poems is most impress" (63). He sent Lax the early version of *Cables to the Ace*. Lax thought they were very crazy cables, but moving, nevertheless, as a meaningful poem after considerable reading and re-reading.

A Catch of Anti-Letters begins in 1962 and ends in 1967. Brother Patrick Hart provides short but most useful background information in his Foreword on the friendship between Merton and Lax, and their college friends and teachers at Columbia University. Merton's poem "Western Fellow Students Salute with Calypso Anthems The Movie Career of Robert Lax" is included as an Appendix. There are references to world politics, innumerable reminiscences of their college days, health problems, as well as Merton's difficulties with the censors and his superiors. "One of the saddest facts of my factual existence is that I am in perpetual trouble with the hoodwinks and the curials . . ." (35) is condensed into "I am hailed before all the councils with a red pencil" (36).

The concluding letters in 1967 express their sorrow and loss over the death of their two close friends, Ad Reinhardt and John Slate. Merton writes: "Make mass beautiful silence like big black picture speaking requiem . . . Sorrows for Ad in the oblation quiet peace request rest" (120). Lax replies: "Oh Chauncey, . . . I sit near the sea & almost fall into it from sorrow. & then I sit (as seldom enough we do) in a church & look at the black & grey squares of the tiles, till the spirit is somewhat mended" (121). They would also mourn Slate's passing. Merton comments: "As each grows old so grows multiple the sorrow" (123). Lax laments: ". . . with passing of Dom John Slate is our generation all dissolved, resolved" (123).

The friendship between Merton and Lax so spontaneously expressed in the anti-letters reminds me of what John C. H. Wu wrote about two Chinese hermits, Han Shan and Shi-Te: "Even hermits have need of like-minded friends for mutual encouragement and consolation. This is what keeps them so perfectly human" (*The Golden Age of Zen*, 279). Brother Hart's description of Merton and Lax as "two supremely free men, free 'with the liberty of the children of God' " is most appropriate.

When Lax was asked how he felt when Merton died, he said: "In specific ways, I certainly felt I'd lost a correspondent; if I had something funny I wanted to tell him about it would be a little more different now . . ." (*Merton By Those Who Knew Him Best*, 74). He said it was one thing to feel that Merton had moved on to another stage and to feel that it was the right time for it. It was another to know that one couldn't drop a letter to Merton anymore.

The book is an entertaining testament of two poets, lifelong friends living life with all its unpredictability and freedom!

Robert G. Waldron. *Thomas Merton in Search of His Soul: A Jungian Perspective*. Notre Dame, Indiana: Ave Maria Press, 1994. 157 pages. $7.95.

Reviewed by Joann Wolski Conn

Robert G. Waldron, whose master's degrees are in English and education, was inspired by years of reading Merton and Jung to view Merton's life as identical to Jung's paradigm of individuation (9). His book uses Jung's analytical psychology to explain the phases of Merton's interior journey.

Waldron's "Jungian Commentary" (9) on Merton's life begins by interpreting Merton's life up to his late thirties as an encounter with his shadow. Whereas Jung defines shadow generically as those aspects of ourselves we would rather not face, Waldron uses this term primarily as synonymous with evil or sin (23) and views Merton's father's death as a wounding of the personality that initiated Merton's entry upon the inner journey to his center, his Self, in which Merton was revolted by what he saw within. Waldron not only identifies Merton's inner journey with Jung's psychological paradigm of individuation but also identifies Merton's faith-journey during this period with Jung's religious vocabulary and assumptions. For example, Waldron judges that "Merton would eventually realize that the ego is not the center of the psyche but the Self which is the Christ, a realization that would lead him into the Catholic church" (35). That is, Merton's conversion to Catholicism is interpreted as manifestation of his inward face, which Jung calls the anima, "the eternal image of the woman . . . an imprint or archetype of all the ancestral experiences of the female, a deposit . . . of all the impressions ever made by woman" (53). According to Waldron, Merton's conversion meant "He had finally found a worthy recipient for his anima projection, Holy Mother Church. . . . His conversion solved his anima problem by finding a bride in the church and by temporarily silencing his shadow" (59). Waldron mentions no other source for this conversion; there is not even an allusion to transcendent grace beyond the psyche. This is one example of the way Waldron consistently adopts one position in an ongoing scholarly debate about Jung's view of Christianity without ever acknowledging that there is a debate or why he prefers the position that he adopts within the debate. I will return to this controversy later.

Merton's struggles in the time between entering Gethsemani (1941) and the early 1950s are seen in terms of a "false self and true self," terms that occur both in Merton and Jung. Waldron assumes that Merton's explanation of a "false self" (*Waters of Siloe*, 349), or the ego that we tend to worship in place of God, corresponds exactly to Jung's belief that in the first stages of individuation the ego considers itself the center of the psyche rather than the Self, which Jung claims is the God within (72). *The Sign of Jonas* reveals Merton beginning to face and accept his shadow, thus opening the way for integration of "the masterpiece of individuation," his anima, which is the theme of Waldron's second part.

A transitional chapter on "Fire Watch" (Epilogue to *The Sign of Jonas*) aims to be a summary of Merton's first phase of individuation. Here Waldron uses Merton to explain Jung's paradigm at least as much as he uses Jung to explain Merton.

Part Two describes Merton's encounter with his anima. This confrontation, according to Waldron, resulted in two events: the "Louisville Vision" and the creation of the prose poem *Hagia Sophia* (97). Waldron links the former event directly to a dream recorded a month earlier in which Merton sees a girl named Proverb (his anima). Merton's Louisville Vision, in which he embraces the human race, "is certainly the result of Merton's embrace of the feminine component of his own personality symbolized in his Proverb dream" (103). The second event is Merton's emotional response to Victor Hammer's painting of a woman crowning a young man. Merton, unconsciously recognizing in these images his own encounter with his anima (106), creates the prose poem *Hagia Sophia*. Waldron interprets it by completely identifying Merton's words "Sister" and "Hagia Sophia" with Jung's term anima, claiming "The Sister (from now on referred to as Anima) is Merton's anima who rises from the depths of the unconscious . . ." (107). "Hagia Sophia is Anima. Anima is Holy Wisdom who invites Merton and all men . . . to live" (108). Waldron explicates Merton's romantic involvement with a nurse, whom the biographer Mott calls S., as Merton's projection of his anima onto a woman (114), and notes that psychically it was probably the best thing that could have happened to him. Why was it best? According to Waldron, because Mary, the Mother of God, is theoretically the only acceptable recipient of all Cistercian monks' anima projections but cannot be the recipient of instinctual longings for all celibate monks (115). This ineffectiveness helps us "understand why so many men fail to take final vows as monks" (115). Waldron's response to this insufficiency is approval of monks' "contact with women who will assist them in getting in touch with the feminine within themselves. Permitting retreats for women at Gethsemani, as is now done, was a bold but wise decision" (115).

The book concludes with a chapter titled "Merton and Jung: Contrasts and Parallels" in which Waldron juxtaposes quotes from each man without context or comment. Again, this reveals Waldron's assumption that the identification between Merton and Jung is self-evident.

For this reviewer, two problems pervade Waldron's book. One is Waldron's uncritical reading of Jung's notion of anima. Most problematic, however, is Waldron's use of Jung's psychology to explain Merton's individuation without giving any critical attention to Jung's assumptions about Christianity. My objection cannot be met by the reply that Waldron's aim is psychological, therefore he need not deal with theological issues. The crux of the matter is whether Waldron can fairly claim Merton's life is identical to Jung's paradigm of individuation (9) without acknowledging how individuation is intrinsically related to Jung's view of Christianity, and at least note the fact that there is a serious debate about the difference between Jung and traditional Christianity. Moreover, in a book that claims Merton's and Jung's search is the same (14), I believe the author owes his readers an explanation of this debate and supporting reasons for his stance in this controversy.

Waldron's position is evident in the way he immediately substitutes anima for Wisdom in his quotations from "Hagia Sophia" and his lack of even the slightest attention to the fact that in Christian tradition Wisdom is a complex symbol associated with Mary and with female characteristics of God. To interpret Merton's poem simply as a meditation upon his anima is to assume the adequacy of the position in the Jung-and-Christianity controversy which claims that all words about Christian experience are and remain completely psychological and that faith does not refer to radical self-transcendence. (On the debate and this position, see Murray Stein, "C. G. Jung, Psychologist and Theologian," in R. L. Moore and D. J. Meckel, eds. *Jung and Christianity in Dialogue* [New York: Paulist, 1990], especially Stein's references to Robert Doran, *Subject and Psyche: Ricoeur, Jung, and the Search for Foundations* [Lanham, MD: University Press of America,

1977]). By interpreting Merton's Christian conversion simply as a projection of his anima (59), I believe Waldron exemplifies his assumption of the adequacy of the view that Jung's psychology is simply a
restatement in psychological terms of the principal tenets of Christian
faith. Waldron emphasizes how Jung, "raised in a Christian family . . .
understood the intrinsic value of religion . . . [and] incorporates religion [in his analytic psychology]" (14). Waldron pays no attention
either to the massive evidence which supports Jung's lifelong struggle
to repudiate Christianity's oppressive claims on his life, or to the ways
in which Jung's interpretation of Christianity was very different from
Christianity's own self-interpretation, an interpretation which was central to Merton's own identity as a Christian monk. (See Peter Homans,
"C. G. Jung: Christian or Post-Christian Psychologist?" in *Jung and
Christianity in Dialogue*: 21–37, especially 23–24.)

A second problem is Waldron's assuming the adequacy of a
standard, uncritical reading of Jung's notion of anima. For Waldron,
following Jung, "the feminine" is a projection within male ego development without reference to this image's social conditioning. In this view,
a male's psychic development is promoted by being able to project his
anima onto a worthy object. Recall that Waldron interprets Merton's
conversion to Holy Mother Church as just such a projection and temporary "solving of his anima problem" (59). There is no mention of
grace or the work of God's Spirit in this conversion. The Church becomes "useful" insofar as She serves to receive this man's anima. Even
more problematic, I believe, is Waldron's view of monks' need to associate with women. This contact, he remarks, will enable these men
to get in touch with the feminine in themselves (115). That is, women
will serve men's development. There is no mention of women's own
gifts seen, for example, in the contribution of contemplative women,
who have been invited to give conferences to the monks of Gethsemani.
Like Jung, Waldron demonstrates a very underdeveloped awareness
of actual women beyond their ability to serve men's needs. This is a
clear example of why feminists find Jung so problematic (see, for example, Naomi R. Goldenberg, "A Feminist Critique of Jung," *Signs*,
2/2 [1976] 443–49).

In short, this book so oversimplifies both Jung and Merton that
I believe it offers no significant contribution to understanding Merton
or spiritual development.

Wendell Berry. *Watch with Me and Six Other Stories of the Yet-Remembered Ptolemy Proudfoot and His Wife, Miss Minnie, Née Quinch.* New York: Pantheon, 1994. 211 pages. $21.00 USA/$28.95 Canada.

Reviewed by Irwin H. Streight

Watch with Me is what literary critics call a short story cycle or sequence. These stories are linked by their setting in Wendell Berry's fictional community, Port William, Kentucky—familiar to readers of Berry's fiction—and, excepting the last story, through a chronology that follows from 1908 up to World War II. Each of the "Six Other Stories" that make up Part I of the cycle was originally published separately, and the individual stories are crafted to be read on their own as well as to form part of a larger interconnected narrative.

Part I is a cycle of six stories that spans thirty years in the large-as-life lives of Ptolemy Proudfoot and his helpmate Miss Minnie. Tol, as he is called, is a farmer, as big-hearted as he is big-bodied (he weighs in at three hundred pounds). In spirit, not in body, he looks up to his petite wife Miss Minnie.

Berry's narrator takes particular relish in telling his Tol tales. The writing style is alive with the humour, loquacity and local turns of phrase of Tol himself. And the stories have a ring of truth to them, an anecdotal quality supported by a coda to every story in which the narrator confirms that he heard the story directly from Miss Minnie or another of the town folk who participated in or took an interest in the doings of the remarkable Tol Proudfoot.

The opening story "A Consent" is told with the engaging humour and overstated action of a good tall tale. We watch Tol, a gentle unkempt Kentucky giant in his bid to win the affections of Miss Minnie, the local school teacher. Tol's characteristic appearance is comically described as he presents himself to Miss Minnie and the town women at the Harvest Festival at Goforth School: "his clothes were damp and wrinkled, his shirttail was out, there was horse manure on one of his shoes. His hat sat athwart his head as though left there by somebody else . . . his hair stuck up and out and every which way." But Miss Minnie loves him. His huge frame and unruly thatch of hair are to her "shelter and warmth." And when Tol smiles at her it is "as though the sun itself had looked kindly at her through the foliage of a tall tree."

The rest of the stories in Part I concern the married life of Tol and Miss Minnie in the turbulent decades of the 1920s and 30s. Their world is an American pastoral, touched yet untouched by the global cataclysms of World War I and the Great Depression. Their profoundly simple lives are punctuated by taking crops and stock to market, attending fall fairs and an occasional missionary society bakesale. The Proudfoots have "stayed home and stayed busy in the leisurely way of people who know exactly what they have to do and how to do it and have got used to doing it, and who don't have to do too much."

Yet in the seeming simpleness of their lives there is a parable to ponder. Tol and Miss Minnie possess a quiet strength rooted in communion with the land and with their neighbours, and that finds expression in their daily living out of the Greatest Commandment. Berry's trademark themes of fidelity to place, language, neighbours and God radiate throughout these tales.

Most compellingly, these stories are filled with the spirit of *hilaritas*: Berry has a gift for the comic insight as well as for telling a humourous yarn. In 1929 Tol buys a Model A, not because he wants or needs one, but as a sign of his affection for Miss Minnie, whom he senses secretly longs for an automobile. But they drive it and conceive of it as a mechanical horse and buggy—"The Trick" Tol calls it. Tol observes of the automobiles parked on Sunday morning outside Goforth Church that they are not lined up at the hitch rail, "but scattered hither and yon, not needing to be tied to anything when you were not using them." And Miss Minnie, we are informed, when riding in an automobile "always hung onto her hat with one hand even when the windows were shut."

The gentle humour rippling throughout these stories occasionally reaches a rollicking pitch. Tol is a man full of laughter, who has "broken the backs of half a dozen chairs rearing back in them to laugh." And the reader may have to be careful of the furniture as well. In "A Half-Pint of Old Darling" Miss Minnie, an ardent supporter of the WCTU in the Prohibition of the 1920s, is unwittingly intoxicated on whiskey Tol bought for medicinal use during lambing season. In "The Lost Bet" Tol plays the bumpkin to uproarious advantage in a fitting act of justice on a condescending city merchant who has belittled him and treated him as a dull-witted hayseed. The chase scene in the tale

of "Old Ant'ny and the chamber pot" told by Tol in the last of the
six stories in Part I, "Turn Back the Bed," is delightfully madcap.

Part II is comprised of a single story, the longest and title story
of the cycle. The tone of this story sets it off from the folksy celebrations of life in the other six. "Watch with Me" is an existential parable
of a human soul's blind journey through a wilderness of lonely and
confused days. In this story, Berry strongly asserts the theme that ani-
mates other of his Port William stories: the importance of a caring community that acts in love to bring its members through times of pain
and spiritual darkness.

Tol and other men of the community leave their chores and
families to follow the suicidal Nightlife Hample; they suffer hunger,
thirst and exhaustion in their desire to save him from the darkness
in his soul and his bent to self-destruction, as emblematized in his
name. This Christ-like concern of the community, aided by an Almighty
thunderstorm, eventually draws the lost and the looking under one
stable roof, where the wanderer is restored to his rightful self and to
a place within the community. The truth of the story is served in the
text of Nightlife's personal sermon in the closing pages of the book:
Matthew 18:12-14—the moral to Christ's parable of the lost sheep.
Old Fetcher—Death—Tol's rifle, with which Nightlife threatened to kill
himself, is disarmed. The women folk have prepared a "small epic"
of a meal, anticipating the hunger of their men, who have been tramp-
ing a day and a night with little to eat. The community is gathered,
a table is spread, and there is feasting and joy.

Through a "precarious interplay of effort and grace," Berry af-
firms, it can be as it will be: in this present world we can have a taste
and sight of "the larger world that lies beyond it and contains it." Echo-
ing Christ's admonishment to his disciples in the Garden at Gethse-
mane, the title *Watch with Me* presents a hopeful imperative. Berry's
seven stories offer to the postmodern reader a "yet-remembered"
re-imagining of the human community in a redemptive act of fiction.

John Dear. *Disarming the Heart: Toward a Vow of Nonviolence.*
Scottdale, PA: Herald, 1993. 192 pages. $11.95 paperback.

Reviewed by Rick Axtell

In the annals of my memory, 1994 will be the year of violence. In May, I sat with a member of my inner city church as he mourned the loss of his son—shot to death in a nearby housing project. During the hot months of summer, I awakened to the sound of gunfire in my neighborhood, just ten blocks from prosperous downtown Louisville. In August, I travelled to El Salvador where I heard the stories of simple people who had endured unspeakable brutalities at the hands of the U.S.-backed military forces. In October, I began new work with homeless men, confronting again the systemic violence that marginalizes increasing numbers of our unskilled population, and the physical violence that so often accompanies that marginalization. Then, in December, during Advent, the same Church member who had lost his son in May, grieved over the fatal shooting of his stepdaughter by an estranged boyfriend. An advocate of nonviolence, I have been enraged by all this violence.

John Dear's book was just what I needed; just what many of us need, I suspect. Dear, a Jesuit priest and internationally recognized activist, calls us to open ourselves to the God of Peace in a way that will "disarm" our violent, enraged hearts. Only then can we be instruments of genuine reconciliation in an alarmingly violent world. Dear calls us to an intense inner journey that leads, necessarily, to an exciting and risky outer journey.

Dear's autobiographical introduction is consistent with Gandhi's reminder that "nonviolence cannot be preached; it has to be practiced." Dear's description of how his pilgrimage to nonviolence turned his life upside down is a moving challenge that sets a solid foundation for the summons that follows. Here, the preacher of nonviolence shows us what the practice of nonviolence looks like. Throughout the book, references to Gandhi, King, Day, Merton, Romero, the Berrigans, and the murdered Jesuits of El Salvador remind us that faithful lives make the strongest argument for nonviolence.

In the first chapter Dear attributes violence to forgetfulness. Violence occurs when we forget who we are—"brothers and sisters of one another, each one of us a child of God" (33). Our forgetfulness reflects a lack of trust, accompanied by selfish pride, anxiety, and fear. Quoting Merton, Dear reminds us that our fear is pervasive because we have "ceased to believe in God" (34-35). Violence reveals the condition of our own hearts.

Dear fruitfully employs the language of addiction in his analysis of violence. Violence has become a self-destructive habit, too ingrained to break. Like addicts, we are out of control and our habit is perpetuated by denial. The analogy is fitting and insightful. Readers may recall Merton's use of the same language in *Faith and Violence* (41–42).

Unwilling to absolve those who are comfortably removed from the most obvious forms of violence, Dear confronts our "silence, apathy, and complicity in the systemic violence of militarism, the nuclear arms race, poverty, starvation, disease, hopelessness, the denial of human dignity and other injustices" (40). We *benefit* from the institutionalized violence of economic exploitation, political domination, and military power. Thus, we share responsibility for the descending spiral of repression and revolutionary violence that traps so much of humanity (41). Dear's insight reflects Merton's critique of the "intrinsically violent" nature of American social and economic structures. I appreciated his potent prophetic challenge. It would have been strengthened with analysis of *how* policies that benefit us actually impoverish others. Americans are not used to systemic thinking that clarifies the links between personal lifestyles and the effects of political, economic, and military policies on the poor.

In chapter 2, Dear defines nonviolence as "the daily act of recalling our basic identities and living out of them" (45). The disarming practice of remembrance creates a nonviolent spirit characterized by active love that is unconditional, non-retaliatory, sacrificial, willing to serve others who cannot reciprocate, and willing to suffer. As Martin Luther King Jr. demonstrated, it takes on the violence of others in the struggle for justice and reconciliation, thereby breaking the cycle of violence and overcoming it. In Merton's "theology of resistance," this is precisely the meaning of the Cross (F&V, 10).

Dear wisely avoids the misunderstood term "pacifism." Far from encouraging passivity, a commitment to nonviolence takes bold and creative *action* that confronts evil and transforms it into good. The goal is real *conversion* in which oppressors recognize the common humanity in the resisters who willingly accept suffering in their uncompromising commitment to truth (50–53, 94–97). Dear cites examples of nonviolent methods of resistance (51, 95–96, 124), but explains that nonviolence is more than just a technique. It is a peaceful spirit; a way of life in which we experience a dynamic process of transformation.

The author adds that nonviolence requires solidarity with the poor (49). The disarmed heart recognizes the face of God in marginalized victims of systemic violence. Only when we relinquish privilege, power, and possessions can we see the world from the perspective of the poor and accompany them in their struggle. This journey into powerlessness releases the power of God (102–105). With his consistently strong emphasis on solidarity, Dear has been careful to avoid the hypocricy exposed by Merton who warned against self-righteously preaching pacifism to those who "suffer the violence which we sweetly impose on them." Suffering love is the responsibility of those who have benefitted from the inherently violent system.

Like Gandhi, who called prayer his "greatest weapon," Dear explains that the demanding life of nonviolence must be rooted in prayer. In solitude, we experience God's presence and nurture the vision of a reconciled world. We confess our addiction, confront our powerlessness and cultivate unwavering trust in the triumph of God's reign. We *remember*. Without such prayer, nonviolence is impossible. Dear quotes Merton's assertion that nonviolence is "nothing more than a living out of a nonviolence of the heart, an inner unity already experienced in prayer" (88). Dear's writings on the spiritual roots of nonviolence (53–54, 97–112) are among his most eloquent. His understanding of prayer as subversive and revolutionary is a much needed correction to the individualistic feel-good spirituality that prevails in today's churches.

In his most significant contribution to Christian literature on peacemaking, Dear calls Christians to profess a *vow* of nonviolence. A vow is "a deliberate, religiously binding, solemn promise made to God concerning some good taken after serious preparation and in full freedom" (56). It is "a pledge to be faithful to a way of life." Dear notes that the vow of nonviolence was an essential element of Gandhi's philosophy. The vow was the foundation that drew him closer to God, strengthened his resolve, and liberated his will. Vows (nonviolence, celibacy, simplicity) provided Indians a disciplined freedom that undermined the ability of the authorities to maintain control. These vows unleashed a remarkable force of love and truth, and gave courage to resist injustice (131–137). Similarly, Dear understands the vow of nonviolence as "a channel of grace," releasing an unpredictable power that transforms evil into good.

Dear reminds us that "baptism itself was a vow to follow Jesus and his way of life and to reject Satan and his way of death" (58). Early Christians understood their baptismal vows as a commitment to a nonviolent way of life, with clear political and social implications. Their pledge of allegiance to Christ as Lord was a radical political act, regarded as treasonous by emperors demanding ultimate commitment. This "sacrament" was a direct challenge to the *sacramentum*, the soldiers' oath of allegiance to the imperial gods of Rome (84).

In the post-Constantinian era, the newly legalized (and soon dominant) Church abandoned nonviolence. Baptism lost its inherent threat to the unjust imperial system. It no longer signified an alternative allegiance. Dear argues that a vow of nonviolence will restore concrete meaning to our baptismal promise to reject sin. The vow makes explicit what is implicit in the baptismal promise: to be a Christian is to be nonviolent; to resist the dominant system; to give total allegiance to God's reign. Dear contends that this understanding will renew a culturally conformist Christianity and restore its public witness.

Chapter 4 is a disturbing reminder of the urgent need for a vow of nonviolence. Like a good dependency counselor, Dear breaks through our denial by confronting us with the serious consequences of our addiction. He presents a sobering catalogue of twentieth-century brutalities, challenges the indifference of Christians who benefit from structured injustice, and decries Christian support for government-sponsored mass murder from Dresden to Hiroshima to Baghdad. This troubling chapter is an essential part of the book. We must face reality with eyes wide open. But thankfully, Dear does not leave us in despair without a vision of hopeful alternatives. As with Francis, Gandhi, and King, the vow of nonviolence can break through our denial and empower us to take stands against all forms of violence. Dear counsels us to count the cost and examines the lifelong implications of the commitment to nonviolence. In beautifully written chapters, he explains the importance of active compassion, truth, prayer, trust in God, powerlessness, purity of heart, humility, forgiveness, and creativity.

The final chapters present Dear's models. First, Dear reviews Gandhi's philosophy of nonviolence. For Gandhi, too, nonviolence was a matter of the heart, concretized in vows, expressed daily in every area of life. The chapter is an accurate and profound reminder of the power and wisdom of Gandhi's life and thought. Dear draws most heavily from Merton's little volume *Gandhi on Nonviolence* (1964) and from Merton's interpretation of Gandhi in *The Nonviolent Alternative* (1971). It is not surprising that Merton saw the connection between

Gandhi's inward and outward journey so clearly: "The whole Gand-hian concept of nonviolent action and satyagraha (soul force) is in-comprehensible if it is to be thought of as a means of achieving unity rather than as the fruit of inner unity already achieved" (144–145).

Dear concludes with a reflection on the life of Jesus as the pri-mary model for nonviolence. He shows how Jesus deliberately broke unjust laws and publicly challenged systemic oppression. Drawing upon the scholarship of Walter Wink, Dear interprets the Sermon on the Mount as "a manifesto on nonviolence" which clearly demon-strates practical alternatives to the structural violence of the Roman/ Sadducean system and the revolutionary violence of the Zealots. Wink's ingenious interpretation of Matthew 5:38-42 is a powerfully per-suasive argument that Jesus advocated creative nonviolent resistance capable of confronting and transforming injustice, while remaining faithful to radically different values. The nonviolence of Jesus included prayer, compassion, trust in God, solidarity with the poor, direct ac-tion to challenge injustice, and redemptive suffering. As a threat to the system, "Jesus suffered the full force of the world's addiction to violence; he died under the full weight of imperial violence" (163). But in the deepest sense, Jesus conquered violence by taking it upon him-self and exposing its true nature. This fact gives his followers the hope and strength they need to continue his work.

Dear's book is deeply challenging and hopeful, especially for those who struggle with despair in this violent age. The profound in-sights outweigh a number of minor frustrations—repetitiveness, lack of factual documentation, avoidance of ethical analysis. It should be noted, however, that the book is primarily a description of the life of nonviolence and its foundations rather than an *argument* for nonvio-lence. From the beginning, the author *assumes* that nonviolence is the only adequate Christian alternative. The idealism here is refreshing. Yet the thoroughgoing realists among his readers might find an almost utopian sentimentality in some of Dear's work. For example:

> When we take this vision of Jesus' nonviolence seriously, wars will end and injustice will cease. The entire weapons industry will close, the Pentagon will become a shelter for the homeless, and all battle-ships and military aircraft will be rededicated to the distribution of food and medicine to the poor of the world. The reign of God's love will extend to everyone (156).

Christian ethicists schooled in Niebuhrian thought (have any avoided it?) will ask whether Dear takes sufficient account of sin and the pervasive power of evil. It is a key issue in the debate between pacifism and just war theory. The persistance of historical evil, after all, is the reality that forces tough ethical choices in frustrating cases like Bosnia and Sudan, where the world has remained helplessly inactive, watching the torturous deaths of countless innocent human beings. Christian peacemakers have agonized about what kind of nonviolent interventions might challenge such calculated brutality. Even Merton, who wholeheartedly affirmed the superiority of nonviolent resistance, was unwilling to reject the right of the oppressed to use force to gain their rights.

Dear does dismiss the possibility of any just war, citing the modern potential for mass destruction (119, 125–126). But Dear also rejects any pacifism that shirks responsibility for defending ourselves and others from evil (129). Consistent with the trend in writings on Christian peacemaking, Dear moves beyond (or before!) the debate between pacifism and just war theory. Following the model of Jesus, nonviolent Christians will accept full responsibility for the world's violence by intentionally entering into situations of injustice and conflict with transforming initiatives that can break the cycle of violence. The true costliness of this stance is clear. And this provides the answer to the inevitable "realist" challenge. Despite the more effusively idealistic passages in Dear's book, his nonviolence is genuinely realistic about evil. It is human sin, after all, that makes the commitment to nonviolence so costly. It is evil (rooted in the sin of forgetting who we are) that nonviolent resistance challenges and seeks to transform. And Dear understands that sin is embodied in social structures. Dear tends to avoid explicit theological/ethical discussion of such issues, but his answers are visible between the lines.

One of the real strengths of this book, however, is that Dear does not give in to the temptation among some ethicists to limit the questions to hot conflict situations. Dear stresses that nonviolence is a lifestyle that arises out of a heart that is being disarmed. Ultimately we must decide whether or not we will participate in the system. I was moved by Dear's call to withdraw cooperation from the structures of violence. His work is a persuasive call to greater intentionality about our inward and outward journey.

Dear notes some necessary elements in the process of preparing to profess a vow of nonviolence. These include Scripture study, self-examination, analysis of political and economic realities, and study of the writings of practitioners of nonviolence, all carried out within a community of faith. Isn't it time for local parishes to develop new structures for their formation programs that will deal seriously with a renewed commitment to nonviolence? Vows have not yet been a part of the process. Dear has convinced me that they should be. This book can serve as an inspiring guide in the formation of Christians whose spirituality is more faithful, prophetic and responsible; more threatening! The exciting and unpredictable journey suggested by Dear really is essential if today's complicit Christianity is to experience genuine renewal.

Matthew Kelty. *My Song Is of Mercy*. Edited by Michael Downey. Kansas City: Sheed & Ward, 1994. 260 pages. $15.95.

Reviewed by Michael Johmann

Quite by accident I stumbled onto a happy word in a Greek dictionary, *monaulia*, "flute solo." But it has another definition as well, "the solitary life," since the root word means both "flute" and "house," and the *monos* characterizes the solo flute and the person living alone, the solitary. It is a beautiful combination, for both are a kind of poetry. Certainly neither has any great practical value, yet the world would be less charming for want of the flute, less tolerable if there were no hermits (*Flute Solo*).

In *The Merton Annual*, volume 6, editor Michael Downey speaks of "the need for a critical turn" after twenty-five years of Merton studies. "Above all else," Downey urges, "it seems that the most pressing task is to connect the discourse within the circle of Merton studies with the discourse in other fields." Although Downey calls in particular for a greater variety of critical hermeneutic, the same might be said of the conversation between monasticism and the contemporary reader influenced by Merton. To many, Merton's writings so dominate the current discussion on monastic life as to become the *only* voice of monastic expression in modern America, yet, as demonstrated by the present volume by Matthew Kelty, there are other voices even at Gethsemani who continue to enrich the dialogue established by Merton and shed needed insight on contemporary issues facing the Church.

Edited by Michael Downey, *My Song Is of Mercy* represents a selection of almost seventy talks and sermons delivered by Father Kelty during his years as a monk at Gethsemani and as a solitary living in Papua New Guinea. Also reprinted for the first time is *Flute Solo*, Kelty's memoir of his life as a monk in New Guinea, Kentucky, and North Carolina, in which the author reflects on the value of solitude in the monastic experience and compares the so-called "primitive" faith of a non-Western culture to our own. The motif of the flute solo, traced by the author to its Greek root *monaulia*, which can also be translated as "the solitary life," underscores Kelty's exploration of the apparent uselessness of eremitism in Western cultures against the necessity of such "uselessness" in traditional cultures and in the deeper life of the historical West. Compared to the "noise" of contemporary society, only in solitude—which does not, by the way, equal physical isolation—can the soul escape into the realm of silence essential to understanding the voice of God in the self and in every person. "It was Thomas Merton who taught me this," Kelty writes, "both in the days I was a novice under his direction, as also in later years in a study of his writings." According to Kelty, "Probably the most significant work of this man [Merton] lay in his return to the solitary aspect of monasticism. The results of this awakening, this rediscovery, have only begun to be manifest. I am sure it is only a beginning." Kelty's own years spent as a hermit monk in New Guinea, along with a three-year stay at a very small and experimental Cistercian community outside Oxford, North Carolina have led him to conclude with Merton that

> Where there is quiet, there is God. And where peace is, and love. If God is dead, we killed him. And we killed him most of all with our noise, the noise of our fuming and agitation. We North Americans love violence and because it is directed against others, it does not lead to the kingdom. I don't think God can stand us when we are this way. He is afraid of us. He runs away. He hides.

By no coincidence, it is the "shyness"—rather than the power or majesty—of God which dominates the best of Kelty's writing. The problem, in his opinion, is not our lack of a search for spiritual values in the twentieth century so much as our frenzied demand for results. Even in the monastery, Kelty argues, the structure of life centers around a discipline and a work ethic devoted to "tangible" results. Some of the most affecting passages from *Flute Solo*, for example, dwell not on the successes of his spiritual wanderings but on his all-too-human failures. "I have been on earth almost 60 years," Kelty writes,

> and the majority of that time in [God's] official service and I don't even know him. I've not begun to begin to understand him, to relate to him. I've spent half a lifetime doing what they told me to do, pouring myself out in a frenzied effort to produce, to deliver, to come up with results.

The point, according to Kelty, is that God, and our awareness of Him deep at work—at rest—in our own lives, has nothing of the practical attached to it whatsoever. Christ himself partakes of the useless: "Christ did nothing worthwhile for thirty years. One carpenter more or less in Nazareth could scarcely have mattered. For all practical purposes, they were wasted years." Contrary to the idea of spiritual abandonment, Kelty argues that the reason for the collapse of spirituality in the West has less to do with abandonment than with exhaustion. "In all of that" Kelty writes in the wake of what he sees as Jesus' largely "failed" ministry during his own life on earth, "I see no justification whatever for the notion that work for God necessarily means a life of feverish action, back-breaking labor, constant tension and concern." Only in solitude, suggests Kelty, can we begin to explore the wholeness of our own being—the anima and the animus which define the whole individual, the silence wherein speaks the voice of God.

Despite the apparent asceticism of Kelty's overall theology, the message itself is often delivered in a surprisingly homespun and deeply humane rhetoric. Moreover, Kelty addresses key issues of the contemporary Church. Kelty often begins his sermons and talks by recalling an article in a secular magazine or by commenting on the rising cost of a cup of coffee at McDonald's—an intentionally disarming strategy for addressing retreatants who might have expected a monastic out of touch with the world. One of the issues consistently raised by the author—as early as 1973 in the case of *Flute Solo*—has to do with the place of gays in the modern Church. Kelty himself admits that, had he not chosen a life of celibacy early on, he would now consider himself homosexual. Yet, in the author's "Epilogue: Celibacy and the Gift of Gay," Kelty asserts that, potentially at least, gays are *better* fitted to a life of monastic celibacy than their heterosexual counterparts to the degree they embody both the masculine and the feminine aspects of their human being:

> For the gay must become comfortable with his being a human, two dimensional, tough and tender, strong and gentle. His search for wholeness is not a search for personality, but for Christ, who cannot be met by anything less than a person, let alone be loved. The love of God is possible in depth only to the whole person, at least the beginnings of one.

Like Merton, Kelty accepts a broadly Jungian approach to the problem of human personality, and his commentary on the ability of gays to combine animus and anima more easily than heterosexuals begs comparison to the once radical ideas on the femininity of deity expressed by his former novice master in such poems as "Hagia Sophia." Given the current atmosphere of fear and embarrassment over homosexuality within the Church, Kelty's words appear at a time when Catholics as a whole must reconsider their longstanding prohibition against considering gays as part of the Church, and find a ground for meaningful dialogue with the last "untouchables" of American culture. "The Gift of Gay" does much to establish that ground for meaningful dialogue—as does the collection of talks and sermons as a whole.

Brian Patrick McGuire, *Brother and Lover: Aelred of Rievaulx.* New York: Crossroad, 1994. 186 pages. $22.95.

Reviewed by Matthew Kelty, O.C.S.O.

Here is a neat piece of work. I write this review with a very specific purpose: to encourage you to take up and read. As one interested in Merton, you are aware of his interest in Aelred, of the life that he wrote. And there is a real similarity between the two Cistercians: both relished talking about themselves, writing about themselves, and used their own experience as point of departure in writing and speaking.

That is why it is possible to write a vivid biography of a man 828 years dead, a life personal, intimate, detailed. Born 1110, died 1167.

Aelred lived in the difficult period following the Norman Conquest. Norman rule and influence were extended north through conflicts that repeatedly disturbed civil life. Celts and Anglo-Saxons and Normans of the nobility intermarried eventually, and this was a major factor in uniting the people.

A charming, engaging, handsome Anglo-Saxon son of priestly family, brought up in the Scottish court, Aelred early on was reckoned worthy of favor and support. Later reform movements removed his father from his parish to enter Durham, a Benedictine monastery. Aelred felt shame at his background, and further guilt at his lapses as a youth at court. On a journey for King David he passed Rievaulx, a recent daughter house of Clairvaux. From then until his death he was a monk. He was Novice Master, Abbot of a daughter house of Rievaulx, and later at that house itself. Abbot from 1143–1167 all told.

This is surely a scholarly work, but I am not qualified to say so with any impact. And though I have no doubt that Aelred was gay, to use the modern term, that too is mere personal opinion. The author is more professional and makes it clear that one does not know and probably never will know Aelred's sexual orientation.

It is not an important matter, save that if what I suggest be true, then Aelred is a superb example of what a man can do with such an endowment, be it viewed as a curse, as gift, as a disordered orientation: he turned it, in the grace of God and the monastic life, to holiness and sanctity.

He lived chaste and celibate as a monk, yet as Abbot and spiritual father, taught his sons warm love and the affectionate expression of that love. This is the important factor. Here he was outstanding and exceptional in thought, word, deed. He is the classic expression of friendship. Rievaulx became famous and loved, widely recognized as a house of compassion, tolerance, a place of beauty.

Perhaps the most significant sentence in this book is the statement: "Twelfth-century monks like Aelred could allow themselves much more physical contact with each other than their nineteenth or early twentieth-century successors" (94). We are more restrained, more controlled and reserved. I daresay we love as much and perhaps as well, but our expression of it is marked by our culture, rather wary of displays of affection among men, any men.

Yet, we must be careful. We are not that unfamiliar with deep love among men. And since Aelred knew only a man's world, it is of men we must speak, at least directly, though celibate love among women is in every sense a Christian and monastic tradition too.

We call deep male love *"bonding."* And the bonding among men in war together, in battle together, is a profound expression of human love. Sometimes it remains the peak experience of a lifetime. We are currently reading David McCullough's *Truman* in the refectory. The love between Truman and his men, their love for one another in a battalion of World War I, remained a lifetime engagement for them all. They remained closely bonded all their lives. Such men literally die for one another. There is something similar among firemen, policemen, who in the course of duty are exposed to great danger. The love is very real, sometimes frankly expressed, after a bit of liquor, for example. Team players can express affection more obviously than others, and there is a real love in a good team. In this bonding, what unites is the common goal: the desire for victory, for courageous action against an enemy, a threat. Their love for one another follows the common pursuit. So, monks love God and the search for God in the monastic context. The common endeavor unites and endears.

Aelred cultivated the commitment to God to foster the warm love for one another. And that love was given tone and quality by its purity and selflessness. So, the ascetical dimension sharpened the experience and added to its beauty.

Western males seem generally to fear intimacy with one another, whatever the reason. This tends to inhibit the practice of celibacy and chills it somewhat. Even so, a monastery for all its sense of austere love is still involved with love, very real love.

One likes to think that the influence of Aelred—Cistericians, after all, unofficially canonized him in 1476—may warm our own chill some, help us acquire a discipline more Christian than Spartan. Judas' kiss of Christ was surely not the only one, and he not the only one to give it.

The book has a map of Aelred's Britain, diagrams of the royal houses of England and Scotland, of Aelred's known ancestors, and a chronology of Aelred's background, life, and work. Footnotes are dispensed with in favor of documentation at the end of the book, a section for each chapter. Plus an index.

Contributors

Rick Axtell is visiting assistant professor of religion and college chaplain at Centre College, Danville, Kentucky.

Claire Badaracco is associate professor in mass communications at Marquette University and was a visiting professor (1994–1995) at the University of Notre Dame. Her book, *Trading Words*, published by The Johns Hopkins University Press (1995).

Christine M. Bochen is professor of religious studies at Nazareth College, Rochester, NY. She is the editor of *The Courage For Truth*, the fourth volume of Merton's letters, as well as the sixth volume of Merton's journals (forthcoming).

Douglas Burton-Christie teaches in the department of theological studies at Loyola Marymount University in Los Angeles.

Angela Collins, O.C.D., is Prioress of the Carmelite Monastery in Savannah, Georgia.

Joann Wolski Conn, professor of religious studies at Neumann College, is the author of *Spirituality and Personal Maturity* (University Press of America, 1994) and editor of a revised second edition of *Women's Spirituality* (Paulist, 1996).

Thomas Del Prete, author of *Thomas Merton and the Education of the Whole Person*, is associate director of the Hiatt Center for Urban Education at Clark University in Worcester, Massachusetts.

Michael Downey is professor of theology at Bellarmine College in Louisville. His publications include the award-winning *The New Dictionary of Catholic Spirituality* and his collected essays entitled *Worship at the Margins: Spirituality and Liturgy.*

Roy D. Fuller holds an M.Div. and a Ph.D. from the Southern Baptist Theological Seminary in Louisville. He is an adjunct instructor at Bellarmine College and Indiana University Southeast.

Roberto S. Goizueta is associate professor of theology at Loyola University in Chicago. His most recent publication is *Caminemos Con Jesús: Toward a Hispanic/Latino Theology of Accompaniment* (Orbis, 1995).

Patrick Hart, O.C.S.O., has been a monk of Gethsemani since 1951. He was Thomas Merton's last secretary and has edited a number of books by and about Merton. Currently he is general editor of the seven-volume series of the Merton Journals.

R. Andrew Hartmans is a student at Louisville Presbyterian Theological Seminary and intern pastor at Buechel Presbyterian Church. His interests include the role of media in facilitating congregational worship.

Michael Johmann holds a Ph.D. in British and American literature from Indiana University. He teaches humanities and English at the University of Louisville and Bellarmine College.

Matthew Kelty, O.C.S.O., is a monk of the Abbey of Gethsemani. He is author of *Sermons in a Monastery* and *My Song Is of Mercy.*

Victor A. Kramer is a founding editor of *The Merton Annual* and editor of the fourth volume of Thomas Merton's journals (HarperCollins) scheduled to be published in 1997. Recently, he edited an issue of *Studies in the Literary Imagination* in contemporary Southern literature (1994) and his *Agee: Selected Literary Documents* (Whitston) is at press.

Gloria Kitto Lewis is the director of the technical writing program and the computers and writing program in the department of English at Wayne State University. She has published in *The Merton Annual* and *The Merton Seasonal.* Her anthology *The Informed Tech-*

nical Reader is forthcoming from Kendall Hunt Publishing Company, 1996.

Thomas F. McKenna, C.M., is a member of the Eastern Province of the Vincentians. He teaches spirituality as an assistant professor in the theology department of St. John's University, New York. He has contributed articles to various theological and spiritual journals.

Matthias Neuman, O.S.B., is a monk of St. Meinrad Archabbey in Indiana. He received his doctorate in systematic theology from the Pontifical University of St. Anselm (Rome). He teaches ecumenical and interfaith theology at St. Meinrad College.

Erlinda G. Paguio is on the staff of Ekstrom Library, University of Louisville, and is serving a second term as treasurer of The International Thomas Merton Society. She has presented several papers related to Merton's study of Meister Eckhart, Kitaro Nishida, D.T. Suzuki, the Carmelite saints, and Sufism.

Parker J. Palmer is an independent writer, teacher, and activist who works in the areas of education, spirituality, community, and social change. He holds a Ph.D. in sociology from the University of California at Berkeley. His most recent books are *The Active Life* and *To Know As We Are Known* (HarperCollins).

Irwin Howard Streight teaches modern and contemporary fiction and writing at Queen's University, Kingston, Canada, where he is an adjunct assistant professor. He has published articles on Flannery O'Connor and on socio-linguistics and has contributed substantially to the *Canadian Guide to English Usage*.

Julia Upton, R.S.M., is professor of theology and director of the Center for Teaching and Learning at St. John's University, New York. She is the author of *A Church for the Next Generation* (The Liturgical Press, 1990) and *Becoming a Catholic Christian* (Pastoral Press, 1993).

Paul J. Wadell, C.P., is professor of ethics at Catholic Theological Union, Chicago. His publications include *Friendship and the Moral Life* and *The Primacy of Love: An Introduction to the Ethics of Thomas Aquinas*.

Index

(Footnotes are not included)

Abbey of Gethsemani, 89, 106, 107, 118, 150, 162–200, 246, 249, 254, 259, 272
ABC of Reading (Pound), 223
"Action and Contemplation in St. Bernard of Clairvaux," 3
Adam of Perseigne, 66, 69
Aelred of Rievaulx, 2, 274–276
Albert the Great, Saint, 19
Al-Hallaj, 22
Andrews, Edward Deming, 251
Anima, 258–261
"Animated Outsiders: Echoes of Merton in Hampl, Norris, Dillard, and Ehrlich" (Badaracco), x, 150–161
Antigone (Sophocles), 117
Appleberry, James, 86
Aristotle, 40, 45–48
Ascent to Truth, 68
Ashbrook, James B., 84
Axtell, Rick, 264–271
Aziz, Abdul, 231, 248

Badaracco, Claire, x, 150–161
Baez, Joan, 219
"Balanced Life of Prayer," xii, 1–21
Bamberger, John Eudes, 109, 110, 187, 199
Bangkok, 167
Bantu philosophy, 116

Basil, Saint, 115
"Bear" (Faulkner), 114
Behara, Gary Charas, 232
Belcastro, David, 230
Bell, Marvin, 78
Bellarmine College (Louisville, Kentucky), ix–x
Bernard of Clairvaux, Saint, 2, 4, 65, 89, 115, 237
Berrigan brothers, 233
Berry, Wendell, 86–87, 262–264
Bloom, Allan, 61–62
Bluefields (Nicaragua), 165, 186, 189
Bochen, Christine M., xi, 162–200
"Boris Pasternak and the People with Watch Chains," 177
Brière, Jacques, 232
Brother and Lover: Aelred of Rievaulx (McGuire), (Review) 274–276
Buber, Martin, 125
Buddhism, 140–149, 233
"Buddhist Emptiness and Christian Trinity" (Corless), 146
Buddhist Sangha Council of Southern California, 146
Burton-Christie, Douglas, 246–254

Cables to the Ace, 256
Camus, Albert, 255
Cardenal, Ernesto, xi, 162–200, 233, 244

Care of the Soul (Moore), 77
Carmelite Monastery (Louisville, Kentucky), xii, 184, 188, 198, 201
Carmelite Monastery (Savannah, Georgia), xii, 201
Carrera Andrade, Jorgé, 181
Carson, Rachel, 238, 248, 250
Casagram, Michael, O.C.S.O., 89, 98–99, 103
Casey, Michael, 229
Cassian, 3
Castro, Fidel, 178–179, 182
Catch of Anti-Letters (Merton and Robert Lax), (Review) 254–257
"Celebration of Friendship" (Clapp), 41
"Celtic Monasticism as a Metaphor for Thomas Merton's Journey" (Pearson), 233–234
Cenobitic monasticism, 248–249
Chamorro, Pedro Joaquín, 193
Charity, 40, 48–58, 72–74
Chittister, Joan, O.S.B., 79
"Christian Humanism," 56
Chuang Tzu, 117
Cistercium, 233
Clapp, Rodney, 41
"Climate of Mercy," 56
Closing of the American Mind (Bloom), 61–62
Cold War Letters, 39, 117, 234–235, 236, 250
Collectanea Cisterciensia, 232
Collins, Angela, O.C.D., xii, 188
Conferences (Merton), 88–102, 118–119
Conjectures of a Guilty Bystander, 71, 242
Conn, Joann Wolski, 258–261
Conner, James, O.C.S.O., 89, 92, 98, 103
Conscience matter letter, 183, 194, 197–198
Consciousness, 140–141

Constitution on the Church in the Modern World, 243
Contemplation, xi, 3, 17–21, 28–33, 79, 154–161, 233, 240
"Contemplation Reconsidered: The Human Way In" (Palmer), ix, 22–37
Contemplative life, 109, 111, 114, 116, 155, 164, 184, 196, 202, 208, 212, 213–214, 217, 222
Coomaraswamy, Ananda K., 74
Corless, Roger, 146
Corn Island (Nicaragua), 181, 186
Coronel Urtecho, José, 192, 195
Council of Ephesus, 16
Council of Societies for the Study of Religion, 145
Courage for Truth, ix, 163
"Courage to Teach" (A retreat), 35
Cuadra, Pablo Antonio, 173, 174, 177, 181, 185, 186, 189, 200
Cuernavaca (Mexico), 165, 166, 168, 174, 180, 185, 186, 249
"Culture and the Formation of Personal Identity: Dilemma and Dialectic in Thomas Merton's Teaching" (Del Prete), ix, 105–121
Cultural Literacy (Hirsch), 60–62
Curriculum reform, 66

Daggy, Robert E., 233
Dakota: A Spiritual Geography (Norris), 157
Dalai Lama, 215
Danielou, Jean, Father, 194, 249
"Daughter of Carmel; Son of Cîteaux: A Friendship Endures. An Interview about Thomas Merton with Angela Collins, O.C.D." (Conducted by Michael Downey), xiii, 201–220
De Waal, Esther, 233
Dear, John, 264–271

Del Prete, Thomas, ix, 74, 81, 89, 105–121, 233
Delacorte, Valeria, 237
Desert fathers, 3, 89, 126–137, 157, 158, 185
Dewart, Leslie, 248
Dhikr, 230–231
Dialogue (Interfaith), 138–149, 231
"Dialogue on Wisdom in Emptiness" (Merton and Suzuki), 139
Dickinson, Emily, 151, 157
Dillard, Annie, 150–161
Disarming the Heart: Toward a Vow of Nonviolence (Dear), (Review) 264–271
Disputed Questions, 81
Downey, Michael, ix–xii, 201–220, 271–272
"Drake in the Southern Sea," 173, 177
Dumont, Charles, 232

Eastman, Patrick, 230
Eckhart, Meister, 141
Eco-feminism, 151–154, 160–161
Education, Higher, x–xi, 59–87
Ehrlich, Gretel, 150–161
Ellul, Jacques, 120
Emerson, Ralph Waldo, 151, 159
Epigrams (Cardenal), 170
"Español en Merton," 233
Exiles from Eden (Schwehn), 64–65

"Faith," 70–71
Faith and Violence, 266
Faulkner, William, 114
"Feast of Freedom," 67, 69
Felipe, León, 176
Feminism, 151–154, 235
Fetzer Institute, 35
Finding Your Centre, A Journey with Thomas Merton (Forest), 225
"Fire Watch," 259
Flute Solo, 271–273

Follow the Ecstasy (Griffin), 209
Ford, John, 237, 250
Forest, Jim, 225
Fox, James, Abbot, 1, 166, 182, 184, 188, 194–195, 197–199, 203, 205, 206, 217, 249
Freedom, 246–254
"Freedom and Spontaneity," 112, 113
Friendships, 38–58
Fromm, Erich, 193, 255
Fuller, Roy D., x, 59–74
Furlong, Monica, 233

Gandhi, Mohandas Karamchand, 265, 267–269
Geography of Lograire, 232
"Get a Life," 28–33
"Gethsemani: The Gift of Faith" (Shannon), 70
Getty, Richard E., 230
"Go, Lovely Rose," (Waller), 119
"God is Shy–And So Am I," 33–37
Goizueta, Roberto S., xi, 162–200
Golden Age of Zen (Wu), 257
"Grace's House," 233
Graham, Aelred, Dom, 138
Griffin, John Howard, 204, 209–210, 212, 219
Griffiths, Bede, Dom, 138
Grinberg, Miguel, 233
Guerric of Igny, Blessed, 2
"Guru," 66–68
Gustafson, James, 70

"Hagia Sophia," 235, 259, 274
Hammer, Victor, 235, 247, 259
Hampl, Patricia, 150–161
Hart, Patrick, O.C.S.O., xii, 1–3, 89, 91, 103, 201, 256
Hartmans, Andrew, 201–220
Havel, Vaclav, 33
"Healing and the Mind" (Moyers), 35

"Herakleitos: A Study," 73
Hermit life, 209, 218, 219, 249, 255
Hermitage (Gethsemani), 165,
    166, 219, 220, 246
Herrero, Jacinto, Father, 178
Hewlett, Sylvia, 83
Hidden Ground of Love (Edited by
    William H. Shannon), 248
Hirsch, E. D., Jr., 60–62
Homosexuality, 273–274, 275
Hopkins, Gerard Manley, 170
Hora O (Cardenal), 170
Hubbard, Barbara, 251
"Human Way Out: The Contem-
    plative Dimension" (A confer-
    ence), ix
"Human Way Out: The Friendship
    of Charity as a Countercultural
    Practice" (Wadell), ix, 38–58
"Humanizing the University:
    Adding the Contemplative
    Dimension" (Upton), x, 75–87
"Humility," 68–71

"Identity Crisis," 118
Individuation, 258–261
"Inner Experience," 22–37, 88,
    229, 255
Inner life, 33–35, 66
Interior life, 169, 172, 196
International Buddhist-Christian
    Dialogue conferences, 145
International Thomas Merton
    Society, 230, 232, 233
Islam, 140, 230–231, 248
Iyer, Pico, 79–80

Jacob, Max, 183
James, Stephen, 251
Johmann, Michael, 271–274
John of the Cross, Saint, 20, 181,
    204, 218, 219, 255
Jung, Carl, 258–261

Kafka, Franz, 122, 132
Keller, Evelyn Fox, 28

Kelly, Timothy, Abbot, 89,
    103–104
Kelty, Matthew, O.C.S.O., 89, 90,
    92, 93, 98, 100–102, 104, 158,
    271–276
Kilcourse, George A., xii, 125
Killing the Spirit (Smith), 62–63
Kirk, David, Father, 252
Kramer, Victor A., xii, 89, 221–245

Landry, Gerald, 250
Latin America, 162–200
Laughlin, Jay, 173, 194, 197, 199,
    244
Lawler, Justus George, 237
Lax, Robert, 170, 177, 195
Lear, Norman, 78
"Learning to Learn," 76
"Learning to Live," 59, 65, 76
"Learning to Live: Merton's
    Students Remember His Teach-
    ing" (Lewis), x, 88–104
le Pennuen, Louis de Gonzague,
    Abbot, 1
Le Saux, Henri, Father, 138
Leclercq, Jean, 244
Lecharlier, Robert, 233
Lemercier, Gregorio, Dom, 165,
    173, 175, 176, 180, 182–187,
    190–191, 194, 195
Leonard, George, 82
Lepp, Ignace, 44
Levertov, Denise, 154
Lewis, Gloria Kitto, x, 88–104
"Life Free From Care," 246
Living Flame (Saint John of the
    Cross), 255
Livingstone, Richard, Sir, 62
Lonely Crowd (Riesman), 120
Los Angeles, Roman Catholic
    Archdiocese of, 146
Louf, André, 232
"Louisville Vision," 259
Love and Living (Edited by Patrick
    Hart and Naomi Burton
    Stone), 76, 88

"Love and Need: Is Love a Package or a Message?" 42
Luce, Clare Booth, 251

McCarthy, Mary, 152
McClintock, Barbara, 27
McGuire, Brian Patrick, 274–276
McKenna, Thomas F., C.M., ix, 122–137
"Making Sense of Soul and Sabbath; Brain Processes and the Making of Meaning" (Ashbrook), 84
Man Against Mass Society (Marcel), 120
Marcel, Gabriel, 120
Maritain, Jacques, 229, 244
Marsden, George, 63–64
Martin, Mary Declan, 65
Martín-Barbero, Jesús, 153, 160–161
Martinez, Angel, Father, 170, 174, 177, 181, 197
Marty, Martin, 125
Mason, Herbert, 248, 253
Mass, 13–21
Massignon, Louis, 22, 241–242, 248
"Mature Conscience," 110
May, Rollo, 80, 85, 87
Measure of My Days (Scott-Maxwell), 29
Mediator Dei (Pope Pius XII), 3, 6, 12–15
Meditation, 17–21, 215
Melleray, Motherhouse of (Brittany, France), 1
Memories of a Catholic Girlhood (McCarthy), 152
"Mental Prayer and Contemplation," 3, 17–21
Menti Nostrae (Pope Pius XII), 3, 4, 6, 12–15
Merton Annual, ix–x, xii, 2, 230, 232, 244

Merton By Those Who Knew Him Best (Edited by Paul Wilkes), 257
Merton Journal, 233
Merton Seasonal, 231–232
Merton Year (1993–1994), ix
". . . Merton's Admiration of Julian of Norwich," 233
"Merton's Notes on 'Inner Experience' Twenty Years Afterwards" (Casey), 229
Milbank, John, 43
"Monastery, the Academy, and the Corporation" (Downey), ix–xii
Monastic curriculum, 109, 113–114, 118–119
Monastic education, 105–121
Monastic Interreligious Dialogue (MID), 146
Monastic life, 165, 234, 249, 252, 271, 275,
"Monastic Orientation Notes," 2
Monastic renewal, 122–137, 212, 217
Monasticism, 90, 228, 252, 275
Moore, Thomas, 77
Morales, Armando, 170, 174, 178, 181, 186, 189, 192, 195
Moyers, Bill, 35
"Mount Athos," 178, 255
Murray, John Courtney, 138
"My Lord God . . ." (A prayer), 102
My Song Is of Mercy (Kelty), (Review) 271–274

Naropa Institute, 145
National Conference of Indian Bishops (1950), 138
Natural religion, 150–161
Neruda, Pablo, 170
Neuman, Matthias, O.S.B., x, 138–149
"Neurotic Personality in Monastic Life," 110

New Man, 49, 55

Nicaragua, 164–165, 170, 179, 181–182, 185, 192

Nicomachean Ethics (Aristotle), 47–48

Niedhammer, Matthew A., Bishop, 186

"Night-flowering cactus," 255

Nishida, Kitaro, 141

No Man Is an Island, 53, 55, 70, 109

Nonviolence, 239, 250, 265–271

Norris, Kathleen, 150–161

"Nuclear Testing" (A conference tape), 117

Objectivity, 24–28

O'Connell, Patrick, 232

O'Connor, Flannery, 157

Olim, Maria Blanca, Sister, 252

Ometepe, 186, 189

"Open Letter to the Hierarchy," 239

Organization Man (Whyte), 113, 120

Orsborn, Carol, 84

Paguio, Erlinda G., 254–257

Pallais, Odilie, 194, 196

Palmer, Parker J., ix, xi, 22–37, 60, 63, 64, 80–81

Parks, Rosa, 32

Passion for Peace (Edited by William H. Shannon), 234

Pasternak, Boris, 81, 82, 170, 177

Paul, Saint, 4, 5, 8, 54, 55, 114

Pearson, Paul, 233

Peck, Scott, 77, 82

Pennington, M. Basil, O.C.S.O., 67

Percy, Walker, 226

Perfectionism, 110, 111

Perón, Juan, 178

Phelps, William Lyon, 62–63

Philippe, Paul, O.P., 2, 166, 249

Pilgrim at Tinker Creek (Dillard), 158

Plath, Sylvia, 154

Pluralism, Religious, 138

Point vierge, 241–242

"Polychrome Face of Contradiction: Assessing Inconsistencies in Thomas Merton" (Getty), 230

Postman, Neil, 76, 87

Postmodernism, 122–137

Pound, Ezra, 223

"Power as life," 54–55

Power of the Cross (Purvis), 54

"Prometheus," 177

"Prophetischer Radikalismus und seine Kritiker" (Remele), 233

Prabhavananda, Swami, 67

Prayer, 1–21, 227, 267

Praying with Thomas Merton (Simsic), 227–228

"Public Prayer and Sacrifice," 3

Purvis, Sally B., 54

Quenon, Paul, O.C.S.O, 89–93

"Quickening of John the Baptist," 217

Rahner, Karl, 125

Raids on the Unspeakable, 228, 256

Ramakrishna, 68

Ranford, Bruno, 233

Ratzinger letter, 149

"Reflections on Thomas Merton's Article: 'Notes for a Philosophy of Solitude' " (Shannon), 230

Remele, Kurt, 233

"Renewal in Monastic Education," 118

"Revisiting *Zen and the Birds of Appetite* after Twenty-five Years" (Neuman), x, 138–149

Riesman, David, 120

Rilke, Rainer Maria, 25, 36

Robert, Thomas, Archbishop, 251

Ruether, Rosemary, 244

Run to the Mountain (Edited by Patrick Hart), 244

Sacred Congregation for Religious (Rome), 165, 166, 195, 249
Saint Bonaventure College [University] (Olean, New York), 106, 107
Saint John's University (Jamaica, New York), ix
Sánchez, Ernesto Mejía, 170, 174, 177, 181, 186, 192, 195, 199
Sardinia, Evora Arca de, 248
Schellenberger, Bernardin, 228
Schema XIII, 248, 251
School of Charity: The Letters of Thomas Merton on Religious Renewal and Spiritual Direction (Edited by Patrick Hart), xii, 2, 201, 248
Schor, Juliet, 83
Schwarzschild, Steven, Rabbi, 251
Schwehn, Mark R., 64–65, 68–73
Schweitzer, Albert, 56
Scott-Maxwell, Florida, 29
Seeds of Contemplation, 109
Selected Poems, 195
Self, 29, 33–37, 41, 43–45, 66, 108, 112, 114–115, 120, 128, 234, 258
"Self-Denial," 71–72
"Self-Impersonation as a Way of Being in the World," 22–28
"Seneca," 256
Seven Storey Mountain, 88, 107
Sexton, Anne, 154
Shannon, William H., xii, 70, 223, 230, 234
Sign of Jonas, 2, 150, 187, 218, 228, 259
"Signed Confession," 177
Silent Lamp (Shannon), 70
Silent Pulse: A Search for the Perfect Rhythm That Exists in Each of Us (Leonard), 82
Simsic, Wayne, 227–228
Smith, Page, 62–63

Society for Buddhist-Christian Studies, 145, 147
Solaces of Open Spaces (Ehrlich), 158
Solentiname, 165, 166, 167
Solitude, 80–81, 165, 166, 183–184, 187, 199, 209, 218–220, 222, 224, 230, 248, 271–273
Somoza-Debayle, Anastasio, 164, 170
Soul of the American University (Marsden), 63–64
Spender, Stephen, 181
Spiritual Canticle (Saint John of the Cross), 20, 255
Spiritual journalism, 151–154, 160–161
Spiritual virtues, 63–64
Spirituality, 91
Stanton, Nivard, O.C.S.O., 2
Stein, Murray, 260
Stenqvist, Catharine, 233
Stone, Naomi Burton, 248
Streight, Irwin H., 262–264
Subjectivity, 24–28
Sufism, 231
Suzuki, D. T., 139, 185, 193
Syncletia, Amma, 157–158

"Teacher Formation Program," 35, 36
Teachers/Teaching, 34–36, 59–74, 88–102, 105–121
Technological Society (Ellul), 120
Technopoly: The Surrender of Culture to Technology (Postman), 87
Teresa of Avila, Saint, 18, 30, 204, 219
Theology and Social Theory (Milbank), 43
Thibodeau, Harold, O.C.S.O., 89, 94, 97, 100–101, 104
Thirty Poems After Fifty Years (O'Connell), 232
Thomas Aquinas, Saint, 19, 40, 47–53, 58, 229

"Thomas Merton and his view on Contemplation" (Stenqvist), 233

Thomas Merton Center (Bellarmine College), ix

Thomas Merton in Search of His Soul: A Jungian Perspective (Waldron), 226–227, (Review) 258–261

Thomas Merton on St. Bernard, 3

"Thomas Merton's *Geography of Lograire:* A Poem of Psychotherapy" (Behara), 232

"Thomas Merton's Interest in Islam: The Example of Dhikr" (Thurston), 230–231

Thompson, Edward, 82

Thoreau, Henry David, 151, 159

"Thousands of Words: A Bibliographical Review" (Kramer), xii, 221–245

Thurston, Bonnie, 230–231

"Time of Transition: A Selection of Letters from the Earliest Correspondence of Thomas Merton and Ernesto Cardenal," 162–200

Times of Stillness (Schellenberger), 228

Tobin, Mary Luke, S.L., 219

Toranzo, Carlos, 178

"Tower of Babel," 177

Transcendentalism, 150, 154, 161

Undivided Heart: The Western Monastic Approach to Contemplation (Casey), 229

University on the Heights, 76

Unsettling of America (Berry), 86

Upton, Julia Ann, R.S.M., x, 75–87

Van Doren, Charles, 195

Van Doren, Mark, 88, 94, 107, 195, 255

Van Waes, Bernard, 233

Vatican Council, Second, 71, 138, 139, 140, 142, 144, 217, 248, 251

"Velvet Revolution," 33

Virgin Time (Hampl), 154, 156

Virtue, Academic, 72–74

Virtue friendships, 45–48

Virtues, 63–65, 109

"Virtuous Teacher: Thomas Merton's Contribution to a Spirituality of Higher Education" (Fuller), x, 59–74

"Vocation and Modern Thought," 72, 118

"Vocation Crisis: 1959–1960," 248

"Vocation of the Cultural Critic" (A symposium), ix

"Voice in the Postmodern Wilderness: Merton on Monastic Renewal" (McKenna), ix, 122–137

Voyage of St. Brendan, 234

Wadell, Paul J., C.P., ix, xi, 38–58

Waldron, Robert G., 226–227, 258–261

Waller, Edmund, 119

Walsh, Dan, 88

"War and Freedom," 250

Wasserman, Anita, Sister, 252

Watch with Me and Six Other Stories of the Yet-Remembered Ptolemy Proudfoot and His Wife, Miss Minnie, Née Quinch (Berry), (Review) 262–264

Waters of Siloe, 259

Weber, Columban, O.C.S.O., 89, 93, 95, 96, 104

"Western Fellow Students Salute with Calypso Anthems The Movie Career of Robert Lax," 256

Whyte, W. H., 113, 120

Wilderness, 126–137

Wilds, 127–137

Wilkes, Paul, 254

William of St.-Thierry, 2

"Wisdom in Emptiness," 139, 147
Wisdom of the Desert, 73, 185
Witness to Freedom: Letters in Times of Crisis (Selected and edited by William H. Shannon), xii, 165, 223, 224, 234, 235, (Review) 246–254
Wolff, Helen, 82
Wong, Frank F., 77
"Working Notebooks," 244

Wu, John C. H., 117, 257

Zeiten der Stille (Schellenberger), 228
Zen, 139–149, 233
Zen and the Birds of Appetite, x, 138–149
Zen Mountain Monastery, 145
Zilboorg, Gregory, 199